Cooperative Language Learning

A TEACHER'S RESOURCE BOOK

Carolyn Kessler

EDITOR
University of Texas at San Antonio

PRENTICE HALL REGENTS
Englewood Cliffs, N.J. 07632

Cooperative language learning / Carolyn Kessler, editor.
    p.   cm.
    Includes bibliographical references and index.
    ISBN 0-13-173618-3
    1. Language and languages—Study and teaching.   2. Group work in
education.   I. Kessler, Carolyn.
    PR2820.A25   1992
418'.007—dc20

                                                                091–29227
                                                                CIP

Acquisitions editor: Anne Riddick
Editorial/production supervision and
interior design: Noël Vreeland Carter
Copy editor: Anne Graydon
Cover design: Wanda Lubelska
Prepress buyer: Ray Keating
Manufacturing buyer: Lori Bulwin
Scheduler: Leslie Coward

© 1992 by Prentice Hall Regents
Prentice-Hall, Inc.
A Paramount Communications Company
Englewood Cliffs, New Jersey 07632

Printed in the United States of America
10   9   8   7   6   5   4   3   2

Permissions appearing on page xiv which constitutes
a continuation of the Copyright page.

0-13-173618-3

Prentice-Hall International (UK) Limited, *London*
Prentice-Hall of Australia Pty. Limited, *Sydney*
Prentice-Hall Canada Inc., *Toronto*
Prentice-Hall Hispanoamericana, S.A., *Mexico*
Prentice-Hall of India Private Limited, *New Delhi*
Prentice-Hall of Japan, Inc., *Tokyo*
Simon & Schuster Asia Pte. Ltd., *Singapore*
Editora Prentice-Hall do Brasil, Ltda., *Rio de Janeiro*

CONTENTS

INTRODUCTION

This is a book about cooperative, sometimes called collaborative, learning—theory, patterns of implementation, and practical classroom suggestions. It is about a humanistic, prosocial form of education that offers second language learners an opportunity to realize new dimensions of achievement.

Educators working either directly with second language learners in the classroom or indirectly with those responsible for design and implementation of English as a second language, bilingual education, or foreign-policy programs form the audience for this book. Many in the audience are educators concerned very specifically with the academic success of language minority or at-risk students. Contributors to this volume address cooperative learning (CL) in the language education of young learners, those in secondary schools, and college students.

The audience also includes those responsible for setting up inservice or staff development programs for educators seeking an understanding of CL applications to second language acquisition as well as those responsible for preparing professionals at the graduate level in second/foreign language education. Contributors give details on providing a cooperative inservice and on designing master's degree courses based on CL theory and practice.

The focus on cooperative learning in second language classrooms with applications for learners representing a wide range of age and experiential levels makes this a unique resource for language educators. Those with interests in second language acquisition for children, adolescents, and adults and with interests in inservice education and graduate programs in bilingual/second or foreign language teaching will find material of theoretical, programmatic, and day-to-day practical interest.

The literature provides a variety of definitions for cooperative learning but certain features are common to all of them. For language learning contexts, CL is a within-class grouping of students, usually of differing levels of second language proficiency, who learn to work together on specific tasks or projects in such a way that all students in the group benefit from the interactive experience. Heterogeneity in the group may include factors other than language—prior experience, first language, culture, level of literacy, personality, learning style, overall academic achievement, to identify a few of the possible variables characterizing a CL team. Utilizing this diversity in specific ways, all learners in the group gain new knowledge of the language together with the social competence that can foster further language acquisition. Learners learn how to take responsibility for their own learning and for that of the other members of the group or team. The positive interdependence resulting from CL activities contributes to creating a community of learners willing to work collaboratively on goals important to the group.

In a number of ways, cooperative learning is not new. The decades of the one-room schoolhouse often found collaborative activities happening in very heterogenous groupings. Older learners helped younger ones and all experienced a sense of cohesion, community, and responsibility for one another. Connections of interdependence made at school continued to foster lifelong learning for many who had shared the experience. I remember this well from the stories my mother told me about attending a country schoolhouse—and I remember how special the friends she made there remained for all of her life. I cherish the memories she shared, too, of how she had learned how to learn there and how she cared about helping others to learn. My mother, her brothers, and sister stand out for me as very strong witnesses to the power of collaborative learning that somehow was lost for a few decades while we adjusted to urban life, large schools, dehumanized learning theories, and competitive endeavors.

Collaborative learning as we know the movement today finds its roots in the 1970s when four research groups, working independently in Israel and the United States, began to design and study CL models for classroom contexts. Now cooperative learning is being implemented and researched all over the world. It is applied in all school content areas and, increasingly, in college and university contexts. The success observed in CL classrooms has led to suggestions for using cooperative learning principles to address a wide array of educational settings and issues (Slavin, 1991). In spite of this, however, there is relatively little material synthesized in a readily accessible place for the application of CL to second language teaching. To provide such a resource for language teachers is the purpose of this text.

As the chapters in this book indicate, the term "cooperative learning" refers to a number of quite different models for structuring collaborative experiences. In spite of this diversity, however, a common thread in patterns of CL implementation is that CL usually supplements teacher instruction by giving students opportunities to integrate their learning through group discussion, discovery experiences, practice of particular skills, and other activities that emphasize *learning* rather than simply *doing* (Slavin, 1991). In summarizing the characteristics of CL models most widely researched, Slavin (1990) points out that most use some form of group goals, require individual accountability, and provide equal opportunities for success of all team members. The most important research finding is that appropriately structured CL classroom organization significantly enhances student achievement.

Overview

This volume is organized into three sections. The focus of the first section is on the foundations of cooperative learning: theory and models for implementation, basis for a communicative curriculum for second language teaching/learning, and relationships to language and cognitive development. The second section addresses CL in content-based language instruction, including science, social studies, mathematics, and the integration of content areas using a Jigsaw cooperative learning model. The third section focuses on the teacher from a variety of perspectives— teacher talk in cooperative and traditional classrooms and the role of the teacher in the cooperative setting. Two chapters treat teacher education specifically, one in terms of teacher preparation in master's degree programs in ESL or teaching foreign languages and the other in terms of teacher inservice education in CL. Finally there is an extensive bibliography for teachers interested in pursuing cooperative learning through further readings from a variety of perspectives.

Part One: Foundations of Cooperative Learning

The first chapter by Olsen and Kagan examines cooperative learning as a resource for language acquisition and academic achievement, especially for students acquiring English as a second language. The authors discuss the benefits to learners of cooperative learning, trace the history of the CL movement, and summarize research results. This chapter also provides a definition of CL, and identifies key elements and major characteristics of CL. Three major CL models are presented, together with an extensive list of structures and procedures. The chapter also reviews some of the published materials available based on a CL model.

In Chapter 2, Coelho provides a sociological, educational, and linguistic rationale for cooperative learning. She addresses the competitive ethic in North American society, how it is manifested in the classroom, and how its counterbalance of cooperation is particularly appropriate for fostering achievement for language minority students. Attention to affective factors and race relations in the classroom points to the benefits of CL and the importance of utilizing CL strategies. Using a Communicative Approach to language teaching, Coelho demonstrates how oral strategies can contribute to effective group interaction. Emphasis is given to how classroom and curriculum organization can provide a culturally appropriate environment for minority students to succeed academically.

McDonell offers a challenge in Chapter 3 to ESL teachers to maximize the language and learning potential of language minority students. This chapter presents a view of language as a collaborative, meaning making process in which children learn to talk as well as learn through and about talk. McDonell points out that conditions for successful language learning pertain to all modes of language learning, including literacy development. The cooperative classroom offers the second language learner a rich and collaborative environment as a foundation for genuine, authentic communication. This chapter stresses that children in a cooperative classroom become better prepared to communicate, collaborate, negotiate, problem-solve, and think critically—all crucial factors in empowering children for school success.

Part Two: Language Through Content

In Chapter 4, Kessler, Quinn, and Fathman examine how CL strategies can serve to integrate science and language learning for ESL learners at the upper elementary, middle, and senior high school levels. The connections given in this chapter, however, are relevant for any special population needing further development in English. Relationships between science learning principles and second language acquisition are discussed, with emphasis given to the role of interactive cooperative groups engaging in scientific investigations. The authors argue that within this context ESL learners can develop access to science and a second language concurrently.

In Chapter 5, Roger Olsen points out that social studies may present particular difficulties for limited English proficient students because the topics are generally abstract, often cognitively demanding, and usually very language dependent. This chapter illustrates different ways to use CL procedures, structures, and related frameworks with social studies content, provided that students have learned prosocial behaviors in team formation, teambuilding, and classbuilding. In applying CL to social studies or any of the content areas, teachers and students need to be at ease with CL. In addition, some form of group and individual accountability needs to take place.

Quinn and Molloy, in Chapter 6, describe a research project using a model of CL in college level mathematics courses with a largely Hispanic population whose academic language in mathematics was not well developed. In small group CL sessions, students learned to talk mathematics—as well as to read and write in a mathematics register. Mathematics came alive for students as they discovered the social support of the group, took responsibility for the learning of others, gained self-confidence in doing mathematics, and met academic success. This achievement has provided access to further mathematics and science study for a population greatly underrepresented in these fields.

Coelho's Chapter 7 provides a synthesis of basic principles of CL applied to content-based instruction, giving attention to various issues including selecting content for the ESL program and subject-specific language. Focusing on Jigsaw as a pattern of curriculum and classroom organization appropriate for integrating language and content, Coelho offers practical suggestions for content-based activities, using published and teacher-made materials.

Part Three: Focus on the Teacher

Although many research findings point to the positive influence of CL on academic achievement, little attention has been given to the nature of teacher talk. In Chapter 8 Harel contrasts styles of teacher talk in classrooms using cooperative learning with teacher talk in traditional teacher-fronted classrooms. Using data gathered from junior high school teachers in Israel, Harel identifies specific features of teacher talk as teachers go from frontal classes to cooperative groups. The style teachers use in CL classrooms more strongly supports the Communicative Approach methodology for ESL teaching and the principles of current second language acquisition theory.

McDonell's Chapter 9 examines the diverse roles of the teacher using CL in a second language classroom. She identifies key elements of the CL teacher's role—inquirer, creator, observer, facilitator, change agent. Additionally, she clarifies the process the teacher needs to follow for effective implementation of CL.

Using cooperative learning as a significant component of a master's degree program in teaching ESL or foreign languages is the focus of Shaw's Chapter 10. As Shaw argues, the case for using CL at the graduate level follows from the belief that the effectiveness of any teacher education program is greatly enhanced if there is close congruence between what is studied and what is done. His position is that CL must be demonstrated and experienced rather than treated solely as an object of study. Benefits derived from this approach include a richer and more enjoyable learning experience, with students better prepared to teach and work collaboratively with other teachers.

In Chapter 11, Judy Olsen examines cooperative learning and inservice education, and the further professional development of educators active in the field. She distinguishes inservice or staff development programs from preservice university-based education and provides an outline of basic issues related to staff development. She addresses participant attitudes, pacing and emphasis of content, and balancing theory with specific activities and procedures. Using variations of Jigsaw, Olsen suggests a format for conducting staff development programs in which participants learn about CL through experiencing CL procedures in meaningful, relevant contexts.

In conclusion, Roger Olsen provides an extensive bibliography organized into three sections. The first is primarily concerned with publications treating CL theory, related research, methodology, and specific procedures. The second focuses on ESL literature, including research, techniques, and strategies incorporating CL. The third section provides selected references on general education, methodology, and classics that relate to cooperative learning.

Cooperative Language Learning: A Teacher's Resource Book is designed for anyone concerned with creating more effective learning environments for language students—those learning English as a second language or any language other than their home or heritage language. Specific audiences include students in either graduate or undergraduate bilingual/ESL or foreign language education courses, educators involved in staff development or inservice programs, curriculum designers, and administrators responsible for language programs. The chapters can be used in any sequence appropriate to the needs of learners. Redundancy is deliberately built into the text to allow for a wide degree of flexibility in using this text.

As Calderon (1990) points out, effective implementation of cooperative learning demands of teachers substantial commitments of time and effort. For teachers working with language learners—whether in ESL, bilingual, or foreign classrooms—an understanding of the processes and strategies that support and encourage second language acquisition is essential for successful integration of CL into the language classroom. The chapters of this text, taken together, provide an integration of cooperative learning principles and procedures with those for second language learning. A resource such as this endeavors to assist teachers drawn to a humanistic, prosocial form of education in organizing their classrooms for student-centered learning.

Carolyn Kessler

References

CALDERON, M. 1990. Training and Coaching Teachers of Language Minority Students for Cooperative Learning. Unpublished manuscript. University of California, Santa Barbara.

SLAVIN, R. E. 1991. Synthesis of research on cooperative learning. *Educational Leadership*, 48: 71–82.

SLAVIN, R. E. 1990. *Cooperative Learning: Theory, Research, and Practice.* Englewood Cliffs, NJ: Prentice Hall.

Acknowledgments

This volume has come to realization because of the many language educators who care deeply about the success of their students and those who provide the network of support for teachers by making texts such as this available to the profession. In particular, I want to acknowledge the vision of Elizabeth Coelho, who is responsible for the genesis of this volume and the design of the framework for it. The unique contribution of each author gives that framework substance. Realization of this book owes much to the support of Roger E. W-B Olsen, whose assistance has been such that one never forgets it. John Duffy gave much support and encouragement during the early stages of development and I am most grateful for it. From Prentice Hall/Alemany I have welcomed the editorial comments and suggestions of Anne Riddick, Noël Vreeland Carter, and the unnamed reviewers and editors who have helped bring this volume to realization. In particular, I want to express appreciation to my colleague Robert Milk, who teaches many of my students how to use CL in bilingual classrooms, and to Curtis W. Hayes, who demonstrates central aspects of CL in our master's degree program for teachers learning how to teach ESL. With special recognition, I want to thank Mary Ellen Quinn, whose own success in cooperative learning endeavors all through her distinguished teaching career has been an inspiration to me. Making available to the profession a book such as this is, indeed, a collaborative effort—one for which I am most appreciative and which I hope is valuable to other educators concerned with meeting the needs of second language learners as efficiently and effectively as possible.

About the Contributors

ELIZABETH COELHO is Program Leader for English as a Second Language/English as a Second Dialect (ESL/ESD) for the North York Board of Education in Metropolitan Toronto where she is responsible for staff and curriculum development to meet the needs of immigrant students in middle and secondary schools. She also teaches in TESL training programs at York University and the University of Toronto. A frequent presenter at local, national, and international conferences, she has authored and co-authored teacher's reference books, professional articles, and classroom materials.

ANN K. FATHMAN is Director of the ESL Program and TESL Certificate Program at the College of Notre Dame in Belmont, California, where she teaches courses in ESL, teacher education, and linguistics. Dr. Fathman specializes in second language acquisition research and the development of ESL content-based materials. She is a frequent presenter at regional, national, and international conferences as well as inservice programs for school districts. Her publications include *The Second Language Oral Test of English,* numerous articles on second language acquisition, and *Science for Language Learners* (co-author).

YAEL HAREL serves as Head of the English Department at Bet Berl College, Tel Aviv University, Israel. In addition to teaching English and American literature, she also teaches a wide range of courses in English as a foreign language (EFL), including cooperative learning in EFL general methodology, and didactics of EFL. Currently, she is a Ph.D. candidate conducting research on the effects of language learning in small groups with particular emphasis on communicative competence in relationship to the speaking skills of EFL learners. She has articles in a number of Israeli publications.

SPENCER KAGAN, Director of Resources for Teachers in San Juan Capistrano, California, is a former professor of psychology and education at the University of California. Dr. Kagan is author of *Cooperative Learning Resources for Teachers* and numerous other books, chapters, and journal articles on the development of cooperative motives and behaviors. He developed the Structural Approach to cooperative learning. Among the extensive contributions he has made to cooperative learning methodology is an array of specific structures, including Pairs Check, Partners, Coop Co-op, Three-Step Interview, and 4S Brainstorming.

CAROLYN KESSLER, Professor of English as a Second Language/Applied Linguistics in the Division of Bicultural-Bilingual Studies at The University of Texas at San Antonio, teaches graduate courses in second language acquisition and ESL methodology. Her research interests include content-based language instruction in ESL and bilingual contexts. Among her many publications are *Literacy con Cariño: A Story of Migrant Children's Success* (co-author) and *The Acquisition of Syntax in Bilingual Children.* She works extensively with school districts throughout the country and is a frequent conference presenter nationally and internationally.

WENDY MCDONELL is Coordinator for ESL/ESD for the City of Etobicoke Board of Education, Canada. She also works extensively with preservice and inservice teachers at York University, Toronto. Currently, she is a Ph.D. Candidate at the University of Reading, England, with studies also at the University of London and University of Toronto. Her research interest is in teacher change with emphasis on teachers as change agents as a result of reflective teaching. She is a frequent presenter and keynoter at conferences in Bermuda, Canada, England, and the United States. Her publications focus on second language acquisition in primary/elementary education.

MARILYN MOLLOY is Professor and Chairperson of Mathematics at Our Lady of the Lake University, San Antonio. Dr. Molloy teaches a wide range of mathematics courses for undergraduate mathematics, math education, and applied mathematics careers. Concerned with helping students gain the self-esteem needed to discover their own creative ability in expressing mathematical ideas, she uses cooperative learning to encourage students to build math vocabulary, critical thinking skills, and problem-solving abilities. Dr. Molloy has received numerous grants in the area of mathematics for minority students as well as awards for her leadership in mathematics and excellence in teaching.

JUDY WINN-BELL OLSEN teaches English as a Second Language at the City College of San Francisco, Alemany Campus, in the noncredit open entry program. A frequent presenter at professional conferences and inservice training sessions throughout the United States, she has also presented in Egypt, Indonesia, Italy, Japan, Palau, Thailand, and Yemen. In 1990–91 she served as the first coordinator for the City College of San Francisco's all-division staff development project for 700 noncredit faculty. She has authored or co-authored *Communication-Starters, Look Again Pictures, Back and Forth,* and *All Sides of the Issue,* among other publications.

ROGER E. W-B OLSEN currently is West Coast Marketing Director for Alemany Press, providing technical assistance and contributions to the ongoing development of ESL publishing programs. In addition, he is a teacher educator in cooperative learning and language acquisition and a frequent TESOL presenter at regional, national, and international conferences. He has particular interest in ESL demographics, including criteria for identification of ESL students for entry to and exit from programs, and high school completion statistics. He has published a number of articles on ESL-related demographics and needs assessment data and analysis.

MARY ELLEN QUINN is Director of Research for the Center for the Advancement of Science, Engineering, and Technology Project at Our Lady of the Lake University, San Antonio. Coauthor of *Science for Language Learners,* Dr. Quinn has authored numerous chapters, journal articles, curriculum guides, and professional reports. Consultant and workshop director in science/mathematics and English as a second language for school districts throughout the United States, she has presented at many international conferences. In addition to her extensive administrative experience, Dr. Quinn has taught at all levels—elementary, secondary, college/university in many parts of the United States as well as in Taiwan.

PETER AMBLER SHAW, Associate Professor of Applied Linguistics, teaches in the master's degree program for teaching English as a second language/teaching a foreign language at the Monterey Institute of International Studies, California. Dr. Shaw has taught English and trained teachers in Europe, Nigeria, Mexico, and California. He incorporates cooperative learning in both the form and content of the courses that he teaches and the workshops that he gives in second/foreign language methodology and curriculum design.

Permissions

The author gratefully acknowledges the following publishers, companies, and individuals for permission to reprint copyrighted materials:

Public Service Commission of Canada for use of sample exercise materials from E. Keller and S. T. Warner, 1976, *Gambits Openers,* Ottawa Public Service Commission.

Thomas Nelson and Sons, Ltd. for permission to adapt the activity "Whose Suitcase?" from Susan Maingay, 1983, *Making Sense of Reading,* London: Harrap.

WAESOL Newsletter for permission to reprint an excerpt from S. Kutrakun, 1989, "The main factors causing LEP students to be at risk in content area classes," WAESOL Newsletter, 14, no. 2, pp. 2, 3, 8.

Judy Winn-Bell Olsen for permission to reproduce art from her book *Look Again Pictures,* 1984, Englewood Cliffs, NJ: Alemany Press.

Globe Book Company for permission to use art from M. Schwartz and J. O'Connor, 1986, *Exploring American History,* Englewood Cliffs, NJ: Globe Book Company, p. 346.

Routledge for permission to quote from D. Pimm, 1987, *Speaking Mathematically,* London and New York: Routledge.

Pippin Publishing Limited for permission to reprint the Jigsaw Word Puzzle, p. 28, from *Jigsaw* by E. Coelho, with permission of the publisher, Pippin Publishing Limited, © 1991. Ontario, Canada. All rights reserved.

ASCD and J. L. Schultz for permission to quote from J. L. Schultz, 1989, "Cooperative Learning: Refining the Process." *Educational Leadership* 47, 4: 43–45. Reprinted with per-

CHAPTER 1

ABOUT COOPERATIVE LEARNING

Roger E. W-B Olsen and Spencer Kagan

Cooperative learning (CL) is a body of literature and research that has examined the effects of cooperation in education. It offers ways to organize group work to enhance learning and increase academic achievement. CL is not general, free discussion; nor are all types of group work necessarily cooperative. Cooperative learning is carefully structured—organized so that each learner interacts with others *and* all learners are motivated to increase each other's learning.

For limited English proficient (LEP) and limited English functioning (LEF) students, CL provides increased interactions between students. This, in turn, increases opportunities for language practice—especially listening and speaking—while using those same interactions to increase comprehension of lesson material. Nonnative English speakers in CL classes show gains in language acquisition and academic achievement that are either equivalent to or superior to gains through traditional whole-class instruction (Bejarano, 1987; McGroarty, 1989).

Carefully structured interactions between students contribute to gains in second language acquisition (Long and Porter, 1985; Pica, Young, and Doughty, 1987) and in academic achievement (Aronson et al., 1978; Bejarano, 1987; Kagan, 1988, 1989a; Johnson et al., 1981; Johnson and Johnson, 1987, 1989; McGroarty, 1989; Sharan, 1989; Slavin, 1983a, 1990; Webb, 1985, 1988). Interactions such as restating, expansions, and contextualizing allow students to clarify their meanings, elaborate explanations, and resolve discrepancies. These interactions enhance comprehension of lesson material (Bejarano, 1987; Kagan, 1988, 1989a; McGroarty, 1989; Slavin, 1990; Webb, 1985, 1988), perhaps by motivating students to clarify in their own minds what they have learned and what they have yet to learn (Sharan, 1989; Webb, 1985, 1988), by offering redundancy or multiple avenues of access to the learning material and tasks, or simply by stimulating students to process lesson material beyond receptive understanding. In addition, interactions can help to develop understanding of the target language (Long, 1983; Long et al., 1984; Long and Porter, 1985; Pica et al., 1987; Pica, 1988) and provide opportunities to practice using the language that is being learned.

Academic achievement is a particular concern for LEP students because they are, by definition, unable to benefit adequately from traditional English-only instruction (Olsen, 1989). Specialized instruction such as English as a second language (ESL), bilingual education, or content-based ESL (Brinton et al., 1989; Crandall, 1987) must be considered. CL strategies may be especially important for LEP students because they provide a variety of flexible options or frameworks for organizing instruction and interaction types so that language and content may be integrated into a wide variety of discourse (and instructional) contexts.

Benefits, History, and Research Base

Benefits

Many benefits of CL are related to student–student interactions that are structured by interdependence and motivated by accountability. The exchanges are generally obligatory or instrumental; that is, students must exchange information in order to complete the CL task. Communication is genuine because students do not already know what information is to be exchanged. The combined effect of instrumental and genuine discourse may be multiplicative, not merely additive. The exchanges not only stimulate necessary clarifications to ensure comprehension, but they also contribute to academic achievement and to language development by increasing the variety of linguistic and academic contexts within which content is encountered, comprehended, verified, and practiced. In addition, activities such as clarifying, paraphrasing, and summarizing can require cognitive elaboration, organizing and sorting ideas, information, and thoughts—all of which contribute to learning (Webb, 1985, 1988).

McGroarty (1989) identifies six primary benefits of CL for students acquiring English. CL offers:

1. increased frequency and variety of second language practice through different types of interaction.

2. possibility for development or use of the first language in ways that support cognitive development and increased second language skills;

3. opportunities to integrate language with content-based instruction;

4. opportunities to include a greater variety of curricular materials to stimulate language as well as concept learning;

5. freedom for teachers to master new professional skills, particularly those emphasizing communication; and

6. opportunities for students to act as resources for each other, thus assuming a more active role in their learning.

Bassano and Christison (1988) identify four kinds of benefits associated with CL classroom management. First, CL can assist with classroom environment and social tasks—for example, arranging the classroom, distributing materials, or generating advice on critical incidents such as greeting new students or dealing with discipline problems. Second, CL can be useful in selecting content and setting goals. Third, CL can help in developing materials such as flashcards and posters. And, fourth, CL can assist in monitoring progress and evaluative tasks.

We recognize three other important benefits. CL classes are often more relaxed and enjoyable than traditional classes. This creates a positive learning environment, with more students attentive to assigned tasks. As a result, academic achievement increases for all students. Another benefit is that CL can help address the needs of heterogeneous classes—diverse in home languages, English-language proficiency, and academic achievement. And, perhaps most important, CL offers a wide variety of techniques, strategies, and considerations for teachers.

Brief History

CL has an extensive history (Johnson and Johnson, 1986). It is described in the Talmud, by Quintilian in the first century, and by Comenius in the seventeenth century. During the late eighteenth century in England, Joseph Lancaster and Andrew Bell developed schools with CL groups. In 1806, a Lancantrian school opened in New York City and the ''common school movement'' emphasized cooperative procedures. CL is associated with Colonel Francis Parker, superintendent of public schools in Quincy, Massachusetts, 1875–80, and with the work of John Dewey, whose group ''project method'' dominated American education through the turn of the century (Dewey, 1957). Theory of cooperative methodology compared with competitive methodology was reviewed fifty years ago by Morton Deutsch (1949).

In the 1960s, during the early days of forced integration of public schools, interest in cooperative learning was reawakened by concern that minority students would fall farther behind when placed in schools with higher-achieving, ''majority'' students. Looking for ways to structure social integration in the classroom and academic achievement for minorities, researchers observed factors associated with improved academic achievement and prosocial behavior such as collaboration and interdependence. Language teachers, who have long recognized the value of group work for language learning, have recently examined and adopted CL procedures to aid in the instruction and management of group activities. This literature on CL is the basis for this chapter.

Research Base

Over one-thousand research studies have investigated the relative effects of cooperation, competition, and individualistic interdependence. Of these, 82 percent have been published since 1960 and 54 percent since 1979 (Johnson and Johnson, 1989). Overall, the results are extremely favorable.

Academic Achievement

A 1981 meta-analysis of 122 achievement-related studies reported that CL promotes higher achievement than competitive or individualistic learning across all age levels, subject areas, and all tasks except perhaps rote and decoding kinds of tasks (Johnson et al., 1981). More recently, Johnson and Johnson (1989) reported a larger meta-analysis of 349 studies involving subjects in public schools (53 percent), college (41 percent), adults (5 percent) and preschool (1 percent), where duration varied from one session (40 percent) to thirty or more sessions (28 percent). The mean effect size of cooperation is 0.66 over competition and 0.63 over individualistic procedures (neutral interdependence). Johnson and Johnson (1989) note that participants in CL, on average, score at about 3/5 a standard deviation above students in competitive or individualistic situations.

Slavin (1983b) analyzed forty-six controlled research studies conducted over an extended time in regular elementary and secondary classrooms. Of these, 63 percent showed superior outcomes for CL; 33 percent showed no differences; and 4 percent showed higher achievement for the traditional groups. Of the studies which used group rewards for individual achievement (individual accountability), 83 percent showed achievement gains. Achievement was about the same as in comparison classrooms when individual accountability was absent.

A number of studies show the greatest gains among minority students (Aronson et al., 1978; Klein and Eshel, 1980; Slavin, 1977; Slavin and Oickle, 1980, 1981) and among medium- and low-achieving students (Armstrong et al., 1981; Martino and Johnson, 1979; Nevin et al., 1982; Sharan et al., 1984; Smith et al., 1981, 1982, 1984; Skon et al., 1981). This suggests that CL is particularly valuable for LEP students.

It is important to note that high-achieving students generally perform at least as well with CL as in traditional classrooms. This is somewhat at odds with common sense—high-achieving students spend considerable time working with weaker students, yet they achieve as well or better than if they were working on their own all the time. This is not surprising to teachers who know how their own knowledge and understanding increases as they teach and reteach academic content. Explaining ideas to teammates enhances understanding, especially when it requires elaborative explanations instead of terminal responses like short answers, or cognitive elaboration work such as organizing thoughts and being certain about concepts (Dansereau, 1985; Webb, 1985, 1988).

Social and Personal Development

Studies also report improved social development (Johnson and Johnson, 1986) and prosocial behaviors (Kagan, 1977), including increased liking for costudents (Slavin, 1979), reduced racial stereotyping and discrimination (Allport, 1954; Cohen, 1980), increased self-esteem (Slavin, 1983a), increased self-direction (Johnson et al., 1976), increased self-expectations (Kagan, 1988), increased sense of intellectual competence (Kagan, 1989a), and increased liking for class (Slavin, 1983a).

Activity related to academic performance and achievement is also improved through CL, such as increased peer tutoring (Cohen and Kulik, 1981), increased frequency and type of practice (Armstrong et al., 1981), increased comprehension of task structure (Stebbins et al., 1977), and time-on-task (Slavin, 1983a). In their meta-analysis of sixty-five peer-tutoring studies, Cohen and Kulik found that 87 percent of studies show participants in the tutoring process, both tutors and tutees, outperform control students.

Language Learning

CL offers more opportunity for language development and for integrating language with content through increased active communication (active use of language both comprehending and producing), increased complexity of communication, and use of language for academic and social functions.

Increased Active Communication   Teachers in traditional classrooms do most of the talking. Cohen (1984) reported that only 25–50 percent of the class may actually listen to the teacher. Less than 20 percent of traditional class time is devoted to student language production (Goodlad, 1984), and low achievers are typically given fewer opportunities to participate (Cooper, 1979). Because student speech in traditional classes is sequential, that is, one student at a time, each has only fractions of a minute to talk during a typical fifty-minute hour in a class of thirty. In contrast, up to 80 percent of CL class time may be scheduled for activities that include student talking. Because this student talk is simultaneous, half the students may be engaged in language production while the others are engaged in language comprehension. This results in increased active communication for all students.

Increased quantities of communication offered through CL can be important for limited English proficient students because more communication is available for intake. LEP students in traditional classes usually receive less teacher and peer communication compared with other students. Moreover, this communication is typically at lower cognitive and linguistic levels (Arthur et al., 1980; Long, 1981; Schinke-Llano, 1983). Increased quantity of communication that is available for intake therefore can benefit LEP students.

Increased Complexity of Communication Linguistic complexity increases through various means, such as increased stating of new information, giving explanations, offering rationales, and showing integration of information. CL groups exhibit greater amounts of discourse that repeats, re-states, or clarifies information (Johnson et al., 1983). Students request and provide clarifications such as expansions, repetitions, explanations, and elaborations to ensure comprehension. Such individualized clarifications and comprehension checks are not possible when speaking to a group, but they frequently are necessary to complete CL tasks. Moreover, increased linguistic complexity is typically accompanied by nonlinguistic or paralinguistic features—for example, gestures such as facial expressions or shoulder movements to convey emphasis. Also, gestures, visuals, hands-on manipulatives, or other realia help clarify meanings. The result of increased quantity and complexity of communication is higher-quality discourse.

Increased Comprehension It is in the interest of each student to make his or her communication understood by other students because the more that is learned by each, the greater the rewards for all. Bejarano (1987) describes this as obligatory multilateral communication . . . needed to perform the group task.

In Jigsaw methods, for example, each student must learn what other group members know, and so English proficient students patiently draw out LEP students (Aronson et al., 1978), ensuring comprehension. Similarly, LEP students must understand English proficient students, so the LEP students are also motivated to negotiate meanings—to verify, explain, clarify, etc. Also, bilingual students may serve as translators, helping students relate what they already know to what they are learning and the information they must share.

Long et al. (1984) and Brock (1986) distinguish between *display questions* and *referential questions.* Display questions are defined as questions for which the speaker already knows the answer, such as "Is the clock on the wall?" In contrast, referential questions are defined as those for which the speaker does not know the answer, such as "Do you like" or "How do you know" questions. Referential questions can motivate students to teach and to learn what the others know. CL offers increased opportunity and need for referential questions and other forms of referential discourse.

In one of the few studies of CL conducted with second language learners, Bejarano (1987) compared Discussion Group (DG) as defined by Sharan and Lazarowitz (1978), Student Teams Achievement Divisions (STAD) as presented by Slavin (1983a), and Whole Class (WC) methods. She found that DG and STAD were superior to WC for developing integrative and discrete language skills according to pre- and postlistening comprehension and discrete-skills assessment with 665 subjects. Both CL groups showed superior content achievement in addition to their language acquisition gains.

Social language development   Many of the prosocial behaviors that are important in CL are very similar to language functions considered important for LEP students, such as asking for and giving clarification (Coelho, 1988). In the CL class, there can be explicit training in skills such as paraphrasing others' ideas, asking for explanations, summarizing group progress, clarifying, indicating agreement/disagreement, and interrupting politely.

Summary of Benefits

In summary, CL offers three major benefits.

1. *CL provides a richness of alternatives to structure interactions between students.* These are important for language development and developing familiarity with new academic content material. Direct teaching does not disappear in CL classes, but the ratio of information-giver to information-receiver does change dramatically, from one to twenty-five or thirty to as low as one to four or even one to one. CL provides a framework for organizing interaction-type according to the kind of information students are learning (such as discrete, high consensus knowledge or low consensus knowledge) and according to the kind of lesson objectives (such as developing awareness or skill mastery).

2. *CL addresses content area learning and language development needs within the same organizational framework.* The effect of combining language learning with content learning may be multiplicative rather than simply additive. For example, emphasizing prosocial behaviors addresses important language functions while increasing content comprehension. And since it is done within a meaningful, highly motivated context, within an instrumental and referential environment, the language functions may be learned more effectively than through traditional direct teaching methods.

3. *The variety of ways to structure student practice with lesson material increases opportunities for individualized instruction, such as peer-provided clarifications.* As a result, lesson objectives may be achieved more readily and more efficiently. The increased quantity and quality of communication apparently bring more benefit than the "risk" that students may receive incorrect information or input of nonstandard varieties of language. Nonnative English speakers show gains in academic achievement and in language

acquisition either equivalent or superior to gains through direct whole-class teaching (McGroarty, 1989; Bejarano, 1987).

Definition, Key Elements, and Characteristics

Definition

No one has proposed a universally accepted definition of CL. Rather, scholars describe elements, characteristics, or principles that contribute to achievement, socialization, and other gains. However, we propose this definition:

> Cooperative learning is group learning activity organized so that learning is dependent on the socially structured exchange of information between learners in groups and in which each learner is held accountable for his or her own learning and is motivated to increase the learning of others.

The interactions may be as simple as having students discuss points of a lecture in pairs; or they may be very complex, based on precise grouping, grading, or specialized tasks. Not all group work or informal collaboration between students is necessarily cooperative. CL is distinctive because it may include attention to: positive interdependence, team formation, accountability, attention to social skills, structures, and structuring of learning (Table 1).

Table 1
Key Elements of Cooperative Learning

Positive interdependence
Team formation
Accountability
Social skills
Structuring and structures

Key Elements and Defining Characteristics

Positive Interdependence

Positive interdependence occurs when the gains for one individual are associated with gains for others; that is, when one student achieves, others benefit, too. Positive interdependence is contrasted with negative interdependence and non-interdependence. Students are negatively interdependent in competitive situations;

that is, the gains of one student are associated with losses for another. Examples of negative interdependence are grading on the curve, posting only a few (the ''best'') papers, or calling on only one student when several raise their hands. Students are noninterdependent during individualized instruction if students are all working alone at their own pace on individual projects or exercises and the grades of each have no relation to those of other students.

Positive interdependence can be created by the task structure, by the way *outcomes* and/or *means* are defined (Table 2). Either goal or reward outcomes can determine positive interdependence. For example, having a single team product such as an essay, mural, or presentation to the class is *goal-structured* interdependence. *Reward-structured* interdependence can result from creating a team score averaged from individual scores or from the sum of the number of individuals reaching a predetermined criterion, among other possibilities. Scores may also be based on extent of gain or improvement, so that students have equal access to rewards (Kagan, 1986).

Student roles, materials, and rules provide means for structuring positive interdependence. *Role-structured* interdependence involves assigning different roles to each student within a group, such as ''explainer'' or ''checker,'' so that each has a specific responsibility. *Materials-structured* interdependence can include limiting resources, such as having only one pencil or worksheet for everyone in the group to use. It can involve designing information or special activity sheets. Students must share information from these to complete the assignment. An example of *rule-structured* interdependence is having a rule that a group cannot progress to a new learning center or project until all students have completed the assignment. Both materials- and rule-structured interdependence stimulate students to interact. Defining specific roles can help specify the ways they will help each other. Table 2 summarizes patterns for structuring positive interdependence.

Table 2
Ways to Structure Positive Interdependence Among Students

> **Outcome structured:**
> Goal structured
> Reward structured
> **Means structured:**
> Role structured
> Materials structured
> Rule structured

Special Role Assignments   Special roles may be assigned and taught to help the group function. For example, one student might be the ''taskmaster'' who makes sure everyone is on task (young children can be told to look at a teammate's eyes instead of worksheets). Another student might be the ''checker'' to make sure all the work is done. Another could be ''secretary'' to record and summarize the team's work for the whole class. Table 3 identifies possible role assignments and

Table 3
Possible Role Assignments and Gambits
(adapted from Kagan, 1989a)

Role	Function	Gambits
Gatekeeper (monitor)	Makes sure each person participates and that no one individual dominates the group process	"What do you think, John?" "Susan, do you agree?" "I would like to hear from Pete."
Cheerleader (encourager)	Makes sure that the contributions of each member and the team as a whole are appreciated	"Let's do a team handshake." "Let's all give Jack a pat on the back."
Taskmaster (supervisor)	Keeps the group on task and attempts to make sure each member contributes; s/he guides discussion or work.	"Have we finished problem 3?" "I think the task is . . . "
Secretary (recorder) (reporter)	Records team answers and supporting material; can also be the team spokesperson in reporting to the whole class.	"Let me make sure I record that right." "Would it be okay if I said . . . "
Checker (explainer)	Checks that everyone agrees before a group decision is made; checks that everyone understands the assignment and what is needed to finish	"Do we all agree on that?" "Everyone together on this?"
Quiet Captain	Makes sure the group does not disturb other groups	"Let's use our 12-inch voices."

gambits, verbal and nonverbal behaviors for fulfilling roles. In a CL class, students are prepared to carry out these functions; they are not left to chance. Role assignments are varied and are rotated, giving each student opportunities to learn and practice many different social skills. Cohen (1990) observes that assigning roles also has the effect of assigning competence to each student, which can enhance esteem for low-status students.

Methods to Create Positive Interdependence Methods to create positive interdependence may be formal or informal (Table 4). For example, students attending a lecture may be directed to discuss specific points with prepared worksheet questions in an Interview procedure (see page 21) or to informally relate lectured information in some fashion. Informal sharing can help students get acquainted and can establish important associations between what they already know and what they are learning. Table 4 summarizes formal and informal ways to structure interdependence.

Table 4
Formal and Informal Ways to Structure Interdependence
(from Olsen and Reer, 1984)

Interdependence Type	Formal	Informal
Goal structured	Class play Debate	Role play Group Discussion
Reward structured	Grading	Privilege
Materials structured	Jigsawed	One pencil per group; one worksheet all must sign
Role structured	Roles assigned	Specific roles not defined; functions occur by chance
Rule structured	Rules defined	Rules not explicitly stated

Team Formation Positive interdependence implies that grouping has occurred, either by assignment or by chance. Students can group themselves; "leaders" can take turns selecting teammates; or teachers can assign students to teams. Informal or spontaneous grouping is less desirable in many situations than formal or planned grouping methods. Four types of formal team formation—heterogeneous, random, interest, and homogeneous/heterogeneous language ability—are described here.

Heterogeneous grouping can vary along several dimensions. The maximally heterogeneous team mirrors the classroom composition. It includes, to the extent possible, achievement level, gender, ethnic, and linguistic dimensions. Heterogeneous teams can be created with a ranked list of students by following three steps;

1. Rank students from highest to lowest achiever using (in order of preference) pretest, recent posttest, past grades, best guess.
2. Assign the top, bottom, and middle two achievers to the first team and remove from the list.
3. Repeat step 2 to create the next teams.

Heterogeneity of achievement levels maximizes peer tutoring and serves as an aid to classroom management. With a high achiever on each team, introduction of new material becomes easier. Low achievers have opportunities to contribute to the group and to seek clarification when needed. Mixed ethnicity can improve ethnic relations among students, such as increased liking for classmates (Kagan, 1985a; Slavin and Oickle, 1981). Linguistic heterogeneity has at least two benefits. First, it promotes cross-cultural understanding, awareness, and appreciation. Second, it increases opportunities for language acquisition, particularly among students learning English.

Random grouping can be based on distributing tokens, such as colored paper, shapes, or playing cards. Students with similar tokens form teams (triangles go together; aces form a team, for example). Numbering off according to group size, or using tables of random numbers also results in random grouping. *Interest grouping* is based on student characteristics other than achievement, gender, ethnicity, race or, language proficiency, although these factors may be considered. Some advantages and disadvantages are in Table 5 (based on Kagan, 1989a).

Table 5
Team Formation Methods
(based on Kagan, 1989a)

	Heterogeneous, Teacher Assigned Teams	Random, Interest Teams
A D V A N T A G E S	Maximum cross-race, cross-sex, and cross-ability Group contact Low achievers carefully placed to maximize tutoring Language ability grouping possible A high achiever for every group Easy management	Class building and networking Built-in roles and teambuilding Can be quick and easy Leadership opportunities for low achievers Many transference opportunities Variety, stimulation, fun Perception of fairness Metacommunication = You can work with anyone!

D I S A D V A N T A G E S	Teacher time
	
	Fewer transference opportunities
	
	No hi–hi and lo–lo contact
	
	Possible teammate overdependence
	
	Possible labeling
	
	Metacommunication = You must be assigned; not all teams work!
		Possible loser teams
		
		Possible intense conflicts
		
		Possible language incompatabilities
		
		Only short-term teams possible with:
		
		    Limited bonding opportunities
		    Weaker team identity
		    Limited opportunities to learn
		    how to learn together

Students with different levels of English language proficiency may need different kinds of materials and interactions. Students acquiring English may need more context and fewer language dependent materials and tasks (Cummins, 1981). Therefore, at certain points of instruction, especially with a wide range of language proficiences and demanding content, homogeneous grouping by English language proficiency may be desirable. Although homogeneous by language, teams are still heterogeneous on other dimensions; hence, the term *heterogeneous/homogeneous language grouping*.

Accountability

Research shows that both individual and group accountability is important for achievement in CL settings, and most scholars (e.g., Slavin, 1990) consider this to be a defining characteristic of CL. Methods which use only a group grade or a group product without making each member accountable do not consistently produce achievement gains (Slavin, 1983b). Students may be made individually accountable by assigning each student a grade on his or her own portion of the team project or by the rule that the group may not go on to the next activity until all team members finish the task. A primary way to ensure accountability is through testing.

Social Skills

Johnson et al. (1986) include teaching social skills as a defining characteristic of CL. Social skills teaching, however, is not always an element in some of the most widely researched CL procedures, such as Student Teams Achievement Divisions (STAD) discussed in Slavin (1983a).

Social skills include ways students interact with each other to achieve activity or task objectives (e.g., asking and explaining) and ways students interact as teammates (e.g., praising and recognizing). Social skills can be emphasized by assigning

Table 6
Task- and Group-Related Social Skills

Task-Related Social Skills	Group-Related Social Skills
Asking for clarification	Acknowledging others' contributions
Asking for explanations	Appreciating others' contributions
Checking understanding of others	Asking others to contribute
Elaborating ideas of others	Praising others
Explaining ideas or concepts	Recognizing others
Giving information or explanations	Verifying consensus
Paraphrasing and summarizing	Keeping the group on task
Receiving explanations	Keeping conversation quiet and calm
Requesting clarification	Mediating disagreements or discrepancies

all teammates to practice specific social skills (Table 6) to ensure that students can fill these functions when required. Social skills behavior may not occur spontaneously with all students (Hertz-Lazarowitz, 1990), and teaching them can have a profound impact on attentiveness, morale, and motivation.

Structures and Structuring

Structures are generic, content-free ways of organizing student interactions with content and with each other. For example, (STEP 1) one student talks while others listen, then (STEP 2) the next student talks, etc. Structures describe different ways students are to interact. Several structures are described in the Structural Approach later in this chapter.

Other Elements

Although there is general agreement on the importance of the above elements, there is considerable variation in the emphasis accorded to size of groups, team building, process/product, awareness/mastery, grading systems, and the role of the teacher.

Group Size   In traditional classrooms, the ratio of information-giver, usually the teacher, to information-receivers, the students, is typically one to twenty-five or thirty. Cooperative groups can provide a dramatically higher ratio of information-giver to information-receivers, including one to one for work in pairs. Team or group size may vary from two to six or more per team. We prefer teams of four to allow for pairwork. Groups of seven or more tend to be cumbersome.

Teambuilding   Teambuilding procedures can include having students choose a team name, symbol, and cheer; or interviewing teammates on topics related to the subject material to be covered. The interviews serve to help teammates get acquainted. They also promote meaningful and important connections to the academic curriculum. Classbuilding methods include building a positive class identity—by creating a class banner, for example—but also include procedures such as Inside-Outside Circle, explained later in the chapter.

Product/Process   Some CL methods emphasize basic skills, while others emphasize higher-order thinking processes. The interactive aspects of CL can be of value even in discrete skill-building tasks. Focus on discrete knowledge allows students to explore the interaction process at hand, such as specific cooperating or language skills. Aspects of the interaction process may be emphasized, as in the use of special "processing" worksheets with which students evaluate how they cooperated, encouraged, and explained.

Another aspect of variation is in the emphasis placed on "high-consensus knowledge" contrasted with "low-consensus knowledge." High-consensus knowledge is generally discrete, known or knowable, and often lends itself to true/false or multiple-choice objective testing. For example, historical dates or mathematical sums are discrete and known (or knowable). Low-consensus knowledge is not described discretely or is not easily described at all. It generally lends itself to essay or open-ended questions. Low-consensus knowledge also includes unfamiliar knowledge as well as experience-based knowledge not readily articulated. Hypotheses not yet well formulated can be one type of low-consensus knowledge.

A note of caution: Emphasizing activities that rely heavily on low-consensus knowledge may initially lead to mixed or inconsistent results for some groups. Teachers experiencing difficulties with low-consensus data might consider designing interactions based on high-consensus data, perhaps with tasks that involve student production or manipulation of discrete items.

Awareness/Mastery   Many lesson objectives are oriented toward mastery of basic skills or other information, emphasizing "final draft" or "public publication" kinds of products. Others emphasize developing familiarity and awareness, encouraging "prepublication" or "rough draft" interactions. A "prepublication" emphasis can increase awareness of content material without the immediacy of pressure to reach mastery levels. Also, a preliminary, prepublication approach may be used to concentrate attention on content rather than on linguistic correctness (Olsen and Reer, 1984). This can be important for students acquiring English.

Grading   Descriptions of grading systems are not uniform (Kagan, 1989a). If grades are based solely on individual performance, reward-structured interdependence may be lacking and interdependence must then derive from other procedures such as goal, roles, or materials. Basing individual grades at least in part on group performance ensures reward-structured interdependence to motivate student–student helping, coaching, or tutoring.

Team-performance grading includes several options, including averaging teammates' individual scores, assigning the lowest individual score to each teammate, or adding individual scores. Improvement scoring—that is, basing the team's grades on improvement measured, for example, with pre- and posttest scores—can be calculated with either grouped or individual scores. Improvement scoring generally means that every student has an equal chance to improve, so each team can do well.

Role of the Teacher   The teacher's role is generally one of facilitating, monitoring students' engagement with process, or clarifying information, rather than primarily one of providing information.

Three Models

Several models and procedures are associated with CL, reflecting different orientations of scholars in this field. The Johnsons' work is referred to as Learning Together cooperative learning. Aronson (Aronson et al., 1978) and Slavin (1990, 1991) are associated with Student Team Learning (STL) such as Jigsaw, procedures of interlocking student materials and tasks to structure interdependence. Kagan

(1985a, 1989b) emphasizes a Structural Approach, with generic procedures that may be adapted to a variety of contexts. Sharan is associated with Group Investigation techniques (Sharan and Sharan, 1976; Sharan, 1980; Sharan and Hertz-Lazarowitz, 1980). This section describes three CL models: (1) Learning Together, (2) the Structural Approach, and (3) Curriculum Packages.

Learning Together

Learning Together is a framework for using CL at any grade level with any subject. It is described at length by Johnson and Johnson (1986). The focus is on basic interdependence principles (Table 2) and decisions teachers must make to apply CL. Eighteen steps, grouped into five categories, represent decision points for lesson planning. The steps also provide the sequence for the lesson itself.

    A.   Specifying objectives.
        1. Specifying academic and collaboration objectives before each lesson begins.
    B.   Making decisions
        2. Deciding on group size
        3. Assigning students to groups
        4. Arranging the room
        5. Planning materials needed
        6. Assigning roles (see Table 4)
    C.   Communicating the task, goal structure, and learning activity
        7. Explaining the academic task
        8. Structuring positive goal interdependence
        9. Structuring individual accountability
      10. Structuring intergroup cooperation
      11. Explaining the criteria for success
      12. Specifying desired behaviors
    D.   Monitoring and intervening
      13. Monitoring students' behavior
      14. Providing task assistance
      15. Intervening to teach collaborative skills
      16. Providing closure, such as summarizing major points of the lesson, asking students to recall ideas, posing final questions, etc.
    E.   Evaluating and processing
      17. Evaluating the quality and quantity of student learning
      18. Assessing how well the group functioned

The teacher's primary in-class emphasis is monitoring and clarifying tasks or teaching collaboration skills. It is not on transmitting information for students to learn.

The Structural Approach

The Structural Approach is based on the use of various distinct sequences of classroom behaviors, called structures (Kagan, 1989b). A structure is a content-free way of organizing distinct sequences of classroom behaviors, including specified types of interactions among individuals at each step. Structures are distinct from activities. Activities are content-bound and specific and usually have a specific objective, such as creating a class banner to build a class identity or finding all the small words possible in a set of words. In our experience, activities cannot be repeated meaningfully many times. In contrast, structures are content-free ways of organizing interactions. They may be used repeatedly with a variety of curriculum materials, at various places in the lesson plan, and throughout the syllabus.

A traditional (competitive) structure may be called Whole-Class Question and Answer (Kagan, 1989b). The steps are as follows: (STEP 1) The teacher asks a question. (STEP 2) Students who think they have the correct answer raise their hands. (STEP 3) The teacher calls on one student. (STEP 4) The student attempts to state the correct answer. (STEP 5) The teacher responds to the student's attempt. This is a competitive structure because as one student is selected the others lose their chance to be called on.

Numbered Heads Together (Kagan, 1989b) is a simple four-step CL structure as follows: (STEP 1) Students number off within groups. If students are in groups of four, every student will be either, 1, 2, 3, or 4. (STEP 2) The teacher asks a high-consensus question, such as, "What is the capital of the United States?" (STEP 3) Students put their heads together to make sure everyone on the team knows the answer. (STEP 4) The teacher calls a number from one to four. Only students with that number can raise their hands if they know the answer. Numbered Heads Together meets the criteria of being a structure because it is a content-free way of organizing social interaction in the classroom. It is a CL structure because student–student interaction is necessary to ensure that everyone in the group knows the answer. High achievers share answers because they know their number might not be called; lower achievers listen carefully because they know their number might be called, so positive interdependence is built in. A CL structure engages positive interdependence, individual and group accountability, motivates individuals to increase others' learning. It can be used with almost any subject matter, at a wide range of grade levels, and at various places in a lesson. Structures allow teachers to focus on the interactional framework rather than on the sequencing of presentation of curriculum material.

Three-Step Interview is a three-step structure: (STEP 1) Students form pairs within their group of four and conduct a one-way interview. (STEP 2) Students exchange roles—interviewers become interviewees. And (STEP 3) each student takes turns sharing within the group of four what was learned in the interview. This contrasts with a traditional group discussion procedure in which the teacher asks a low-consensus question and then tells students to talk it over. Three-Step Interview ensures that each student will talk, listen, and summarize for the team. Three-Step

Interview might be combined with Numbered Heads, so the fours or the threes are called on to summarize the team's interviews for the class.

Structures have different domains of usefulness. They are effective for some but not all steps in a lesson and for certain but not all kinds of cognitive and social growth. Some structures are more appropriate for discrete, high-consensus knowledge. Others are more appropriate for developing awareness rather than mastery of content or skills. Sequencing or chaining structures can create multistructural lessons (Kagan, 1989a, 1989b).

Structures may be categorized in several ways:

1. by function or domain of usefulness such as classbuilding, teambuilding, communication skills mastery, or concept development;
2. by complexity such as simple and complex or mini- or megastructures;
3. by the type of interdependence they promote between teammates and teams (positive, negative, or none);
4. by the type of cooperation promoted between teammates, such as encouraging, tutoring, sharing information, dividing up of labor, or coordinating work on a cooperative project.

This is a partial list of CL structures organized by function or type of cooperation. Some structures fill more than one function. For example, Inside-Outside Circle is useful for review and classbuilding. For additional discussion of these and other structures, see Kagan (1989a), Coelho (this volume) and Shaw (this volume).

Classbuilding

Similarity Grouping

(1) Teacher announces a dimension such as hair color or birthday month or categories, such as food and seasons; (2) everyone with the same answer forms a group; (3) students then discuss positive and negative aspects of that characteristic.

Line-ups

Students line up according to height, birthdays, alphabetical order, distance from school, etc.

Teambuilding

Roundtable

Each team has one piece of paper and one pen. One student writes a contribution and passes the paper and pen to the student on the left. Roundtable can be used to introduce a new topic or theme, (list key words or concepts from a lesson or reading), or just to liven up practice.

Round Robin

Same as Roundtable, but student contributions are oral, not written.

Communication Builders

Talking Tokens

Each student must "spend" a token to speak. To talk, the student places a token in the center of the table. The student cannot talk again until all tokens are in the center of the table, when everyone has taken a turn. Tokens are then retrieved. The process begins again. Variations include limiting talk to a one-minute turn; allowing yes/no questions and answers for free; using more than one token per student; coding different tokens for different kinds of discourse such as seeking clarifications, asking for or giving examples, encouraging and praising.

Paraphrase Passport

One student makes a statement. The next student must paraphrase that statement correctly before talking.

Match Mine

Each student has an identical set of figures. A barrier is set up or students sit back to back. One student puts the figures in a pattern and describes it to a partner. The partner recreates the same pattern. Variations include using a grid; using content-related figures or illustrations; using fewer or more figures; providing sample communication patterns for requesting clarification, checking understanding, or describing; describing a picture so well that teammates can draw it; taking turns describing the picture; giving commands; restricting drawing to circles, squares, and lines for beginners. Describers cannot look until illustrators are finished. (Thanks to Judy Winn-Bell Olsen for introducing these to us.)

Mastery

Numbered Heads Together

Students number off (in teams). Teacher asks a question (usually high-consensus data). Students literally put their heads together to make sure everyone knows the answer. Teacher calls a number. Students with that number raise their hands to be called on, as in traditional classrooms.

Pairs Check

Students work in pairs with one worksheet, taking turns doing the problems. (1) One student is "coach" while the other is the "solver" and completes the problem; (2) the coach praises the solver; (3) they switch roles; (4) teams compare answers after both pairs in the team have finished all the problems.

Review

Inside-Outside Circle

(1) Students stand in two concentric circles with the inside circle facing out and the outside circle facing in; (2) they make a quarter right turn; (3) teacher tells them how many steps to rotate, or advance, to face a new partner; (4) students share information; and (5) students rotate again.

Color-coded Co-op Cards

(1) Pretest. (2) Each student makes flashcards on specific problems s/he missed. (3) Pairs use flashcards with questions on one side, answer on the other side. At every round, the tutor gives praise and returns the card if the answer is correct or tutor gives a ''helper'' and puts the card on the bottom of the pile to try again. Three ways to use flashcards are: (a) With maximum cues, the tutor shows and reads both sides; tutee writes, says, or traces the answer; tutor shows question and asks for answer. (b) Giving few cues, the tutor shows question only; tutee gives answer from memory. (c) No cues are given; the tutor asks question without showing the card. (4) A practice test is based on the flashcards to focus only on the problems practiced. (5) Color-coded Improvement Scoring. (6) Repeated practice. (7) Final Test. (8) Final Improvement Scoring. (9) Recognition based on improvement individually, by teams, and for the whole class; teams are recognized for having advanced the class overall, not for ''beating'' other teams. (10) Processing: students ''debrief'' by discussing processes such as how they felt giving or receiving help and praise, what kinds of help were useful, how well they worked together, or how they could improve working together.

The Co-op Card method is useful because it: (a) focuses each student on his or her most needed learning tasks; (b) provides immediate, frequent, tangible, and social feedback on improvement; (c) gives all students equitable access to rewards; and (d) converts dull drill into fun.

Student Teams Achievement Divisions

STAD (Slavin, 1990) has five major components: class presentations, teams, quizzes, individual improvement scoring, and team recognition. Steps include introducing STAD procedures to the class. (1) Using direct teaching methods, teach the first lesson; prepare a quiz on the lesson material and worksheets based on the quiz. (2) Introduce team assignments, explain group scoring, and start team practice on worksheets. Teams can enter Group Discussion, Pairs Check, or just work informally until each member is sure that all on the team will make 100 percent on the quiz. When students have questions, they ask teammates before asking the teacher. Teammates explain answers. (3) Review and continue team practice. Teacher reviews the lesson; students then review in pairs with worksheets, then change partners to ensure every teammate knows the answers. (4) Quiz (individually, not one quiz per team). (5) Improvement scoring, that is, teacher bases scores on improvement from pre- to post-test scores. It applies to either individual or group situations.

Teams-Games-Tournaments (TGT)

This replaces quizzes with academic tournaments. Improvement scoring is replaced by a bumping system akin to spelling bee tournaments (see Slavin, 1990 for details). WE DO NOT RECOMMEND TGT. TGT rewards high achievers and may allow extra points for challenging classmates, which may explain decreased self-esteem and decreased feeling of intellectual competence found with TGT procedures (Kagan, 1989a). The bumping system moves the winner at a tournament table to a higher-level table, the loser to an easier table, ensuring that winners and losers are identified individually.

Concept Development

Group Discussion

(1) Teacher presents a topic or question; (2) students discuss in small groups; (3) a group representative summarizes the group's discussion for the class. Variations are endless and can focus on roles within groups (such as a monitor to keep everyone talking about the assignment, a recorder to take notes, a researcher to get information from outside the group when needed, and a reporter to summarize), on kinds of summary reporting (such as giving best ideas only, sharing best or worst ideas, teams exchanging reporters, using Numbered Heads to assign reporters), and on kinds of topics or information (such as high- or low-consensus information, guessing what the next unit will cover, or predicting a reading passage based on headings and subheadings).

Three-Step Interview

(1) Students are in pairs; one is interviewer and the other is interviewee; (2) students reverse roles; (3) each student shares with the team what s/he has learned during the two interviews.

Think-Pair-Share

(1) Teacher poses a question (usually a low-consensus question); (2) students think of a response; (3) use Interview procedure to share answers. An advantage to TPS is that students have increased wait time (Budd-Rowe, 1974), the opportunity to think about their answers before thinking about who they will share with. Low-consensus information, unfamiliar topics, or ''higher-order'' analysis, synthesis, or evaluation applications may require more thinking time

than high-consensus information. (Thanks to Frank Lyman for this structure. See Lyman [1981, 1989] for several interesting and useful variations.)

Solve-Pair-Share

(1) Teacher poses a problem (a low- or high-consensus item); (2) students work out solutions individually (a Checker may be needed); (3) students enter Three-Step Interview or Round Robin to explain *how* they solved the problem. SPS can be very powerful with high-consensus data when students share *how* they used the available information (such as how they set up and solved a word problem in math). SPS can develop awareness of problem-solving strategies, decrease learner anxiety about symbolic reasoning, and increase motivation to learn new ways to solve similar problems (Olsen and Reer, 1984).

Brainstorming

(1) Teacher presents a topic or problem; (2) students give as many ideas as possible individually, in pairs or in teams; (3) the ideas are shared, using Group Discussion, Roundtable, etc. For variation, students brainstorm individually, in pairs, or in teams, writing each idea on a different slip of paper. Teams categorize the ideas. Students then walk around the room to see each team's categorized ideas.

Division of Labor

Telephone

(1) One student from each team steps out of the room; (2) teacher presents information to the class, such as reading a short story; (3) absent students return; (4) teammates teach absent students everything they can about the information presented. (Thanks to Barbara Chips for this idea.)

Partners

(1) Form partners with teams; (2) class divides so topic-one partners and topic-two partners sit separately; (3) students master learning assignment; (4) partners consult with same-topic partners to check for correctness, completeness, and different points of view; (5) partners prepare to teach their topic, deciding what critical elements are to be presented and how; (6) teams reunite and partners share and tutor; (7) teams process how they did as teachers and as learners; (8) individual assessment is used, such as quiz or essay; (9) improvement scoring, that is, basing scores on improvement from pre- to post-test scores.

Jigsaw

(1) Each individual becomes expert or source of unique information; (2) individuals then share in a structured form. Several variations of Jigsaw exist. Kagan (1989a) identifies thirteen varieties. Jigsaw I, the original, assigns different material to students (Aronson et al., 1978). A variation called Jigsaw II assigns different tasks based on the same material (Slavin, 1983a). Students can

be given different worksheets based on the same reading (such as analysis or application kinds of questions) and they then share their questions and answers. Jigsaw III may use bilingual learning materials and emphasize social-skills activities such as wrap-up processing for students to examine whether they allowed others to speak, listened well, and treated each other with kindness and respect.

In Team Jigsaw, students form temporary "mastery teams" or "expert groups" with different learning assignments to master. Students then return to their original or "home" teams and share new knowledge with teammates. When students work primarily within their "home"-team group, it is called Within-team Jigsaw. Expert Partner Jigsaw uses expert partners instead of expert groups.

Other variations include Double Expert (using more than one expert group for more than one function), Jigsaw Twins (in which pairs, such as a higher- and a lower-achieving student or a new student and an "old hand," might share a responsibility). Partner Expert Group Jigsaw combines "partners" (for initial learning), "expert groups" (for preparing and practicing presentations), and Three-Step Interview or Roundtable for sharing and learning with original teammates (Thanks to Billie Jean Telles for emphasizing the effectiveness of this with students acquiring English). For other variations, see Aronson et al. (1978), Johnson and Johnson (1986), Kagan (1989a), or Slavin (1983, 1990). Jigsaw is one of the most highly researched forms of CL and perhaps the most flexible of the complex forms.

Cooperative Projects

Co-op Co-op

(1) Students discuss as a whole class what they already know and what they would like to know about a topic; (2) students are assigned to teams; (3) team members participate in teambuilding activities; (4) teams select a topic from the topics listed in step one; (5) teams divide into subteams (individuals or partners) to select minitopics for further study; (6) individuals research minitopics and prepare presentations to their teams; (7) minitopic presentations; (8) teams prepare presentations about their topic for the whole class. (9) teams present to whole class; (10) evaluation may be assessment, improvement scoring, processing, etc. See Kagan (1985b) for fuller discussion.

Group investigation

(1) Identify topic(s) and organize research groups. (2) Groups plan their learning activities. (3) Individuals carry out the investigation, emphasizing "multilateral communication" as students communicate with collaborators, teacher, other groups, and resource persons. They gather, analyze, and evaluate data, reaching conclusions in ways that they decide are appropriate. (4)

Groups prepare the final report. (5) Groups present the final report. (6) Evaluation. For more discussion, see Sharan and Hertz-Lazarowitz (1980).

Multi-structural Lessons

Individual structures may be sequenced or chained throughout a lesson, so each structure creates a learning experience that builds on experience from previous structures. For example, a unit on math word problems might begin with Solve-Pair-Share, a structure to develop awareness of ways to approach or set up problems; then students enter Three-Step Interview, Pairs-Check, or Partners as the unit progresses. Subsequent lessons in the unit might utilize Color-coded Co-op Cards or Jigsaw, and some of the class might be taught in traditional ways.

Curriculum Packages

Several sets of materials have been published that incorporate CL procedures to varying degrees. The more elaborate packaged materials are highly curriculum and age-grade specific, so that they are not wholly appropriate at all grade levels nor for all curriculum topics. *Finding Out/Descubrimiento (FO/D),* (De Avila et al., 1987) for example, is a general math/science program for elementary schools targeted primarily for bilingual or ESL settings. Its organization can provide insight for adaptations and variations to meet other needs.

FO/D assigns teams to learning centers, and each team member must complete the entire assignment before the team is allowed to move on to the next set of problems or learning center. Students who complete the assignment rapidly help slower students. Everyone completes the assigned material. Cooperating skills, such as giving and asking for help, are emphasized. In addition, FO/D offers student material in Spanish as well as English, so students can learn the content in either language. Students learning English or Spanish as a second language may consult material in their primary language only after first seeking clarifications or explanations from teammates.

A second package approach is *Comprehensive Integrated Reading and Composition (CIRC),* which combines CL procedures and process writing with specific basal programs. CIRC is developed at the Johns Hopkins University by Dr. Robert Slavin and colleagues (Madden et al., 1986; Stevens et al., 1987). CIRC uses mainly Jigsaw, STAD, and improvement scoring. The Johns Hopkins team has also developed Team Accelerated Instruction (TAI) materials for mathematics (Slavin et al., 1986).

Some published materials do not depend upon highly sequenced series of lessons. Among these are works by Palmer et al. (1988), Olsen (1984), and Coelho et al. (1989). These materials use structured interdependence, basic task structures in various ways, and a blackline master format with permission to photocopy. Olsen uses high-consensus data (visual), and an interesting problem for student pairs to solve, with barriers and interview-type structures. Students are to identify, as the primary task, eight differences between picture pairs. Tasks are designed for different kinds of language practice, often integrated with life skills.

Palmer uses discrete data in four kinds of tasks: describing pictures, listening to descriptions of pictures, listening for a word, and listening for cues to a scripted dialogue. Students listen to their partners to discover the correct choice. In the case of the cued dialogues, students listen to choose between two possible replies.

Coelho and colleagues emphasize low-consensus data, including controversial issues such as environmental pollution. Each unit is presented with four "sides of the issue" available for the teacher to duplicate and distribute to teams. Up to four-way debates can emerge. Andrini (1989) and Stone (1989) feature multistructural lessons that sequence or chain structures, providing learning experiences that are designed to build on each other. Andrini integrates all eight strands of the national mathematics framework and provides multistructural lessons on each strand at each grade level. Students reach predetermined learning objectives with minimal verbal instruction from the teacher.

Other published material can be easily adapted, such as collections of role play or simulations for use with Three-Step Interview or Think-Pair-Share structures. For example, Ford and Silverman (1981), Olsen (1981), and Messerschmitt and Cui (1984) present scenarios and up to four different ways the scenarios may be resolved. Students select one of the proposed solutions, explaining their decisions. Jew and colleagues (1988) present job interview situations designed for role play. In addition to being useful in Three-Step Interview or Think-Pair-Share, these materials provide processing worksheets for students to evaluate their interviewing.

Variations and Getting Started

Teachers who are unable to redesign their entire curriculum or who simply wish to use CL as a way to structure student–student interactions can get started with CL by consulting the key elements to decide which to introduce into their lessons. They may select a structure to use within a mostly traditional lesson (such as Think-Pair-Share during a lecture), or try out one of the many sample lessons elsewhere in this book.

We recommend training and consulting with other teachers who are using CL. At the very least, one may collaborate with another teacher who is also interested in developing skills with cooperative learning. Many resource books are available, but nothing substitutes for classroom experience!

REFERENCES

ALLPORT, G.W. 1954. *The Nature of Prejudice*. Reading, MA: Addison-Wesley.

ANDRINI, B. 1989. *Cooperative Learning and Math: A Multi-Structural Approach*. San Juan Capistrano, CA: Resources for Teachers.

ARMSTRONG, B., D.W. JOHNSON, and B. BALOW. 1981. Effects of cooperative versus individualistic learning experiences on interpersonal attraction between learning-disabled and normal-progress elementary school students. *Contemporary Educational Psychology,* 6: 102–9.

ARONSON, E., N. BLANEY, C. STEPHAN, J. SIKES, and M. SNAPP. 1978. *The Jigsaw Classroom.* Beverly Hills, CA & London: Sage Publications.

ARTHUR, B., R. WEINER, M. CULVER, Y.J. LEE, and D. THOMAS. 1980. The register of impersonal discourse to foreigners: Verbal adjustments to foreign accent. In D. Larsen-Freeman (ed.), *Discourse Analysis in Second Language Acquisition.* Rowley, MA: Newbury House.

BASSANO, S., and M.A. CHRISTISON. 1988. Cooperative learning in the ESL classroom. *TESOL Newsletter,* 22, no. 2: 1, 8–9.

BEJARANO, Y. 1987. A cooperative small-group methodology in the language classroom. *TESOL Quarterly,* 21, no. 3: 483–504.

BRINTON, D.M., M.A. SNOW and M.J. WESCHE. 1989. *Content-Based Second Language Instruction.* New York: Newbury House.

BROCK, C. 1986. The effects of referential questions on ESL classroom discourse. *TESOL Quarterly,* 20, no. 1: 47–60.

BUDD-ROWE, M. 1974. Pausing phenomena: Influence on the quality of instruction. *Journal of Psycholinguistic Research,* 3: 203–23.

COELHO, E. 1988. Cooperative group learning: A theoretical and practical overview. Colloquium presentation at TESOL, Chicago.

COELHO, E., L. WINER, and J. W–B. OLSEN. 1989. *All Sides of the Issue.* Hayward, CA: Alemany Press.

COHEN, A. 1984, March. Introspecting about second language learning. Paper presented at the Ninth ILASH Conference, Netanya, Israel. (Cited in Bejarano 1987: 496)

COHEN, E.G. 1980. Design and redesign of the desegregated school: Problems of status, power, and conflict. In W. G. Stephan and J. R. Feagin (eds.), *Desegregation: Past, Present, and Future.* New York: Plenum Press.

————. 1990. Keynote Speech, International Association for the Study of Cooperation in Education, 5th International Convention, Baltimore, MD.

COHEN, P.A., and J.A. KULIK. 1981. Synthesis of research on the effects of tutoring. *Research Information Service,* 39: 227–29.

COOPER, H.M. 1979. Pygmalion grows up: A model for teacher expectation, communication, and performance influence. *Review of Educational Research,* 49: 389–410.

CRANDALL, J. 1987. *ESL Through Content-Area Instruction.* Englewood Cliffs, NJ: Prentice Hall Regents.

CUMMINS, J. 1981. The role of primary language development in promoting educational success for language minority students. In Office of Bilingual Bicultural Education, California State Department of Education (ed.), *Schooling and Language Minority Students: A Theoretical Framework.* Los Angeles: Evaluation, Dissemination, and Assessment Center, California State University.

DANSEREAU, D.F. 1985. Learning strategy research. In J. Segel, S. Chipman, and R. Glaser (eds.), *Thinking and Learning Skills: Relating Instruction to Basic Research, Vol. 1.* Hillsdale, NJ: Erlbaum.

DE AVILA, E.A., S.E. DUNCAN, C. NAVARRETE. 1987. *Finding Out/Descubrimiento.* Northvale, NJ: Santillana.

DEUTSCH, M. 1949. A theory of cooperation and competition. *Human Relations,* 2: 129–52.

DEWEY, J. 1957. *Experience and Education.* New York: Macmillan.

FORD, A.M., and C. SILVERMAN. 1981. *American Cultural Encounters.* Hayward, CA: Alemany Press.

GOODLAD, J.I. 1984. *A Place Called School: Prospects for the Future.* New York: McGraw-Hill.

HERTZ-LAZAROWITZ, R. 1990. Observing students' interaction within an integrative classroom-context. Paper presented at the International Association for the Study of Cooperation in Education, 5th International Convention, Baltimore, MD.

JEW, W., R. TONG, and W. LEFKOWITZ. 1988. *Job Interview Practice Pak.* Hayward, CA: Janus Books.

JOHNSON, D.W., and R.T. JOHNSON. 1986. *Learning Together and Alone* (2nd ed.) Englewood Cliffs, NJ: Prentice Hall.

————. 1987. *Cooperation and Competition.* Hillsdale, NJ: Lawrence Erlbaum.

————. 1989. *Cooperation and Competition: Theory and Research.* Interaction Book Company, 7208 Cornelia Drive, Edina, MN 55435.

JOHNSON, D.W., R.T. JOHNSON, and E.J. HOLUBEC. 1986. *Circles of Learning: Cooperation in the Classroom (revised).* Edina, MN: Interaction Book Company. (See JOHNSON AND JOHNSON, 1989.)

JOHNSON, D.W., R.T. JOHNSON, and G. MARUYAMA. 1983. Interdependence and interpersonal attraction among heterogeneous and homogeneous individuals: a theoretical formulation and a meta-analysis of the research. *Review of Educational Research,* 53: 5–54.

JOHNSON, D.W., G. MARUYAMA, R. JOHNSON, D. NELSON, and L. SKON. 1981. Effects of cooperative, competitive, and individualistic goal structures on achievement: A meta-analysis. *Psychological Bulletin,* 89: 47–62.

JOHNSON, D.W., R. JOHNSON, J. JOHNSON, and D. ANDERSON. 1976. The effects of cooperative vs. individualized instruction on student prosocial behavior, attitudes toward learning, and achievement. *Journal of Educational Psychology,* 68: 446–52.

KAGAN, S. 1977. Social motives and behaviors of Mexican-American and Anglo-American children. In J.L. Martinez (ed.), *Chicano Psychology.* New York: Academic Press.

————. 1985a. The dimensions of cooperative classroom structures. In R. Slavin, S. Sharan, S. Kagan, R. Hertz-Lazarowitz, and R. Schmuck (eds.), *Learning to Cooperate, Cooperating to Learn.* New York: Plenum.

————. 1985b. Co-op co-op: A flexible cooperative learning technique. In R. Slavin, S. Sharan, S. Kagan, R. Hertz-Lazarowitz, C. Webb, and R. Schmuck (eds.), *Learning to Cooperate, Cooperating to Learn.* New York: Plenum.

————. 1986. Cooperative learning and sociocultural factors in schooling. In California State Department of Education (ed.), *Beyond Language: Social and Cultural Factors in Schooling Language Minority Students.* Los Angeles: Evaluation, Dissemination and Assessment Center, California State University.

————. 1988. *Cooperative Learning Resources for Teachers.* San Juan Capistrano, CA: Resources for Teachers.

————. 1989a. *Cooperative Learning Resources for Teachers.* San Juan Capistrano, CA: Resources for Teachers.

————. 1989b. The structural approach to cooperative learning. *Educational Leadership,* 47, no. 4: 12–15.

KLEIN, Z. and Y. ESHEL. 1980. *Integrating Jerusalem Schools.* New York: Academic Press.

LONG, M.H. 1981. Input, interaction, and second language acquisition. In H. Winitz (ed.) *Native Language and Foreign Language Instruction. Annals of the New York Academy of Sciences,* 379: 250–78.

————. 1983. Linguistics and conversational adjustments to non-native speakers. *Studies in Second Language Acquisition,* 5: 177–93.

LONG, M.H., and P. PORTER. 1985. Group work, interlanguage talk, and second language acquisition. *TESOL Quarterly,* 19, no. 2: 207–28.

LONG, M.H., E. BROCK, G. CROOKES, C. DEICKE, L. POTTER, and S. ZHANG. 1984. The effect of teachers' questioning patterns and wait-time on pupil participation in public high school classes. Technical Report No. 1. Center for Second Language Classroom Research. University of Hawaii at Manoa.

LYMAN, F. 1981. The responsive classroom discussion. In A.S. Anderson (ed.), *Mainstreaming Digest.* College Park, MD: University of Maryland.

LYMAN, F. 1989. Rechoreographing: The middle-level minuet. *The Early Adolescent Magazine,* 4, no. 1: 22–24.

MADDEN, N.A., R.E. SLAVIN, and R.J. STEVENS. 1986. *Cooperative Integrated Reading and Comparison: Teacher's Manual.* Baltimore: Johns Hopkins University, Center for Research on Elementary and Middle Schools.

MARTINO, L. and D.W. JOHNSON. 1979. Cooperative and individualistic experiences among disabled and normal children. *Journal of Social Psychology,* 109: 177–83.

McGROARTY, M. 1989. The benefits of cooperative learning arrangements in second language instruction. *NABE Journal,* 13, no. 2 (Winter 1989): 127–43.

MESSERSCHMITT, D.S., and Z. CUI. 1984. *American University Encounters.* Hayward, CA: Alemany Press.

NEVIN, A., D.W. JOHNSON, and R. JOHNSON. 1982. Effects of groups and individual contingencies on academic performance and social relations of special needs students. *Journal of Social Psychology,* 116: 41–59.

OLSEN, J. W–B 1984. *Look Again Pictures for Lifeskills and Language Development.* Hayward, CA: Alemany Press.

————. 1981. *American Business Encounters.* Hayward, CA: Alemany Press.

————. 1989. A Survey of limited English proficient (LEP) student enrollments and identification criteria. *TESOL Quarterly,* 23, no. 3: 469–88.

OLSEN, R.E. W–B, and L.J. REER. 1984. An introduction to cooperative learning. Presentation at California Reading Association, Anaheim, CA.

PALMER, A.S., T.S. RODGERS, and J. W–B. OLSEN. 1988. *Back and Forth: Pair Activities for Language Development.* Hayward, CA: Alemany Press.

PICA, T. 1988. Interlanguage adjustments as an outcome of NS-NNS negotiated interaction. *Language Learning,* 38, no. 1: 45–73.

PICA, T., R. YOUNG, and C. DOUGHTY. 1987. The impact of interaction on comprehension. *TESOL Quarterly,* 21, no. 4: 737–58.

SCHINKE-LLANO, L.A. 1983. Foreigner talk in content classrooms. In H.W. Seliger and M.H. Long (eds.), *Classroom Oriented Research in Second Language Acquisition.* Rowley, MA: Newbury House.

SHARAN, S. 1980. Cooperative learning in small groups: Recent methods and effects on achievement, attitudes, and ethnic relations. *Review of Educational Research,* 50: 241–71.

———. 1989. Cooperative Learning Presentation at the First Annual National Symposium for Cooperative Learning and School Change, San Francisco, CA.

SHARAN, S., and R. HERTZ-LAZAROWITZ. 1980. A group-investigation method of cooperative learning in the classroom. In S. Sharan, P. Hare, C.D. Webb, and R. Hertz-Lazarowitz (eds.), *Cooperation in Education.* Provo, UT: Brigham Young University Press.

———. 1978. *Cooperation and Communication in School* [in Hebrew]. Tel-Aviv and Jerusalem: Shocken. (Cited in Bejarano, 1987: 488).

SHARAN, S., and Y. SHARAN. 1976. *Small-Group Teaching.* Englewood Cliffs: Educational Technology Publications.

SHARAN, S., P. KUSSELL, R. HERTZ-LAZAROWITZ, Y. BEJARANO, S. RAVIV, and Y. SHARAN. 1984. *Cooperative Learning in the Classroom: Research in Desegregated Schools.* Hillsdale, NJ: Erlbaum.

SKON, L., D.W. JOHNSON, and R. JOHNSON. 1981. Cooperative peer interaction versus individual competition and individualistic efforts: Effects on the acquisition of cognitive reasoning strategies. *Journal of Educational Psychology,* 73: 83–91.

SLAVIN, R.E. 1977. How student learning teams can integrate the desegregated classroom. *Integrated Education,* 15: 56–58.

———. 1979. Effects of biracial learning teams on cross-racial relationships. *Journal of Educational Psychology,* 72: 381–387.

———. 1983a. *Cooperative Learning.* New York: Longman.

———. 1983b. When does cooperative learning increase student achievement? *Psychological Bulletin,* 94, no. 3: 429–45.

———. 1990. *Cooperative Learning: Theory, Research, and Practice.* Englewood Cliffs, NJ: Prentice Hall.

———. 1991. Synthesis of research on cooperative learning. *Educational Leadership,* 48: 71–82.

SLAVIN, R.E., M.B. LEAVEY, and N.A. MADDEN, 1986. *Team Accelerated Instruction: Mathematics.* Watertown, MA: Charlesbridge.

SLAVIN, R.E., and E. OICKLE. 1980. Effects of learning teams on student achievement and race relations in a desegregated middle school. Presentation at the American Educational Research Association, 1980.

———. 1981. Effects of learning teams on student achievement and race relations: Treatment by race interactions. *Sociology of Education,* 54: 174–80.

SMITH, K., D.W. JOHNSON, and R. JOHNSON. 1981. Can conflict be constructive? Controversy versus concurrence seeking in learning groups. *Journal of Educational Psychology,* 73: 651–63.

————. 1982. Effects of cooperative and individualistic instruction on the achievement of handicapped, regular, and gifted students. *The Journal of Social Psychology,* 116: 277–82.

————. 1984. Effects of controversy on learning in cooperative groups. *Journal of Social Psychology,* 122: 199–209.

STEBBINS, L.B., R.G. ST. PIERRE, E.C. PROPER, R.B. ANDERSON, and T.R. CERVA. 1977. *Education as Experimentation: A Planned Variation Model, IV-A, An Evaluation of Follow Through.* Cambridge, MA: Abt Associates.

STEVENS, R.J., N.A. MADDEN, R.E. SLAVIN, and A.M. FARNISH. 1987. Cooperative integrated reading and composition: Two field experiments. *Reading Research Quarterly,* 22: 433–54.

STONE, J.M. 1989. *Cooperative Learning & Language Arts: A Multi-Structural Approach.* San Juan Capistrano, CA: Resources for Teachers.

WEBB, N. 1985. Student interaction and learning in small groups: A research summary. In Slavin et al. (eds.), *Learning to Cooperate, Learning to Learn.* New York: Plenum.

————. 1988. Small group problem solving: Peer interaction and learning. *International Association for the Study of Cooperation in Education Newsletter,* 9, nos. 3 and 4: 11–12.

CHAPTER 2

COOPERATIVE LEARNING: FOUNDATION FOR A COMMUNICATIVE CURRICULUM

Elizabeth Coelho

Competition or Cooperation?

What is the competitive ethic? How is it reflected in classroom procedures and student interaction? What are the educational outcomes of a competitive orientation in the classroom? What are the effects of introducing a cooperative learning environment? This section will examine these questions in order to provide a rationale for the implementation of cooperative learning.

The Competitive Ethic in Society

North American culture values competition as a motivational factor in learning. The whole education system is based on the premise that competition brings out the best in us, providing a challenge that good learners are eager to meet. There is a strong belief in society generally that competition—often called "healthy competition"—promotes excellence in business, politics, and education. Acceptance of competition as the major motivator for human progress is so widespread and ingrained that "the competitive instinct" is often believed to be innate, "part of human nature," and the concept of "survival of the fittest" is used to rationalize this belief.

This belief is reflected in media messages all around us. A recent advertisement for the *Encyclopaedia Britannica* uses these slogans: "Today, I've got a big advantage . . . " (child sitting at front of class, beaming over his A+ paper); "Give your child the competitive edge with the most valuable home learning centre in the world;" "What puts some kids head and shoulders above other kids in their class and makes them first with the right answer every time?" and "The Britannica advantage . . . an invaluable study aid that can help your child compete successfully in school today—and compete just as successfully in life tomorrow." Private schools and tutoring programs often attract the parents of students who are already failing to "keep up," who are "falling behind," or "not making the grade" in the educational competition. This advertising message (for automobiles) was recently seen emblazoned on some buses run by the Toronto Transit Commission: "Designed to Compete, Priced to Win."

This kind of advertising reflects a societal preoccupation with competition, getting ahead, and seeking advantage over others. Aronson and his colleagues (1978) observe that winning has become a religion in American society, which asserts its allegiance to winners and its contempt for losers. This emphasis on winning can be very harmful, especially when the stakes are high.

Competition as the principal motivation for excellence is not borne out by research in social psychology. Kohn (1986), reviewing some of this literature, notes that competition requires some individuals to fail in order for others to succeed. He concludes that, contrary to popular assumptions, competitive behavior is learned, not innate, and that competition does not promote superior performance. Debunking the notion of "healthy competition," he analyzes the psychologically and socially damaging effects of competition on individuals and groups in family relationships, education, and business. He makes a convincing case for the value of cooperation in business, in the arts, in leisure activities, in personal relationships, and in education.

The Competitive Ethic in the Classroom

How does competition work in education? In the classroom, students compete for a limited number of good grades and teacher approval. It is commonly accepted, especially at the secondary level, that some students will fail; in fact, there is an expectation in many educational institutions that there will be a distribution of grades that places a few students at the top, the majority bunched around the average, and a few students in the failing range. Teachers are at times challenged by their administrators if all their students pass, or if too many achieve marks in the high range. The conclusion is that the course is too easy.

A typical classroom scenario will illustrate the often damaging effects of the competitive ethic in education. A teacher has just finished making a presentation and is beginning to ask questions of students to check their comprehension of the material presented. The teacher poses a question to the whole class, and waits for volunteers to raise their hands. In most classes, the same few students invariably raise their hands eagerly, anxious to demonstrate their knowledge and gain the teacher's approval. A few others raise their hands tentatively, knowing that the appearance of willingness will also win teacher approval. And there is another group of students who seldom or never volunteer to answer questions in class, maybe because they really can't answer or because they don't care to join in the contest. Perhaps they have already learned that it is too risky, or they are so alienated that they are not interested in the teacher's approval.

Meanwhile, the teacher selects one of the eager students to answer. Others anxious to display their knowledge are disappointed that they are not chosen. Some of them would like the student who was selected to "get it wrong," thus giving *them* a chance to shine. Most teachers must have observed how the disappointed students reluctantly lower their hands, only to wave them vigorously in the air again if the responding student begins to falter. In other words, it is to their advantage if that student fails. Sometimes the student does falter. In concentrating so hard on winning in this contest for teacher approval, when the time comes to answer, the student has forgotten the answer—and possibly the question as well. Kohn (1986) observes that there is a difference between trying to do well and trying to beat others, and that the emphasis on competition often produces inferior results.

The competitive structure of most elementary classrooms does not provide a social environment that promotes respect, trust, or altruism. Goodlad (1984), in his remarkable study of schools in the United States, concludes that classroom life does not encourage group cohesion and cooperation for the achievement of common goals. Aronson (1978) describes the negative and stereotypical attitudes that the students who seldom or never fail hold towards those less successful than themselves. Conversely, unsuccessful students may resent high achievers, grouping together to ostracize those whose academic success reflects unfavorably on themselves. Thus academic success in the competitive classroom carries a penalty: lack of peer approval. Many teachers of adolescents have seen high achievers reject academic success in favor of peer acceptance: a tragic choice for young people to have to make. These are some of the socially and psychologically damaging effects of "healthy competition."

Minority Achievement in the Cooperative Classroom

Clearly the prevailing ethic of competition does not motivate the lower achievers in the class. Who are these lower achievers? It is known that certain groups in North America are particularly at risk. In the United States, Black and Hispanic students are underachieving in the school system, and drop out of high school in disproportionate numbers. In Canada, the same phenomenon has been observed and documented with regard to Greeks and Haitians in Montreal, Blacks and Portuguese in Toronto, and francophone students in the anglophone provinces. Across Canada and the United States it is clear that the school system is still searching for ways of meeting the needs of Native American students. The children of poor families of all racial and ethnic backgrounds do far less well in school than the children of middle-class parents.

Is it possible that the competitive culture of the school is one of the factors in these students' underinvolvement and alienation? Some of the literature on cooperative learning suggests that this is so. According to Spencer Kagan (1986), the competitive structure is culturally biased against minority and low income students. There is considerable evidence that the traditional mode of instruction, which sets students to compete against each other for good grades and teacher approval, is culturally inappropriate for many minority groups. Sharan and Shachar (1988), reporting on recent studies of the effects of cooperative learning experiences on the academic achievement, social integration, and linguistic development of students in multiethnic classrooms in Israel, conclude that cooperative learning experiences equalized the status between ethnic groups, and that this kind of classroom environment promotes integration in the multiethnic or multiracial classroom.

Noting the achievement gap between minority and majority students in U.S. schools, Kagan remarks that this phenomenon is often attributed to lower intelligence or motivation among minority students. He suggests that minority students lack motivation to learn in culturally inappropriate environments that promote competition and individual achievement, and that the deficits in basic skills can be overcome by transforming the social organization of the classroom. Research studies over the last twenty years indicate that restructuring the classroom to provide opportunities for students to work together and learn from each other in carefully structured, heterogeneous learning groups has many positive outcomes for *all* students in terms of academic achievement, and that for minority students the academic gains made in a cooperative environment are outstanding. Reviewing these studies, Robert Slavin (1983) also suggests that some ethnic and racial groups are culturally more predisposed to cooperate, and that they learn best in a learning environment that supports and promotes their cultural values.

For minority students in particular, then, a competitive learning environment cannot be said to be "healthy." The cooperative classroom, fostering peer assistance and peer approval for achievement, provides a more culturally appropriate learning environment: interactive, democratic, and supportive. Many teachers interested in improving the academic performance of minority students are adding cooperative learning to their repertoire of strategies in order to provide this kind of environment.

Affective Development in the Cooperative Classroom

Another factor in the lower achievement levels of minority students is a poor sense of self-worth. Which comes first, low self-esteem or poor performance? It is a self-perpetuating negative cycle that is exacerbated in a classroom situation that isolates students from each other and builds an aversion to learning in countless young people. In contrast, cooperative learning experiences almost always promote higher levels of self-esteem. Does improved self-esteem foster improved academic achievement, or vice-versa? There is a cycle here that is extremely important to students' academic and affective development—both areas of concern for school systems.

We know that many of today's youth are increasingly alienated from school and from society at large. William Glasser (1986) identifies the need to belong as one of the chief psychological needs of all people. This is one of the needs that adolescents seek to satisfy at school and elsewhere in their interactions with others. If it is not satisfied within the academic program, the student becomes alienated from the classroom. Some students find that sense of belonging only through involvement in the sports program, which may partly account for the overrepresentation of some groups; others turn for support and affirmation of self-worth to an equally alienated and disaffected peer group. As we have seen, even the high achievers in the class may experience alienation; their success reflects badly on others, and sometimes brings peer rejection.

In contrast, peer support and acceptance for learning in the cooperative classroom occurs because each student's success is to the benefit of the group. Students feel more in control of their own learning; display more on-task behavior; show improved attendance; like their classmates, the class, the school, the subject, and the teacher better; and become more cooperative and altruistic as a result of cooperative learning experiences. These positive attitudes are likely not only to improve academic performance but to prepare students for effective and nonconfrontational interaction with the community and the world beyond.

Race Relations in the Cooperative Classroom

Most teachers in multicultural, multiracial schools see daily evidence of what Kagan (1986) calls "progressive racism." As children get older, racial and ethnic preferences become stronger. In Canada and the United States, we have only to observe what happens in our classrooms, cafeterias, and schoolyards to confirm this. The traditional school environment and methods of classroom organization do not foster positive race relations. The competitive nature of the classroom may even exacerbate racism by pitting students against each other rather than enabling them to learn to work together. It can be argued that this is a reflection of a social problem wider than an educational one, but it is only within the school setting that it can be addressed. School may be the only place where students have opportunities for daily contact with people of different racial and cultural backgrounds.

According to Gordon Allport (1954), students will not unlearn prejudice simply by going to the same school or sitting in the same class as those of other racial or cultural backgrounds. Specific measures must be taken to equalize status within the school and within the classroom.

Cooperative learning provides an environment that equalizes the status of students. The shared goals of group members result in a common sense of identity and purpose. Shared goals foster positive interpersonal interaction; frequent, meaningful, and mutually supportive contact assists students to view each other in non-stereotypical ways. By assigning students to work in heterogeneous groups, the teacher makes a strong statement about expectations that students can and will work effectively and cooperatively with people of different backgrounds. In fact, more may be achieved by this kind of organizational change in the classroom than by any amount of reading, writing, and talking overtly about race relations. Many studies have revealed that intergroup relations improve dramatically after cooperative learning experiences in heterogeneous groups, and that the improvement in race relations has long-term effects. Slavin (1980) concludes that classrooms promoting interracial cooperation provide the most effective environment for improving students' racial attitudes and behaviors.

Talking to Learn in the Cooperative Classroom

The traditional, competitively oriented classroom is essentially undemocratic and teacher dominated. The importance of talk as a tool for thinking and learning is frequently underestimated, and students spend a lot more time listening in class than talking. According to Flanders (1970), reporting on his studies of interaction patterns in the classroom organized around teacher-led presentation and discussion, the usual distribution of talking time is about 68 percent to the teacher and 20 percent to the students with the remaining 12 percent given to "silence and confusion." In a fifty-minute lesson, therefore, the students as a whole have ten minutes of talking. If there are thirty students in the class, each student talks for twenty seconds—if all students choose to do so. Goodlad's (1984) survey of classrooms in the United States indicates that the ratio of teacher talk to student talk has not improved since Flander's study: teachers still do about 75 per cent of the talking.

In reality, some students say nothing at all during a whole lesson, especially the language learner in the class for whom oral participation in front of the whole class, in a language which does not allow them to display everthing they know or can do, is often very intimidating. For those students who do participate in teacher-led classroom discussions, what is the quality of the interaction? Is the exchange teacher- or student-initiated? How many of the questions are intended to elicit factual recall of information rather than exploration of ideas? How extended are the students' responses? Is there a genuine exchange of information, or is it merely a comprehension check? Students realize that the teacher already knows the answers to the question. They simply must display the same answer. This is testing, not talking.

Flanders (1970) asserts that when classroom interaction patterns favor more initiation and exploration of ideas by the students, they will have more positive attitudes toward the teacher and the curriculum, and academic achievement will be higher. Britton (1970) observes that talk is an important tool for learning; participants benefit both from their own verbalization of ideas and from the contributions of others. Cooperative, small-group instruction provides the kind of structured, organized opportunities that encourage exploratory talk among nonjudgmental peers: a forum for restating, rehearsing, and internalizing new ideas and concepts. The research literature on language and learning suggests that this kind of classroom talk assists students to develop higher-level thinking skills, such as analysis, evaluation, and synthesis of information and ideas. Barnes and Todd (1977) emphasize the importance of talk in clarifying ideas and assisting the understanding of others. In a situation where some of the students have a language other than English as their first language, or are more proficient in a variation of English significantly different from that of the school system (and possibly devalued by it), this kind of oral rehearsal is especially valuable.

Cooperative Learning in the Language Classroom

What are the benefits of cooperative learning to the second language learner? How do the social skills required for cooperative group work support the linguistic objectives of a communicative curriculum? How can cooperative learning strategies be implemented in the second language classroom? This section analyzes the cooperative classroom as a language learning environment and describes some cooperative activities for developing social skills, thinking skills, and functional oral language.

Student Interaction in the Cooperative Classroom

Lack of proficiency in the language of instruction is an important factor in the lower achievement of minority students, whose language is often identified by teachers as "deficient" in some way. Cummins (1986) attributes the failure of many minority students to develop language necessary for academic success to the teacher-centered, transmission-oriented methodology that prevails in many classrooms. An interaction model, on the other hand, develops higher level cognitive skills and meaningful, communicative language skills.

A primary requirement for second language acquisition is the provision of opportunities for frequent and extended interaction in the target language. Language learners need to interact on meaningful tasks with one another and with native speakers of the target language. In the situation where the language of instruction is English, and English is a second language for some or all of the students in the class, there is great value in providing the ESL students with opportunities for interaction with native or more proficient speakers of English. In heterogeneous groups where a range of proficiency in English is represented, from fluent speaker to beginning learner of English, the ESL students interact with peers who serve as language models. There are increased opportunities to question and negotiate meaning. The fluent speakers modify their own language to provide comprehensible input, and the English-language learners model their own language on that of their peers in order to produce comprehensible output. *All* students are learning and extending their language while using it. They become successful communicators because they have a real need to communicate.

Cooperative techniques dramatically increase the amount of time for oral interaction available to each student. Furthermore, the quality of that interaction is greatly improved. Cooperative group work fosters purposeful, task-oriented communication. The task to be completed or the problem to be solved is the students' main focus, but the information-sharing and discussion process assists students in acquiring more of the language and refining their language competence. All students, native speakers or second language learners, benefit from increased opportunities for peer-group interaction on learning tasks. The more opportunities students have for talk, practice, or experience, the better is the retention of new information and ideas. Cooperative learning strategies provide such opportunities.

Cooperative Learning and the Communicative Approach

In recent years, ESL curricula have developed communicative objectives for language learners. Students learn how to communicate effectively in the second language, rather than learn about the language. The focus is on the communicative functions of language: how to use the language in order to carry out specific intentions, such as apologizing or persuading, and to signal the organization of ideas by using rhetorical patterns, such as classification, comparison, or sequence.

If we compare the literature on communicative curriculum design and the literature on cooperative learning, we begin to see some striking parallels. The functional categories described by applied linguists look remarkably similar to the social skills or cooperative group skills described by cooperative learning experts.

Among various taxonomies of language functions are these examples of functional categories given by Finocchiaro (1983):

Referential	**Interpersonal**
paraphrasing/summarizing	indicating agreement/disagreement
asking for explanation	interrupting politely
explaining	sharing feelings
clarifying	
reporting facts	
evaluating results	

The literature on cooperative learning, particularly that of the pedagogical handbooks, emphasizes the need to teach cooperative skills. After years of socialization in the competitive/individualistic mode of learning, students need assistance in learning to work cooperatively. Many of these skills can be regarded as oral communication skills. For example, Kagan's (1987) list of cooperative skills includes specific communicative acts:

Communication Skills	**Conflict Resolution**
active listening/paraphrasing	checking for consensus
relating to ideas and the reactions of others	seeking basis for lack of consensus
	expressing disagreement constructively
checking for understanding	polite, proactive disagreement
asking for clarification	
maintaining eye contact [a culturally based behavior]	

The many parallels between linguistic functions and cooperative group skills suggest that cooperative learning can provide the foundation for a communicative curriculum design. In providing opportunities for students to develop specific group skills, we can focus on the corresponding language functions. We can elicit realizations of these functions or provide examples of the oral strategies needed in their realization.

Oral Strategies for Effective Group Work

What are some of the oral strategies students need for effective interaction in cooperative group work? Do these strategies have application in other kinds of interaction: with friends and co-workers, with employers and other authority figures, with service providers, among others?

Gambits (Keller and Warner, 1976), published by the Public Service Commission of Canada many years ahead of its time in 1976, is a three-book series intended for use with francophone civil servants. The series was developed as the result of some pioneering research on conversational discourse strategies in a variety of formal and informal situations. Eric Keller, then a consultant with the Language Training Branch of the Federal Government of Canada, reports that a classification of 500 oral strategies was developed from data gathered in this research (Keller, 1979). These strategies consist of semi-fixed expressions or oral *gambits* that allow a speaker to initiate or enter a conversation and take turns effectively, signal intent, assert some control over the tone and direction of an oral transaction, and terminate the exchange smoothly. This series focuses on four general categories of gambits: Openers (phrases that open up or initiate a conversation or topic), Links (transitions from one aspect or topic into another), Responders (responses that provide commentary or feedback), and Closers (expressions that terminate the interaction). Each gambit performs certain language functions according to the sociolinguistic context in which it is used. The *Gambits* books provide activities and exercises that allow students to practice the use of these gambits in realistic contexts.

Developing Oral Strategies Through Group Interaction

The following activity, from *Gambits 1: Openers,* practices some oral strategies for interrupting politely: a skill important in many contexts and essential for effective group work.

In a cooperative learning situation, activities like the "Interrupting Game" can be used to help students develop the oral strategies required for effective group interaction. At some point in a cooperative learning activity, the focus shifts away from content to analysis of the process of information sharing. In providing opportunities for students to identify and develop specific group skills, we can focus on the

Interrupting Game

Levels 2–4, class, speaking, game, 10 minutes

Sorry, but

Excuse me for interrupting, but

I might add here

I'd like to comment on that

May I add something?

May I say something here?

I'd like to say something

May I ask a question

The teacher (or a volunteer student) starts to talk on any topic. Anyone in the class can interrupt him or her, using one of the openers suggested at the left. The speaker then answers the person who interrupted, but after that he or she quickly brings the discussion back to the original topic. Try to interrupt as often as possible and in a variety of ways to try to sidetrack the speaker.

Examples

"Last night I went to a hockey game . . . "

"*Excuse me for interrupting, but* which one?"

"The one between the Boston Bruins and the Montréal Canadiens. Anyway, so I went to the game and got to my seat . . . "

"*Sorry, but* where was your seat?"

"In the red section, As I was saying, I got to my seat . . . "

etc.

TO RETURN TO THE TOPIC:

Anyway

In any case

To return to

To get back to

Where was I?

Going back to

TOPICS

what you did last night

a funny thing that happened at work

a joke you heard recently

an argument you've had with someone

how you get to work or to school

a fabulous meal you've cooked recently

corresponding strategies used to realize these intentions orally. For example, while the students are working in groups—exchanging, analyzing, and evaluating information—the teacher as language observer can take note of specific functions the students need to develop in order to make their interaction more effective and satisfying. The teacher chooses a function and matches it to a list of appropriate oral strategies; the *Gambits* material will be helpful.

The following example illustrates how a teacher might use a cooperative learning activity to introduce and practice clarification strategies. The class has not been together very long and some of the students still have difficulty understanding one another. Nevertheless, students need to receive information from one another in order to complete the task or solve the problem that the teacher has assigned. While the students are working, the teacher decides to observe clarification strategies. These include some nonverbal signals (eyebrow-raising, snatching the paper from one another, etc.) and a number of linguistic signals such as the following:

> "Huh?"
> "What?"
> "Whaddaya say?"
> "Did you say . . . ?"
> "Would you spell that?"
> "Would you repeat that?"
> "What did he/she say?"
> "Are you speaking English?"

After the students have completed the task, or that phase of it, the teacher points out that some students were having problems in understanding one another, and writes on the board a list of the nonverbal behavior and oral expressions students used to get around the problem. Then the teacher asks students to brainstorm with their groups in order to add to the list. (At this point there is no evaluation of the appropriateness of certain behavior and language to this situation.) Then each group in turn suggests an addition to the master list on the board until there are no more suggestions to be made. The teacher can assist students in extending the list with some strategies that were not thought of but that would be useful in the classroom and in interactions with others. Students may even recognize expressions that are not yet part of their own productive language. It is the more formal expressions and the idiomatic phrases that probably need extending:

> "I'm sorry, I didn't get that. Would you repeat it, please?"
> "Would you mind going over that again?"
> "I missed that."
> "Would you run that by me again?"
> "Come again?"

The teacher points out that some of the strategies are likely to hinder rather than facilitate the group process. In the list of observed behavior above, expressions such as, "Are you speaking English?" or turning to another student to ask, "What did he/she say?" are put-downs. Using them is likely to inhibit the other student from participating again. Groups should discuss which strategies are more cooperative and less "blaming" than others. As part of this evaluation process, each group makes a list of verbal and nonverbal strategies considered acceptable in the group.

Finally, students need to consider the sociolinguistic rules that govern the choice of one strategy over another, when both perform the same function. In their groups, students discuss which they would (or would not) use, for example, when asking a teacher to repeat or clarify something in class, when speaking to a friend, or when speaking to an unknown person on the phone.

Gambits: Responders, Closers, and Inventory, the third book in the series, has several activities to develop "Incomprehension Responders and Cross-check Gambits." These could be used or adapted as a reinforcement activity the following day.

A list of some of the strategies can be posted in the classroom for future reference and the students reminded to use some of them the next time they work in groups. The cooperative classroom focuses strongly on the process. Groups ask: How did we work on this task? Could it have been better? What kind of language will help? By the end of a school year, the classroom wall will be covered with lists of oral strategies used to realize specific skills. Students will have internalized many of the strategies and incorporated them into their productive language.

Conversational skills such as effective turn-taking, disagreeing, and paraphrasing employ a set of linguistic strategies to convey the intentions of participants in the group process. Ability to recognize and use these strategies can provide students with the tools for interacting effectively with peers and adults in a variety of relationships. With such strategies, students can take more control of daily language transactions and learning experiences. In most classrooms where the students and teacher are native speakers of the same language, the teacher assumes that students know how to realize language functions such as asking for clarification. In situations where some or all of the students are native speakers of a language other than English, or speak a variation of English that does not match that of the teacher, this assumption does not hold true. It is probably not true for all of the native speakers either. The teacher may be looking for a repertoire of middle-class language registers or styles not available to many students. If we want to empower students so that they can interact effectively with peers, teachers, and employers, we have to make sure they do have access to this repertoire of language.

Integrating Cooperative Skills, Language Functions, and Language Structures

The following activity, "Whose Suitcase?" is adapted from an exercise devised by Maingay (1983) on reading labels and making inferences about the owners of the items. This adaptation will demonstrate how we can match functions to group skills, and focus on discrete grammar items as well.

- Students work in groups of four.
- For the first phase of this activity, they form two pairs within each group.
- Each pair receives one of the following discussion tasks and works separately from the other pair in the group.

One pair receives the following student handout.

Whose Suitcase?

At the end of a long day at Toronto International Airport, there are some suitcases left behind. This is a list of the contents of one of them. Use the contents to help you make some inferences about the owner of the suitcase:

> What sex do you think this person is?
> How old do you think this person is?
> What is this person's occupation and income level?
> What is this traveler's destination?
> What is the purpose of the trip?
> What is this person's first language?

The Suitcase: Navy blue suitcase, real leather, excellent condition. No nametags.

The Contents:
1 Pierre Cardin beach towel, navy and beige striped
1 pair of Vuarnet sunglasses
1 Walkman cassette player with several cassettes: American rock music
1 hairdryer with adapter
3 paperback books in Spanish
2 computer magazines
1 pad of artist's paper: unused
1 box of water color paints and brushes: new
1 pair of black pants, waist size 30
1 pair of white shorts, waist size 30
2 T-shirts, size L: 1 red, 1 white
1 pair of jogging shoes, size 9
leather case containing a razor and shaving cream
a bottle of "Chanel for Men" cologne, still in its box
1 bathing suit
5 pairs of underwear by Calvin Klein
5 pairs of socks

The other pair receives the following version:

Whose Suitcase?

At the end of a long day at Toronto International Airport, there are some suitcases left behind. This is a list of the contents of one of them. Use the contents to help you make some inferences about the owner of the suitcase:

> What sex do you think this person is?
> How old do you think this person is?
> What is this person's occupation and income level?
> What is this traveler's destination?
> What is the purpose of the trip?
> What is this person's first language?

The Suitcase: Navy blue suitcase, real leather, excellent condition. No nametags.

> **The Contents:**
> 1 white jacket, 100 percent silk
> white silk pants, size 30
> 1 dictionary: Russian/English
> 1 guidebook: Moscow
> 1 Nikon camera, with two interchangeable lenses, light meter, and tripod
> 20 boxes of film
> soft bag containing heavy silver jewelery
> cosmetics: several brands, including Charles of the Ritz, Helena Rubenstein
> women's underwear: 5 sets
> a bottle of "Chanel No. 5" perfume, half-full
> two fashion magazines: *Vogue*
> 1 hairbrush, real bristle
> two pairs of leather sandals: size 9
> ten Bruce Springsteen cassette tapes, all the same
> five pairs of Levi's blue jeans, different sizes

- When students have reached consensus in their pairs, the teacher informs the class that both suitcases are assumed to belong to the same person.
- Students rejoin the other pair, stating the conclusions reached. Each pair is likely to differ on some of the questions; for example, they will almost certainly have different opinions about the person's gender. The task is to reconcile their inferences with the contents of both suitcases.
- It is not necessary for students to reach consensus. In an attempt to reach consensus some students will opt out of serious discussion, going along with whatever the most dominant member of the group decides is the "right" answer. In fact, there is no answer; all opinions that can be rationalized with reference to the contents of both suitcases are "right." This may be a problem for some students whose previous school experience has taught them that there is only one right answer, and the teacher always has

it. For these students, this kind of problem-solving activity helps to develop a different attitude toward knowledge. They learn that knowledge and opinions are based only on available information. An open mind accepts more information and, if necessary, revises previous hypotheses.

• During discussion, the teacher circulates from group to group, observing and helping. Because this task produces conflicting opinions, the observation should be of how students express disagreement.

• The teacher also acts as a linguistic and cultural consultant. There is a great deal of cultural information in this task. For example, students may miss the significance of a Pierre Cardin beach towel, as opposed to just a beach towel. The teacher emphasizes the importance of asking a cultural informant to explain this kind of detail so that learners may have access to all the information.

Follow-up Activities

1. *Group skills/functions/oral strategies: expression of opinion; how to rationalize an opinion*
   After students have reached their conclusions, the teacher provides a list of opinion openers and rationalization links:

Opinion Openers	**Rationalization Links**
I think	because + verb phrase
I would say	because of + noun phrase
I'm sure	although + verb phrase
It's possible that	in spite of + verb phrase
I guess	
In my opinion,	
It's clear to me that	
Without a doubt	
It's possible that	

   Students write down the inferences they have made about the traveler, using an opinion opener and rationalization link in each sentence.

2. *Group skills/functions/oral strategies: managing disagreement*
   The teacher shares observations about how the students handled disagreement when they had different opinions. Students work together to develop a list of oral strategies. The task below is from *All Sides of the Issue* (Coelho, Winer, and Winn-Bell Olsen, 1989).

Cooperative Skills Sheet:
Managing and Expressing Disagreement

When you are working in a Jigsaw group, each person has different information on the same topic. Sometimes that information is so different that you may have a very different opinion from other members of the group.

Directions: Read the information and questions below. Then work with your group to add to each list. Follow the examples.

1. **Listen to the information that others have.**
   Information from other people may cause you to change your opinion. What can you say to get someone to explain to you why they have a different opinion?

   I don't understand why you think so. Would you explain your reason?

2. **Disagree politely, giving reasons for your opinion.**
   You may have information that will cause others in your group to reconsider their opinion. What can you say to introduce a disagreement or a different opinion?

   I don't agree with you, because

3. **Reach a compromise.**
   Try to find an opinion that everyone can accept. Maybe everyone has to change his or her mind a little bit. If you have listened to everyone, and everyone has listened to you, you may be able to find an opinion on which everyone can agree. What can you say to try to reach a compromise?

   Let's find the points we agree on.

4. **Agree to disagree.**
   If it seems impossible for you to reach a compromise maybe you can agree that it is not necessary for everyone to agree this time. Everyone can have a different opinion as long as they can give good reasons for their opinion. What can you say to close the discussion without forcing everyone to accept the same opinion?

   I guess we all have to make up our own minds about this.

All Sides of the Issue, © 1989, Alemany Press, Hayward, CA. Permission granted to reproduce for classroom use.

The procedure just outlined for "Clarification Strategies" can be used to synthesize and extend the lists of oral strategies for managing disagreement.

3. *Grammar focus: modals to express degrees of certainty*
   The teacher explains and posts a list of modal verbs used to express degrees of certainty (see left-hand list below) and asks students to select modal verbs to comment on some statements about the traveler. Students rehearse their comments orally in groups before writing them down:

Modal Verbs	Degree of Certainty	Rationalization
must be		
got to be	very sure	because/becauseof/
has to be		although/in spite of
may be		
might be	possible	
could be		
can't be	impossible	

Use the pattern above to comment on these statements about the traveler:

The traveler is a man.
The traveler is going to a country in Latin America.
The traveler is over sixty years old.
The traveler is a photographer.
This person's first language is Spanish.
This person is traveling during the summer.
This person is very organized.
This person is traveling first-class.
This person enjoys swimming.
This person is very status conscious.

4. *Adaptation of the activity*
   Students are told that a third suitcase, identical to the other two, has been found. They write a list of contents of the third suitcase, giving reasons for including each item.
   This kind of activity can be adapted for different age groups. Two different lists are made of, for example, the toys in a toybox, the contents of bags of groceries in a shopping cart, the contents of different rooms in a house, or the contents of a school locker or schoolbag. Each list should seem to point toward different inferences.
   Young children or preliterate students work with pictures or real objects.

Older students will enjoy creating a problem like this: Each group writes a problem, prepares two lists (or draws pictures, or gathers realia), and gives the problem to another group to solve.

As an independent assignment or test, students receive a single list and make written inferences from it, using the rhetorical and grammatical patterns practiced in class.

The activity can be adapted to specific curriculum areas. Content-area tasks might include characteristics or properties of a living organism, a historical figure, a character from a novel, a geographic region, or a contemporary politician/writer/musician/scientist, for example. Each list should leave "information gaps" so that students need the information from the other list in order to make positive identification.

Conclusion

Cooperative learning is relevant to all teachers and students, particularly in multiracial, multicultural classrooms where some or all of the students are still learning the language of instruction. This kind of classroom and curriculum organization provides a culturally appropriate learning environment that can raise the levels of academic achievement of minority students, promote the affective development of students, improve race relations, and encourage the kind of exploratory talk that assists students in comprehending and internalizing new ideas and information. The cooperative classroom also provides a supportive and empowering language learning environment where students can develop and rehearse the language they need for effective interaction in a variety of contexts beyond the classroom.

REFERENCES

ALLPORT, G. 1954. *The Nature of Prejudice*. Reading, MA: Addison-Wesley.

ARONSON, E., N. BLANEY, C. STEPHAN, J. SIKES, and M. SNAP. 1978. *The Jigsaw Classroom*. Beverly Hills and London: Sage Publications.

BARNES, D., and F. TODD. 1977. *Communication and Learning in Small Groups*. London: Routledge & Kegan Paul.

BRITTON, J. 1970. *Language and Learning*. Coral Gables, FL: University of Miami Press.

COELHO, E. 1991. *Jigsaw*. Revised edition. Markham, Ontario: Pippin Publishing Limited.

COELHO, E., and L. WINER. 1991. *Jigsaw Plus*. Revised edition. Markham, Ontario: Pippin Publishing Limited.

COELHO, E., L. WINER, and J. W-B. OLSEN. 1989. *All Sides of the Issue*. Hayward, CA: Alemany Press.

CUMMINS, J. 1986. Empowering minority students: A framework for intervention. *Harvard Educational Review,* 56, no. 1: 18–36.

FLANDERS, N.A. 1970. *Analyzing Teaching Behaviour.* Reading, MA: Addison-Wesley.

FINOCCHIARO, M. 1983. *The Functional/Notional Approach: From Theory to Practice.* New York: Oxford University Press.

GLASSER, W. 1986. *Control Theory in the Classroom.* Harper and Row.

GOODLAD, J. 1984. *A Place Called School: Prospects for the Future.* New York: McGraw Hill.

KAGAN, S. 1986. Cooperative learning and sociocultural factors in schooling. In *Beyond Language: Social and Cultural Factors in Schooling Language Minority Students,* (pp. 231–98). Los Angeles: Evaluation, Dissemination, and Assessment Center. California State University.

———. 1987. *Cooperative Learning Resources for Teachers,* 4th ed. Riverside, CA: Resources for Teachers.

KELLER, E. 1979. Gambits: Conversational strategy signals. *Journal of Pragmatics,* 3, nos. 3–4: 219–38.

KELLER, E., and S.T. WARNER. 1976. *Gambits: Openers; Gambits: Links; Gambits: Responders and Inventory Closers.* Ottawa: Public Service Commission.

KOHN, A. 1986. *No Contest: The Case Against Competition.* New York: Houghton Mifflin.

MAINGAY, S. 1983. *Making Sense of Reading.* London: Harrap.

SHARAN, S., and H. SHACHAR. 1988. *Language and Learning in the Cooperative Classroom.* New York: Springer-Verlag.

SLAVIN, R. 1983. *Cooperative Learning.* New York: Longman.

SLAVIN, R.E. 1980. Cooperative learning. *Review of Educational Research,* 50, no. 2: 315–42.

CHAPTER 3

LANGUAGE AND COGNITIVE DEVELOPMENT THROUGH COOPERATIVE GROUP WORK

Wendy McDonell

Introduction

The challenge for English as a second language teachers is to maximize the language and learning potential of our students. All teachers know that language plays an important role in education. Language is the means of expression and communication, the medium of thought and a central tool for learning. It pervades all aspects of the educational experience and is directly linked to academic success in schools. The role of teachers who themselves are empowered becomes one of empowering learners and, in turn, one also of empowering their nation. Educators who promote children's proficiency in two languages empower minority students, their parents, and contribute to creation of a linguistically competent nation. (Cummins, 1989).

Equally important is the fact that one of the aims of education is to assist students to achieve a high degree of language competence so that they may achieve personal fulfillment, reach their potential, and participate in society in a meaningful way. For minority students, becoming an effective language user gives access to mainstream culture. In this regard, language serves as a liberating tool.

In the past, second language teaching focused on the learning of grammar and vocabulary. A later shift to a communicative approach to language teaching was further refined in the distinctions made between *social communicative proficiency* and *academic communicative proficiency* (Cummins, 1981b). Although the ability to communicate with native speakers of English for social purposes—social communicative proficiency—is critical for the adjustment of immigrant students to the schooling situation, it does not necessarily lead to academic success. For that reason second language learners must develop language for academic purposes—academic communicative proficiency. This language of instruction is difficult because it is context-reduced, cognitively demanding, and draws on literacy-related features of reading and writing in academic settings.

Another important issue in language teaching is an understanding that effective language users are not those who speak "correctly" but rather, those who speak "appropriately" (Klein, 1981). In other words, second language learners must know when and how to adjust the structure and form of language to a variety of contexts and how to fulfill a variety of functions. These purposes and uses of language are central to the development of meaning.

This chapter presents a view of language as a collaborative, meaning-making process shaped by social contexts and the purposes for which language is used (Dwyer, 1989). It concentrates on talk, the basic form in which language is manifested. It looks at how children learn to talk, learn through talk, and learn about talk in a cooperative classroom. Specifically, this chapter on language and learning considers language and thinking in the context of their functional use; the image of the learner in the learning process; the connection between talk and learning; and lastly, the reasons why collaborative group work helps the language learner to learn language, learn through language, and learn about language.

The Nature of Language Learning

Learning a First Language

How and why do children learn to talk? It is necessary to begin with this question because the how and why of language development are inseparable. The reason why children learn language at home can be answered by simply saying that they have a need to communicate and a desire to get things done.

According to Frank Smith (1988), infants have a sense of what spoken language does. Young children learn language and its uses simultaneously. (Halliday, 1973). Smith further notes that language uses engage every human endeavor—physical, cognitive, emotional. All of these uses must be demonstrated to those learning language. It is from these language demonstrations that children make sense of the speech they hear and learn how to mean as the society around them does (Halliday, 1975).

Children discover "how to mean," that is, how to make sense of their world, because parents or family members interact with them in purposeful activities. All the opportunities for the social basis of talk are provided when the adult and child interact with one another. Talk initiated by the child, turn-taking, the giving of new information, responses, and attention to each other's meaning are all part of child–adult discourse.

Smith (1988), in his book *Joining the Literacy Club,* directs our attention to the role of expectation in learning to talk. He says that children are admitted to the spoken language club on one criterion: You are one of us. The adult members do not doubt that children will speak. Rather they know that the junior members will attain competence in time. They expect mistakes; there are no labels of discrimination against children for their levels of language development. The role of parents or other family members, friends, and caregivers is critical. Adults help the child to say what the child is trying to say and help the child to understand what the child is trying to understand. The communicative partners acknowledge the child's contributions, sustain and extend the talk initiatives, and provide a scaffold that supports and encourages talk (Bruner, 1981). The help and support that is given is always appropriate and makes sense.

Throughout this whole process of negotiation of meaning and shared experiences children are involved in a purposeful range of activities that make sense to them. It is obvious from this account that the discovery of how language works is essentially a collaborative process.

Most of what we learn, we learn through language even before schooling begins (Halliday, 1989). By the time children enter school, they have learned a lot about language and all seem to have acquired a basic linguistic repertoire in their first language, although the uses of language may differ. They have learned language by actively constructing an internalized grammar, rather than by imitating language to form a set of habits.

Learning a Second Language

The same basic conditions for learning a first language apply when students are learning English as a second language. That is, a second language is learned when there is an emphasis on meaning-making in the context of purposeful activity, as well as the presence of learning language, learning through language, and learning about language (Halliday, 1979).

Enright and McCloskey (1988), summarize the current theoretical position in second language education by noting that second language acquisition is a highly interactive and collaborative process. Second language learners actively construct and test out hypotheses about how language works as they communicate with others in meaningful activities. This would appear to be very similar to what has been described in learning a first language.

In the field of second language acquisition theory, the emphasis on meaning is greatly supported by Krashen's work. His *Input Hypothesis* (1985) provides a rationale for why second language learners gain language competence better with a small-group approach rather than through a methodology that emphasizes the memorizing of vocabulary words, drill exercises, and grammar work in isolation. Second language acquisition is successful because the focus is on the message rather than the form.

According to Krashen, second language learners acquire language by understanding language that is a bit beyond the learner's current level. That is, they go for the essential meaning of the communication. Even when the language contains structures that are unfamiliar, the learner can use context, extralinguistic information, and knowledge of the world to decipher the meaning. As long as the language is not too far beyond the learner's capacities, it functions as ''comprehensible input'' for second language learning.

The instructional implication is that ESL learners gain from being involved in genuine communication with first language users of English. In this situation they will more likely receive comprehensible input, because by *focusing on communication,* native speakers will make use of nonverbal and contextual support to assure that their meaning is understood (Krashen, 1981).

The Functional Approach to second language acquisition theory also endorses cooperative learning methodology. This approach provides children with the language functions essential for academic success (Chamot, 1983). Language functions refer to what the learner can do with language, such as giving and receiving information, asking for clarification, and expressing agreement or disagreement. Cummins' (1981a, b; 1984) model of language proficiency reflects this theoretical orientation as well with its identification of two aspects of language proficiency—social communicative proficiency and academic communicative proficiency. The objective of Cummins' approach is to help children learn the functions that are part of decontextualized language proficiency in order that they may succeed in the classroom.

Again the implication for instructing minority language children is to make use of the collaborative group process. From the discussion in Chapter 2 on cooperative learning as a foundation for a communicative curriculum, we can see many parallels between cooperative group skills and linguistic functions associated with academic uses of language. This supports that view that cooperative learning is ideal for providing a foundation for communicative curriculum design.

From the literature on first and second language learning, certain basic principles about language learning for children find agreement. The following list adapted from *Readers and Writers with a Difference* by Rhodes and Dudley-Marling (1988) articulates these principles:

1. Children learn language by using language.
2. The focus in language learning is on meaning and social function rather than form.

3. Language learning is personally important, concretely based, and free from anxiety.
4. Children learn to use language in an ever-widening variety of contexts and to vary their language for the context in which it occurs.
5. Knowledge of language rules is largely intuitive. Children form rules from language input and employ these rules to use language.
6. Language learning is largely self-directed.
7. The conditions necessary for language learning are similar for all children, although the rate of development may vary.

The conditions that make for successful language learning have been identified by Brian Cambourne, an Australian researcher on learning and literacy (Cambourne, l988). These conditions are relevant to all kinds of language learning—for example, learning to read and write and learning a second language. Cambourne also believes that these conditions are transferable to classroom practice. The conditions are as follows (Cambourne, 1988):

1. **Immersion**: All children are immersed in purposeful, meaningful, and whole language from birth.
2. **Demonstration** of how the medium is used. This can make use of either actions or artifacts.
3. **Engagement** with the demonstration is made available once the learners see themselves as able to do the demonstration and see it as purposeful to their lives.
4. **Expectations** are communicated to learners in subtle ways. These expectations, implicit or explicit, work against or in favor of learning.
5. **Responsibility** for one's own learning. Children are left to decide what they will learn about their language.
6. **Use:** Learners need time and opportunity to use and practice their developing language skills.
7. **Approximations**: Learners are not expected to display adult competence from the beginning and are free to approximate or "have a go." These attempts at using the new language are received in a positive way.
8. **Response**: The mutual exchange between expert and novice is meaning-centered, nonthreatening, functional, and relevant to the child's needs.

To summarize this section, language is learned when it is real, natural, whole, sensible, interesting, relevant, purposeful, part of a real event, accessible to the learner, and allows for learner choice. More importantly, the learner has the power to use it (Goodman et al., 1987; Goodman, l986).

How We Learn

Children learn long before they come to school. Every child who learns language learns through language. Language and thinking develop together and are nurtured through both personal and social forces. The work of Vygotsky has provided us with the understanding that thinking is not an individual act (Moll, 1988). Vygotsky's (1978) theory of learning supports the collaborative approach because it analyzes how we are embedded with one another in a social world.

In many ways, Vygotsky's view of language and learning is similar to that of Halliday (1983, 1979). Both view language and learning as a process of making sense and as a social activity. In Vygotskyan terms, human learning is always mediated through others—parents, peers, and teachers—and these interactions themselves are mediated (Moll, 1988). In other words, learning is a collaborative enterprise in which the adult engages in a dialogue with the child in such a way that the child is enabled to solve a problem that he or she was unable to manage alone.

Vygotsky (1978) proposed his concept of the "zone of proximal development" in order to make sense of the relationship of society and the individual and social and cognitive development. He defined the zone as the distance between what a child can do in isolation—that is, the actual *developmental* level—and what the child can do in collaboration with others. This he called the *proximal* level. The distance between these points (the actual and the proximal) is the zone of proximal development. Good learning for Vygotsky is always that which advances development to the next zone.

Vygotsky made this proposal in reaction to the use of IQ testing as a way of finding out about the child's cognition. He advocated that more information could be acquired about the child's thinking if educators were to concentrate on the child in social activities. If we look at the child in a collaborative setting, the processes and activities that remain hidden in individual tasks are revealed to us. This perspective offers ESL teachers a means to increase the range of competence of second language learners. Implicit in the notion of zone of proximal development is the assumption of how we learn. The main path of learning proceeds from the social to the individual. The individual is actively involved at all times. Hence, what is the proximal level today in collaboration with others will be the actual developmental level tomorrow.

Vygotsky places a great deal of emphasis on the nature of the interaction between the child and the teacher. These communicative interactions between adult and child are basic to the expanding and extending of language. He also suggests that the quality of these interactions in specific problem-solving environments are in direct relation to the intellectual skills that the children will acquire. One element that is essential to these interactions is cooperation (Moll, 1988).

This theory also presents a view of teaching as a process of mediation, which is consistent with the cooperative learning approach. In the chapter on the role of the teacher, a more detailed account of the teacher as a facilitator of learning is given.

As mentioned previously, Vygotsky views the learner as an active participant in the learning process. This is consistent with the image of the learner envisioned by many educators who support a child-centered approach. The learner is a self-motivated, self-directed problem solver who derives a sense of self-worth and confidence from a variety of accomplishments as pointed out in a document from the Canadian Ministry of Education (1980). For fear that this image of the learner be viewed as too idealistic or holds true for only some students, it should be stressed that this image applies potentially to all learners.

What do learners do, then, during the learning process? To begin with, learners are always learning. They actively construct knowledge for themselves as they search for meaning. In order to construct this knowledge, learners draw on what they already know. Learning does not occur in a vacuum. Drawing on prior knowledge, learners generate hypotheses about the new, which they test out, alter, or refine on the basis of their experiences. These experiences include social exchanges with others, learner reflections, and demonstrations of learning. It is important to note that learning is not neat and sequentially ordered. Rather it is likely to be spiral in nature, and this spiral is both self-regulating and self-preserving.

Clearly this learning theory has implications for educators. In order to facilitate learning, we must start with learners, finding out what they know so that we can plan meaningful learning experiences. Learners will also need opportunities to learn from and to teach one another. They must have freedom of choice so that they can investigate from their own perspectives. They will come to value their own experiences and thoughts as they learn new information. Teachers can encourage a variety of learning styles and multimodal sources of information to achieve the learning outcomes. There is no need for extrinsic rewards because the motivation to learn—the desire to make sense—lies within the child. Learning experiences become whole, purposeful, and negotiable. Teachers trust the learners and respect the fact that they are responsible for their own learning. Lastly, the climate for learning is collaborative, cooperative, natural, authentic, useful, anxiety free, nonjudgmental, and meaningful to the learner.

The Role of Language in Learning

Language is a tool for learning. Traditionally, much emphasis has been placed on using language for learning language. What has not been stressed is that learning to use language and language for learning are inseparable. In the last decade there have been many educational reports written in the United States, England, and Australia that have endorsed the value of talk as a means of student learning and assessment. Among recent reports is that from England, Department of Education and Science (1988), the *National Curriculum Council: English for Ages 5–11*. It observes that interactive spoken language is recognized as a powerful means of learning across an increasingly wide spectrum of society. It also urges that children be able to demonstrate ability to use spoken language effectively in a variety of contexts, matching style and response to audience and purpose.

Before we discuss how to achieve this goal, we must clarify what is meant by talking to learn and why it is a valuable tool for learning. Talking to learn is speculative or thinking aloud talk. This exploratory talk is important because it helps learners to:

- sort out their thinking
- clarify meaning
- explore their ideas
- think up questions
- suggest possible answers
- negotiate meaning and intention
- link events in some way
- look for causes and reasons
- shape understanding
- interpret and reflect on experiences
- exercise imagination
- define who they are to others and themselves.

To best illustrate the point that simply talking aloud results in more effective learning than just passively listening, think how often you have been engaged in a natural conversation and you, the speaker, have realized that you gained more from that conversation than the listener. In this circumstance you were not really talking to communicate; rather, you were talking to learn.

Young children demonstrate this process naturally at home while engaged in play or some other concrete experience. For them talking and thinking are inextricably intertwined. To silence them would inhibit their thinking.

I am also reminded of the time that I overheard an ESL fifth grader say to herself after many hesitations, pauses, rephrasings, and change of directions, ''Now I really understand it.'' As I observed her in the group process I knew that she was simultaneously monitoring what she was saying and thinking ahead to what she wanted to say next. Finally, she had fixed the ideas firmly in her mind and had personalized her knowledge.

Group work fosters talking to learn. Pairs or small groups provide nonthreatening situations so that each child talks readily and is often encouraged to talk. It is important to remember that talk does not take place in a vacuum and for that reason students need to talk about something. They need real problems to solve and real situations to explore. The subject matter should be linked to their experience in order that their prior knowledge can be used.

Since listening, too, is a means of learning, much attention must be given to listening as well. This is acknowledged in the Department of Education and Science report from London (1988), which stresses that the ability to listen actively is crucial to effectiveness in using the spoken language appropriately.

The opportunities best suited for talk-for-learning are problem solving, such as in math or science, making decisions, brainstorming, project work, and role-play. Of course, these opportunities are part of every subject and organic to a unit, theme, or integrated learning.

Learning through cooperative group work is a gradual process. Teachers must be patient and not force the pace. Children need to come to trust and value one another as learning partners. As mentioned before, they need to learn how to listen to one another and be encouraged to talk in an exploratory manner in the group process.

Sometimes talk in the small-group process is affected by the membership of the group. This could be a result of personalities, attitudes toward race and culture, and the relationship between boys and girls. That is why cooperative group work is useful and appropriate: Group members learn how to work together as they practice social and cooperative skills. During the reflection stage, group members have a chance to look closely at the group process and their role in it.

Learning through cooperative group work allows second language learners the opportunity to:

- generate more ideas and be exposed to different points of view
- develop tolerance for ambiguity
- experience incidental and planned opportunities that use language as a tool for learning
- learn from and teach one another in a supportive environment
- ask their own questions so that they own their learning and have better retention
- make use of exploratory talk; offer possible suggestions and tentative ideas
- realize the fact that their talk helps them to understand better
- gain confidence while learning as a result of peer support and encouragement
- acquire higher-level thinking skills (for example, to speculate, hypothesize, and generalize) because of the potential for *what if* questions to occur
- develop short- and long-term recall of information
- experience genuine intellectual inquiry that cultivates moral and intellectual autonomy
- value their thinking and experiences during the learning process
- become more responsible for their own learning and the learning of others
- see how others learn and how they themselves learn
- have shared experiences that become the basis for learning
- present what they know and reflect on how they learned it (i.e., develop metacognitive knowledge)

- build on what they know already with increased motivation in order to get more information that makes use of critical thinking skills
- develop problem-solving strategies
- attain better academic achievement
- learn in a context compatible to their culture
- develop empathetic perspectives as a result of working together
- learn how to work together (i.e., acquire social skills)
- develop a liking for self and others.

In concluding this section I would like to address a significant factor for talk in the classroom—the teacher variable. Teachers committed to talk for learning do the following:

- listen to what the children have to say; take seriously what they say
- encourage learners to talk with each other
- minimize their own teacher talk
- accept the children's questions and comments
- allow learners to speak and think for themselves
- encourage learners to find out what they know and want to know
- value and respect the language of each child

The Cooperative Classroom and the Second Language Learner

What does the cooperative classroom offer the second language learner? Research informs us that the greatest growth in language and cognitive development is made by a child who is in a rich and collaborative environment with an informed teacher. The cooperative classroom is such an environment because it provides the foundation for a communicative classroom and is organized for collaboration, purpose, student interest, previous experience, holism, support and variety (Enright and McCloskey, 1985).

Learners become more proficient in language as a result of group work because they:

- have more comprehensible input through peer interactions
- have better listening skills as a result of responding and acting on what has been said
- receive immediate response to their participation
- build on the talk of others through elaboration and/or restatement

- have longer conversational turns than in the whole-class teaching situation
- consult with each other to seek opinions and information
- initiate their own questions, articulate their needs and interests
- become aware of audience, purpose, and social context
- exchange information about ideas, feelings, and needs
- have access to a more varied and complex use of language
- focus with conversational partners on meaning and what is appropriate, rather than on accuracy
- have continual comprehension checks and clarification requests
- relate new information about language to existing information
- experience individually appropriate language with extralinguistic support (e.g., facial expression, diagrams) to aid understanding
- make use of their own natural learning power in a positive and accepting environment

In addition to these opportunities for language development provided through a cooperative group process is the fact that second language learners acquire school-information talk critical for academic success. This highly valued information-related talk dominates life in the classroom and in the workplace (Brown et al, 1984). The purpose of such talk is to transfer information to a listener who needs it. Samples of school talk include: recounting an anecdote, paraphrasing, justifying a position, describing or explaining a process, or giving instructions (see Appendix for a more complete list). Research of Joan Tough (1977) found that many children, first and second language users, do not engage in school talk. They do not use language to recall, reason, anticipate, or predict outcomes, analyze events and consider alternatives, project into new situations, develop imaginative situations, and hypothesize.

Once teachers become aware of the range of language functions needed for effective school talk, they can plan appropriate learning experiences to facilitate use of such language. This knowledge also enables teachers to assess spoken language. Teachers can provide appropriate demonstrations of how language is used in school to get things done—for example, how to ask someone for more information.

Simply putting learners into groups is not going to guarantee that they work and learn cooperatively. Gains in language are facilitated by attention to the learning climate, group process, and social skills. Learners succeed in their verbal exchanges with one another because they are concerned about the performance of all group members and know they are accountable to each other. Group members talk about how they worked together, reflect on what they learned, and identify the social skills that they want to practice.

During the processing stage for cooperative learning, I have often observed that children ask more questions and make comments about language as they become more proficient with language. It would appear that metalinguistic awareness is a by-product of language development. Directly linked to this metalinguistic knowledge is the development of metacognitive strategies. These are strategies that involve thinking about the learning process, planning for learning, monitoring of learning while it is taking place, and self-evaluation after the learning experience.

Conclusion

This chapter offers an explanation for why a cooperative classroom works so effectively for children learning language. It articulates a theory of language and cognitive development to help teachers know how children learn concepts and learn language. Such knowledge greatly influences the quality and quantity of learning in the classroom.

If teachers are not informed by theory, they cannot communicate their goals or reflect on their decisions to use appropriate teaching strategies within their program. They will be easily swayed by every technique, strategy, idea or approach that comes their way. Their ability to empower second language learners with language can be limited by a lack of theoretical knowledge. Not being rooted in an educational foundation that balances theory and practice is to be somewhat like tumbleweed blown about by the wind.

The message of vital importance in this chapter is that children who learn within a cooperative classroom will be better prepared for the challenge of the future because they will be better able to communicate, collaborate, negotiate, problem solve, and think critically. If we are to achieve our goal of empowering our children with language so that they can be successful in school and the world in general, can we afford not to commit ourselves to a pedagogy that could transform our classrooms and assist us in realizing our goal?

Appendix

Language Uses in the Classroom:

analyze	express likes/dislikes
anticipate	give/respond to instructions
argue	hypothesize
ask for help	imagine
brainstorm	interview
clarify	justify judgments/actions
define	make choices
describe	make comparisons
draw conclusions	make requests
explain	organize ideas

paraphrase	reflect
predict	refuse/offer alternatives
project	report
question	solve problems

REFERENCES

BROWN, G., A. ANDERSON, R. SHILLCOCK, and G. YULE. 1984. *Teaching Talk: Strategies for Production and Assessment.* Cambridge, England: Cambridge University Press.

BRUNER, J. 1981. The pragmatics of acquisition. In Deutsch, W. (ed.), *The Child's Construction of Language,* (pp. 39–55). New York: Academic Press.

CAMBOURNE, B. 1988. *The Whole Story: Natural Learning and the Acquisition of Literacy in the Classroom.* Auckland, New Zealand: Ashton Scholastic Limited.

CHAMOT, A.U. 1983. Toward a functional ESL curriculum in the elementary school. *TESOL Quarterly,* 17, no. 3: 459–71.

CUMMINS, J. 1981a. *Bilingualism and Minority-Language Children.* Toronto: The Ontario Institute for Studies in Education.

————. 1981b. The role of primary language development in promoting educational success for language minority students. In *Schooling and Language Minority Students: A Theoretical Framework.* Los Angeles, CA: Evaluation, Dissemination, and Assessment Center, California State University.

————. 1984. *Bilingualism and Special Education: Issues in Assessment and Pedagogy.* San Diego: College-Hill Press.

————. 1989. *Empowering Minority Students.* Sacramento: California Association for Bilingual Education.

Department of Education and Science, 1988. *National Curriculum Council: English for Ages 5–11.* London, England.

DWYER, J. (ed.) 1989. *A Sea of Talk.* Rozelle, NSW, Australia: Primary English Teaching Association.

ENRIGHT, D.S., and M. MCCLOSKEY. 1985. Yes talking! Organizing the classroom to promote second language acquisition. *TESOL Quarterly,* 19, no. 3: 431–53.

————. 1988. *Integrating English: Developing English Language and Literacy in the Multicultural Classroom.* Reading, MA: Addison-Wesley.

GOODMAN, K. 1986. *What's Whole in Whole Language?* Richmond Hill, Ontario: Scholastic TAB Publications.

GOODMAN, K., E.B. SMITH, R. MEREDITH, and Y. GOODMAN. 1987. *Language and Thinking in School.* New York: Richard C. Owen Publishers.

HALLIDAY, M.A.K. 1973. *Explorations in the Functions of Language.* London: Edward Arnold Publishers.

————. 1975. *Learning How to Mean: Explorations in the Development of Language.* London: Edward Arnold Publishers.

————. 1979. Three aspects of children's language development: Learning language, learning through language, learning about language, in Y. Goodman, M. Haussler, and D. Strickland (eds.), *Oral and Written Language Development Research: Impact on the Schools.* Urbana, IL: National Council of Teachers of English.

HALLIDAY, M.A.K. 1989. *Spoken and Written Language,* Oxford: Oxford University Press.

KLEIN, M. L. 1981. Key generalizations about language and children. *Educational Leadership:* 446–448.

KRASHEN, S.D. 1981. Bilingual education and second language acquisition theory. In *Schooling and Language Minority Students: A Theoretical Framework.* Los Angeles: Evaluation, Dissemination, and Assessment Center, California State University.

———. 1985. *Inquiries and Insights.* Hayward, CA: Alemany Press.

Ministry of Education, 1980. *Issues and Directions.* Toronto: Ministry of Education and Ministry of Colleges and Universities.

MOLL, L.C. December 1988. *Teaching second-language students: A Vygotskyan perspective.* Paper presented at Whole Language and Literacy Processes Seminar. Tucson: University of Arizona.

RHODES, L.K., and C. DUDLEY-MARLING. 1988. *Readers and Writers with a Difference.* Portsmouth, NH: Heinemann Educational Books.

SMITH, F. 1988. *Joining the Literacy Club.* Portsmouth, NH: Heinemann Educational Books.

TOUGH, J. 1977. *The Development of Meaning: A Study of Children's Use of Language.* London: Allen & Unwin.

Vygotsky, L.S. 1978. *Mind in Society.* Cambridge, MA: Harvard University Press.

CHAPTER 4

SCIENCE AND COOPERATIVE LEARNING FOR LEP STUDENTS

Carolyn Kessler, Mary Ellen Quinn, Ann K. Fathman

Nobel prizes in science—great breakthroughs in understanding the wonders of the universe—are almost always the result of cooperative learning. Working together, sometimes across oceans and continents, often through using English as a second language, scientists learn from one another, and together make discoveries that ultimately benefit us all. In a very real sense, science and cooperative learning have a long historical relationship, one that is growing stronger with advances in global telecommunication. Scientists, no matter what their first language and culture, understand clearly the relevance of team work in problem solving, in probing new avenues of inquiry.

This chapter addresses how cooperative learning strategies can serve to integrate science and language learning for limited English proficient (LEP) students, particularly upper elementary, middle, and senior high school students. LEP students are those learners coming from a variety of linguistic and cultural backgrounds without sufficient access to English to succeed in a mainstream English-only classroom (Lessow-Hurley, 1990). The connections between cooperative learning, science and language learning given here also are relevant for any special population needing further development in English as a second language (ESL). This development can occur in heterogeneous groupings with learners at different levels of English language proficiency working together on the same science activity.

For English to serve as a medium of science learning for LEP students, integration of language and science content requires organizing science experiences in specific ways to facilitate development of both language and cognitive processes. An overview of principles associated with science learning/teaching and language learning/teaching provides the framework that supports the integration of science and language instruction in a cooperative setting.

Science Learning

Science is defined by what it does, by how it is done, and by the results it achieves. It is a way of thinking and doing, as well as a body of knowledge (AAAS, 1989). Science is generally defined as a set of concepts and relationships developed through the processes of observation, identification, description, experimental investigation, and theoretical explanation of natural phenomena (Kessler and Quinn, 1987a).

Cooperative learning provides an ideal instructional starting point for science learning. It provides a means to engage science learners in concrete experiences, to help them work together as they learn to think critically, analyze information, and link concepts that build on the structural foundations of science.

Aware of the widening gap between genuine science inquiry and science education in the United States, science educators have called for profound reform. Science education in the schools is undergoing major curriculum changes, described in the report of the American Association for the Advancement of Science, *Science for All Americans* (AAAS, 1989); the National Center for Improving Science Education report, *Science and Technology Education for the Elementary Years* (Bybee, 1989); and the National Science Teachers' Association's 1991 Scope, Sequence and Coordination program.

Today's science teaching is becoming thematic. Hazen and Trefil (1991) have selected twenty "Great Ideas in Science" that draw upon concepts common in all of natural science. Concepts build upon a structure of the major ideas that connect the disciplines of science. Integrating physics, biology, chemistry, earth/space science as well as other disciplines fosters thematic teaching. It is meant to foster the intellectual ability to connect ideas both within the broad fields of science and across to other subjects. Thematic teaching is closely linked to constructivist teaching, a model of learning borrowed from cognitive psychology (Clemson, 1990; Sachse, 1989). It takes into account prior experiences, knowledge, and ideas that students have about a particular theme. Assessment of and sensitivity to student worldviews contribute to the shaping of science teaching, of doing what is needed to change misconceptions often highly resistant to change. Science educators recognize cooperative learning as an excellent instructional procedure for constructivist teaching.

Heterogeneously grouped students can together design and conduct experiments to test their ideas, to build new ideas on existing intellectual foundations. The teacher's role is to create blueprints for learning and monitor execution of the design. In other words, the teacher serves as an instructional leader for inquiry rather than as a transmitter of facts given in a linear textbook approach to science teaching. When students are set free to follow different routes or find multiple solutions, Sachse (1989) observes that there are no slow learners in science. All students have views on how the world works and want to share those views.

Linking Science and Language Learning

Science for All Americans (AAAS, 1989) provides an overview of principles of learning and teaching that form the basis for the new science core curriculum. Of importance to second language teachers and learners is the remarkable similarity between science learning principles and those widely recognized for second-language learning. The following science *learning principles* adapted from AAAS (1989: 145–47) are related to those for second language acquisition (Richard-Amato, 1988; Krashen, 1987; Ellis, 1985):

Learning Is Not Necessarily an Outcome of Teaching

This principle, based on results of cognitive research, holds that even the best of students understand less than expected, that good instruction does not necessarily correlate with student understanding, that the quality of understanding is more critical than the quantity of information presented.

From a language learning point of view, this principle supports the position that language learners are not able to process all that language instruction presents. The depth of comprehension or meaningful understanding of concepts is far more important than a superficial, high quantity of information about the language structure.

Prior Knowledge Influences Learning

This principle holds that learners must construct their own meanings regardless of how well concepts are presented to them. To be understood and remain in memory, concepts—the essential units of human thought—need multiple connections to the learner's worldview. Furthermore, effective learning often requires the restructuring of one's thinking to accommodate new ideas. It may even mean discarding old beliefs to make way for new or changed connections. Students need encouragement to develop new views, through understanding how the new ones help them make better sense of the world.

So, too, it is with the language learner. ESL learners bring cross-cultural sets of beliefs and worldviews to the language learning setting. Prior experiences, personal and cultural, shape worldviews that enter into the language learning process. Learning a second language requires restructuring within the brain in ways not yet understood. We know it happens because we see the effects. But learning the second language is very much a process of making new connections, discarding old ones, changing or resetting parameters already in place (Cook, 1989). Second language learners, just as science learners, need encouragement to develop new views about a new language, a new culture. They need encouragement in trying to make sense out of the new linguistic and cultural demands presented to them.

Learning Usually Moves from the Concrete to the Abstract

Concrete experiences—visual, auditory, tactile, kinesthetic—help learners of all ages to understand abstract concepts and to develop relevant conceptual structure or schemata.

Successful language learning relies very heavily, certainly at the earlier stages of proficiency, on concrete experiences, the use of manipulative materials in a here-and-now context. The facilitative effect of using sensory materials, everything from charts and diagrams to objects that can be touched and manipulated, occurs for language learners of all ages.

Learning Requires Practice in New Situations

Learning to think critically, analyze information, communicate ideas, argue logically, and work on a team requires practice in applying science concepts in new, realistic situations. And it requires many of them.

Language learning also requires practice, not through repetitive drilling or pattern practice, but in applying the new language system to genuine, real-life communicative situations—and many of those situations.

Effective Learning Requires Feedback

Learning often takes place best when students can express ideas and get feedback from their peers. Feedback, to be most useful, needs to be more than just correct answers. Rather, it needs to be analytical or suggestive of other ways of thinking. Timing is important. Feedback needs to come when learners are interested in it. Learners then need time to reflect on it, make adjustments, and try again.

Current second language learning research emphasizes the value of peer correction and interaction. Error correction for its own sake has little value. But given at a time when a learner wants it, it can trigger internal adjustments that alter the language system. Peer feedback in language learning can be more powerful than teacher feedback. Peer–peer interactions on topics of interest and relevance, in situations requiring negotiation of meaning, strongly facilitate language learning. Success in communicating provides its own positive feedback.

Expectations Affect Performance

Learners respond to their own expectations of what they can learn. If they believe that they can grasp a complex science concept, the probability is very high that they will. Self-confidence engenders success. Learners also assess the expectations made about them by teachers and peers, among others. If learners are expected to perform poorly in science, they probably will do so.

Language learners are also very strongly affected by their own expectations of success or failure in learning a second language. ''Good language learners'' expect success of themselves and that teachers and peers hold similar expectations of them. Self-confidence is a personality variable that facilitates the process of language learning, just as low self-esteem works against it (Brown, 1987).

The parallels or links between science learning and second language learning are remarkably strong. Principles for effective science learning are also those that support second language learning. The case for using science contexts for second language learning is strengthened when we examine these principles in the light of their similarities.

For science teaching, the learning principles direct the ***teaching principles***. Again, the similarities between the principles for science teaching and for second language teaching become apparent. *Science for All Americans* (1989: 147–51) outlines science teaching principles, all of which relate closely to those for language teaching.

Teaching Should Be Consistent with the Nature of Scientific Inquiry

Effective science teaching usually starts with investigation of phenomena interesting and familiar to learners, not with abstractions or events beyond their experiential range. Learners need concrete experiences with things around them as they learn to make observations, collect data, raise questions, make predictions. Learning to make sense out of many and varied experiences requires being given problems at levels appropriate to the learners. Students need guidance and encouragement in activities that have an intellectually satisfying payoff. At the same time, science teachers encourage effective use of oral and written language because of the crucial role clarity of language plays in expressing and understanding scientific procedures, findings, and ideas. Related to this is a deemphasis on the memorization of technical vocabulary. Teachers introduce technical terms only as they are needed to clarify thinking and promote meaningful communication.

The collaborative nature of work in science and technology is emphasized by frequent group activity in the science classroom. Science students need experience in sharing responsibility for learning with each other. To come to common understandings, they must give information, argue over findings, make assessments. In the context of team responsibility for accomplishing a meaningful task, learners experience the relevance of feedback and the necessity for communicating accurately.

For second language teaching, the same principle of consistency applies. Language teaching needs to be consistent with what we know about language learning. We know that taking into account the language learner's prior knowledge and experience helps the process. We know, too, that students need many and varied opportunities to try out their new language. Only in using the new language in genuine communication can learners begin to make sense out of the language data coming at them. Problem-solving experiences, under the guidance and support of the teacher, lead to those payoffs that say 'I like this' and lead students to seek more. Language teaching, of students from the earliest levels of proficiency on, encourages use of both oral and written modalities. Vocabulary is learned as the need arises, in meaningful contexts.

A collaborative setting facilitates second language acquisition (McGroarty, 1989). When second language learners share responsibility for learning connected with meaningful tasks, such as those of science, they gain the language needed to express information, arguments, and evaluations related to those tasks.

Science Teaching Should Reflect Scientific Values

Science teaching encourages curiosity, rewards creativity, and fosters a spirit of questioning. Students learn to recognize science as a process for extending their understanding, not as a set of truths or correct conclusions. Science teaching also means establishing a learning environment where students broaden and deepen their responses to the beauty of science in its many facets.

Likewise, effective second language teaching draws on the natural curiosity of learners, encourages investigation and questioning. Effective language teachers help learners understand the process of second language acquisition and recognize that errors are part of the process. They also provide a learning environment that promotes multidimensional aesthetic responses.

Science Teaching Aims to Counteract Learning Anxieties

For many students, science learning creates anxiety. By making sure that students have successful experiences in learning science and by emphasizing group learning, teachers can reduce anxieties. Rather than creating a competitive environment, group approaches help learners value their own contributions and recognize that all can contribute to the attainment of common goals.

Anxiety is a critical variable in second language learning. Successful teachers use a variety of activities for lowering the affective filter, making learners feel less on the defensive (Richard-Amato, 1988). Science experiences done in a cooperative learning setting are ideal for counteracting language learning anxieties.

In summary, not only does the restructuring of science education hold the potential for more effective science learning for native speakers of English, but it also offers the potential for integrating the LEP student into the science class. When this happens, the concurrent learning of science and English as a second language can take place.

From the perspective of second language acquisition theory, the focus on themes that have direct meaning to everyday lives provides a source of meaningful input. According to Krashen's (1987) view of language acquisition—defined as a subconscious process of getting a language through focus on content rather than on linguistic structures—relevant input in a challenging learning situation is a causative variable for the acquisition of a second language. In a heterogeneous group with varying levels of English language proficiency and science understanding, LEP students can participate in ways that simultaneously contribute to effective language and science learning.

Cooperative Learning in Science and Language Learning

Cooperative learning is a powerful approach to integrating science and language learning for LEP students. It permits crucial elements facilitating both science learning and language learning to come together. Small-group interactions not only provide meaningful input for language acquisition but also provide the sociocognitive conflict necessary for science learning.

Cooperative science experiences also make use of both oral and written language. Spoken discourse in the interactions within the group normally leads to written reports or other forms related to the experience.

In the small-group interactions of cooperative learning, positive affective conditions needed for second language learning can be established. Working together in heterogeneous groups, peer tutors can function effectively and at the same time make gains in their own language proficiency (Long and Porter, 1985).

Cooperative learning groups provide the focus for negotiation of meaning in which a wide range of language functions appear. Among them is the function of defining, a central function for science. In group work on science tasks, giving and requesting information are basic functions. Discussing findings and arguing, in a positive sense, result from group attempts to arrive at a common understanding. This involves suggesting and expressing opinions, agreeing and disagreeing. Evaluating results often involves comparing as well as classifying. All of these language functions are important to the use of a second language and essential to its use in a science context. Along with the language functions associated with science, learners also acquire necessary vocabulary and the syntactic structures needed for scientific discourse.

The Language of Science

The language of science is complex and much is yet to be analyzed in its relationship to the needs of ESL science learners. Some basic principles to keep in mind for the LEP student include:

- Acquisition of new terminology, new syntactic structures, and new discourse patterns is contingent on putting items to be learned in context, not on isolation of items in lists or exercises for conscious, overt attention.
- Language acquisition occurs more quickly when students are physically engaged in hands-on activities, talking about concepts in a genuine communicative context (Mohan, 1986).

Fortunately, much of the terminology and symbol system used in science is recognized internationally, a facilitating factor for the older ESL student with prior science instruction in the first language. However, the development of the language of science, or the scientific register, still remains a major consideration in relating science and ESL learning.

In science discourse, abstract ideas are logically developed and linked with one another through a number of linguistic devices: repetition of key words, use of paraphrase or semantically similar terms, and use of logical connectors such as *because, however,* and *consequently.* These connectors carry out a number of semantic functions in making connections between ideas. Connectors typically signal addition or similarity, contradiction, cause/effect or reason/result, and chronological or logical sequence notions (Celce-Murcia and Larsen-Freeman, 1983). Although little investigation has been done on identification of the difficulties that logical connectors present to the ESL student in science contexts, a study of 16,530 students enrolled in grades 7–10 in Australia showed a significant number of students experiencing difficulty with connectives in logical reasoning (Gardner, 1980). Therefore, we can expect logical connectors in the language of science to present difficulty for ESL students.

An important component of science instruction, especially as it applies to older learners, aims to promote activities in which students actively engage in discussion with one another over the truth of hypotheses presented and the meaning of data gathered. The ability to ask questions, generate tentative answers, make predictions, and then evaluate evidence as supporting or rejecting those answers develops in part as a result of attempting to carry on discussions. Internalization of linguistic elements of argumentation appears to be a prerequisite for aspects of proportional reasoning and other types of advanced reasoning used in science. The ability, for example, to raise questions about a problem, generate hypotheses, make predictions, and design an experiment to test those hypotheses rests on the gradual internalization of the linguistic elements involved (Lawson et al, 1984). To the extent that science students do not have access to these linguistic abilities, they cannot successfully engage in science inquiry demanding this kind of reasoning. ESL students who do not have access to linguistic structures for these processes may be expected to have particular difficulty in science reasoning.

Specialized vocabulary is closely tied to the specific content of science. While the extreme focus on terminology in science teaching is undergoing change in the new science curriculum, new words, terms, and definitions pose problems for the ESL learner. This is particularly crucial in light of recent evidence of the importance of vocabulary knowledge in learning academic content through a second language.

In a study of factors affecting academic achievement in ESL, Saville-Troike (1984) found that knowledge of vocabulary is a crucial variable in learning academic content through a second language. Vocabulary knowledge is more important than knowing English morphology, such as plural markers on nouns or past tense on verbs or even syntactic structures for sentence formation. In fact, Saville-Troike concludes that vocabulary is the most important part of linguistic structure that the ESL student needs for school success.

Access to science concept definitions and their verbal labels is a feature of science communication. Lynch and his colleagues (Lynch, Chipman, Pachaury, 1985) studied a set of key concept words used in defining the nature of matter (e.g., *atom, solid,* and *element*). In administering equivalent tests to tenth graders in Australia, using English, and in India, using Hindi, they found identical scores for both groups. Test item analysis, however, revealed variations in the recognition order for specific terms. In one paradigm dealing with spatial and relational notions, for example, the order for English speakers was *area* develops before *mass*. For Hindi students the reverse order of *mass* before *area* appeared. In another paradigm on the physical form of matter, English students scored consistently higher than the Hindi students on the set of terms about the states of matter: *solid, liquid, gas*. Hindi students, on the other hand, showed higher scores for terms dealing with the substructure of the atom: *electron, proton, neutron*. Differences in the recognition order for science vocabulary are attributed, at least in part, to linguistic and cultural variables in the first languages. Findings such as these have implications for teaching science to LEP students. Learners' first language and culture may play a role in acquisition of scientific language more than is currently acknowledged.

In addition to linguistic structures and vocabulary, specific discourse and textual patterns characterize the use of language in science discourse, spoken or written. Five major patterns (Horowitz, 1985) are particularly relevant: time order, list structure, compare/contrast, cause/effect, and problem/solution. Although originally identified as text patterns for written discourse, they are also central in spoken science discourse. Time order frequently appears in a set of directives, given orally or in writing, of what to do procedurally. List order, or attribution, often with qualifications such as *in addition, then* or *finally,* is used in listing materials needed for a science investigation. This pattern can also be found in the list of data recorded during the activity and/or in a final science report. Compare/contrast, cause/effect, and problem/solution patterns are central to scientific investigations. Found in charts and diagrams in written science reports, these patterns serve as a means for organizing data or information. They are critical for successful scientific inquiry.

Cognitively, patterns drawing on comparing and contrasting events, making cause and effect connections, and problem solving require higher-order thinking than the patterns of time order and list structure. Observing similarities and differences, noting cause and effect relationships, understanding the problem, and hypothesizing or offering a solution are thinking processes basic to scientific inquiry. The ability to engage in the thinking processes underlying science discourse patterns indicates high levels of both cognitive and linguistic functioning. This interlocking of cognitive and language development is central to second language learning in the context of science (Kessler and Quinn, 1987b).

Organizing Science Experiences
for Cooperative Learning

Cognitively, engagement in science activities is an interactive endeavor between learners and content to generate new understanding. Participation in science experiences requires access to basic processes in expanding conceptual knowledge. Working cooperatively, LEP students utilize thinking processes such as observing, describing, classifying, inferencing, hypothesizing, and evaluating. Science experiences appropriately structured can utilize the prior experiences of learners to build new meanings and understandings.

One way to structure a unit integrating science concepts and language makes use of the following elements (Fathman and Quinn, 1989):

- Teacher demonstration: preparation for small-group work
- Group investigation: set-up for cooperative learning
- Independent investigation: follow-up to cooperative learning work

Within this structure, the teacher initially presents a science concept such as *light* or *electrical energy*. During the demonstration, the teacher has multiple opportunities to relate concrete objects and actions with meaning. For LEP students not familiar with the language associated with a particular concept, the demonstration provides the first source of meaningful input. This preparation for working cooperatively in small groups helps even the least proficient language learner make meaningful connections that facilitate participation in the small group.

An example of a teacher demonstration based on light energy illustrates how the teacher introduces concepts and sets the stage for group interaction (Fathman and Quinn, 1989: 2–3). Students have a work sheet as a guide and follow-up to the demonstration.

Light That Bends

SCIENCE CONCEPT: A beam of light changes direction as it passes from one kind of material into another.

LANGUAGE FUNCTIONS: Directing and requesting

Watch and Listen

What to Do: Watch the teacher and listen to him or her explain how light bends.

Words to Study
At this point, two lists of relevant words are given, one for a beginning proficiency level, the other for advanced learners. Relevant words include, among others, *beam, bend, surface, path, image, prism, refraction.*

What to Discuss
1. Tell another student how to make light bend.
2. Request several classmates to: turn on the flashlight; wave the flashlight to the right or left. Use a polite form of speech.
3. Discuss these questions: Does light bend? When does it bend? Does it always bend when it goes from air to water? How do we hold the flashlight to make its beam of light bend? Which way does the beam bend? What do you think would happen if the beam traveled from the water into the air?

What to Record
1. Match the columns. Write the correct letter next to each picture in the space provided. (For this activity, diagrams in one column are to be matched with appropriate words or phrases, such as *beam of light, entering the water at a slant.*
2. Draw pictures of: *a tank of water; a tank of water with a beam of light going straight down into the water.* (Spaces are provided for the drawings.)
3. Use these words to fill in the blank spaces: *beam, surface, path . . .* (Students complete a set of related sentences requiring completion with vocabulary from the study list.
4. Answer these questions in writing. (A set of questions the teacher asks orally is given in written form.)

During this demonstration, students have the chance to develop concepts about light energy together with related vocabulary. They listen to the teacher, participate in spoken discourse, read directions and questions about what to record, and write answers to questions based on the demonstration. The demonstration integrates science concepts and language learning. It makes use of both spoken and written discourse.

The group investigation utilizes a cooperative learning model with all students helping one another to carry out the investigation. Heterogeneous grouping with multilevel language proficiency provides a setting for peer tutoring and taking responsibility for one another's learning.

An example of a group investigation based on inquiries into electrical energy is the following on electricity based on the format for *Science for Language Learners* (Fathman and Quinn, 1989). Targeted to language learners, it also includes specific attention to certain language functions used in scientific investigations. It is an appropriate activity for upper elementary and junior and senior high school students or for any special populations who need help in developing English proficiency.

Electricity

SCIENCE CONCEPT: The electrical energy that causes lightning also causes balloons to do some interesting things:

> Groups of electrons move and repel each other.
> They also attract positive charges.

LANGUAGE FUNCTIONS: Agreeing and disagreeing

Investigate Together

What to Use
1. Balloon
2. Rubber band
3. String
4. Paper torn into very small pieces

What to Do
1. Blow up the balloon.
2. Fasten the balloon closed with a rubber band.
3. Rub it rapidly across your clothing six or seven times in the same direction.
4. Touch the balloon to the wall.
5. Tear up some paper into very small pieces.
6. Rub the balloon across your clothing again.
7. Dip the balloon into the small pieces of paper.
8. Try to explain why the paper sticks to the balloon.
9. Agree or disagree with your team members.
10. Tie the string to the balloon.

11. Rub the balloon across your clothing again.
12. Let it float near the balloon of another group. What happens?
13. Agree on something else that you could do with the inflated balloons.
14. Try out your idea. What happens? Why do you think it happens?

Words to Study

electrons	electricity	electrical energy
attract	repel	charge

What to Record

1. I agree that _____
2. We disagree about why _____
3. I think we could agree to _____
4. Another thing we could do with our balloons would be to _____

This group investigation taps processes in scientific thinking and cognition. It requires making observations and descriptions about the balloon in reference to the pieces of paper, the wall, another balloon. It provides for comparing and contrasting. Comparisons are made about the similarity of attraction between the balloon and paper and between the balloon and the wall. This is in contrast to the way that two balloons initially repel each other after they are rubbed against clothing. The investigation also involves classifying or analyzing. Furthermore, it requires inferencing—arriving at understandings that combine observations with the learner's prior knowledge or schemata. In addition, the small-group interaction is directed toward hypothesizing about why the balloon attracted some objects and not others, as well as why two rubbed balloons repel one another. Finally, the group is asked to design an experiment, which draws on the cognitive process of evaluating.

An independent *Investigate on Your Own* section uses the same format, directing students in what to use, do, study, and record. This section is designed to be used by individual students as a follow-up to the cooperative learning section.

Specific language activities follow each section of the unit: teacher demonstration, cooperative learning activity, independent work.

Language Activities for Cooperative Learning in a Science Setting

Cooperative work in a science setting is an ideal environment for students to learn to understand and use a new language. Language will be acquired naturally as students are encouraged to listen to others and express themselves while working interactively in groups. Communication, both oral and written, is necessary for successful interaction in science. A language will be learned by the need and desire to communicate with others. Teachers can, however, enhance language learning by using certain strategies incorporating language activities and exercises into science investigations.

In designing language activities for groups, some of the strategies that teachers can use as well as encourage aides or peers to use also are:

- repeat or paraphrase whenever possible
- focus on what is said, not how it is said
- encourage students to experiment with language without fear of making mistakes
- have students talk about what they are doing
- encourage students to ask for help
- use concrete objects/visuals in explanations and discussions
- make all students feel a part of the group activities.

The incorporation of language activities into a science setting can be effectively achieved if teachers are aware of what students need to know linguistically to understand and express themselves in group science investigations. Teachers need to be aware of the proficiency level of students in order to design language activities that can be flexibly adapted to motivate and involve students at all levels—beginning, intermediate, and advanced. All students can benefit from multilevel groups, but expectations and demands of the students in groups should vary according to language ability.

Language activities appropriate for the beginning level might include: following simple "action" commands, identifying the names of objects, answering simple *yes/no* questions, reporting results involving numbers of short answers, reading simple words related to visuals or concrete objects.

Intermediate level students can be encouraged to: talk about actions, objects, pictures; ask and answer simple questions; write simple descriptions of what they have done or observed; write short answers to questions; read simple directions; read what they have written.

During language activities, advanced students should interact with lower-ability students, providing encouragement and help in dealing with the comprehension of science concepts and linguistic structures. Advanced students should be capable of following detailed instructions, giving explanations, asking and answering complex questions (*how/why*), talking about abstract ideas, summarizing, expressing opinions in writing, and understanding, from a language point of view, most of the material presented in science texts.

An interactive learning setting and appropriate teacher management strategies can greatly enhance language learning. In the science classroom, teachers need sensitivity to the language skills for understanding science concepts. The development of cognitive strategies is closely related to the development of language learning strategies. Language activities fostering the development of necessary vocabulary, linguistic structures, and language functions can be integrated into science investigations as an introduction, supplement, or review. Specific activities can be designed to encourage use of specific vocabulary, functions, and relevant structures.

Exercises that may be used to supplement lessons as a support for vocabulary learning are:

1. *Drawing/picture exercises:*
   Students work with labeled pictures, color specific parts of pictures, or draw their own labeled diagrams or pictures related to science concepts.

2. *Matching exercises:*
   Students match names with pictures/objects/actions, identify words with meanings, combine sentence parts that contain key vocabulary.

3. *Classifying and ordering exercises:*
   Students classify words into specific categories, fill in charts, unscramble the letters of new vocabulary words, or order sentences in correct sequences.

4. *Short-answer exercises:*
   Students complete sentences, write the correct vocabulary words when given a definition or description, answer questions using key vocabulary.

5. *Creative expression exercises:*
   Students use key vocabulary to answer *how/why/what* questions, summarize information from readings/observations, draw conclusions, or state opinions.

Vocabulary practice with these types of exercises can be done cooperatively in groups or by individuals. Students of different proficiency levels within a group can be given different kinds of exercises, ranging from drawing for the lowest levels to creative expression for the more advanced levels.

Teachers should identify the relevant vocabulary words for a science lesson, as has been done in the ''Light'' and ''Electricity'' investigations described in this chapter. The meanings of the new words can be discussed in class or small groups, looked up by individual students, or provided by the teacher or peers. Then students should be required to use the vocabulary within the context of the science investigation.

In addition to vocabulary, teachers will also want to give attention to language skills needed to participate effectively in science investigations. For example, in group activities, students need to be able to:

- ask for repetition/meaning/information
- tell others what/how to do something
- check/compare information
- enter/participate in discussions
- provide feedback

- report findings/results
- express opinions
- summarize/draw conclusions

Specific language functions may be emphasized in science experiences, such as requesting, defining, comparing, agreeing/disagreeing. This can be done through oral and written activities associated with the science lesson, as shown in the "Light That Bends" and "Electricity" investigations in this chapter. In the "Light" demonstration, the language focus is directing and requesting, and students are required to carry out specific oral and written activities that require them to follow directions and to tell or request others to do something. Students follow the teacher's directions and, in oral activities, interact with others by telling how to make light bend and requesting information. In written activities, students are asked to change written commands to polite forms, request results from other students, and record data (Fathman and Quinn, 1989).

The "Electricity" investigation in this chapter focuses on agreeing and disagreeing. Through modeling by the teacher or peers, LEP students can be shown the most commonly used statements for expressing agreement, as well as linguistic structures associated with the verbs *agree* and *disagree*. Oral language activities include sharing information about observations and agreeing or disagreeing with others about why balloons attract or repel one another. Written language activities include recording results and agreeing or disagreeing with written statements given by the teacher or by other students.

In summary, oral and written language activities can be designed to focus on specific vocabulary, structures, and functions throughout science investigations. Science group activities, involving brainstorming, problem solving, investigating, experimenting, discovering, designing, or creating provide rich opportunities for language development.

The strong natural relationship between science group activities and opportunity for language development is evident in the following sample activities from a unit on plants (Fathman and Quinn, 1989):

Students work together in groups to:

1. Name as many plants as possible and develop lists, clusters, or semantic maps (vocabulary development through brainstorming).
2. Decide how plant germination times can be determined (suggesting / expressing opinions while problem solving).
3. Germinate different kinds of seeds and observe germination times (discussing/recording observations while investigating).
4. Determine the height of plants on days following germination (sharing information after discovering).
5. Design other germination systems to determine how light and space affect growth (suggesting new alternatives while creating and designing).

Different kinds of linguistic strategies are needed to participate in these activities. Students can learn these strategies together with the structures and functions associated with them through high interest, interactive, nonthreatening communicative activities while exploring together in the science setting.

Summary

This chapter has focused on the interrelationships between science and language learning in cooperative learning contexts. It has examined the principles of science and language learning and the related ones of science and language teaching. An overview of the language of science illustrates the interdependence between linguistic factors and scientific thinking. Analysis of the linguistic features of science discourse and the processes involved in scientific reasoning provide direction for organizing and structuring science investigations and related language activities. In so doing, the learning of science and language can take place concurrently.

Emphasis is given to the role of interactive cooperative learning groups carrying out scientific investigations together. Within this context, ESL learners can develop access to science and a second language. The excitement of making these connections is perhaps best expressed in the words of middle-school LEP students carrying out science inquiry according to the model presented in this chapter. A science investigation on plants and seeds done in an ESL class, using cooperative learning, triggered enthusiastic comments.

> I liked the experiment because it help learned new words. also I would have liked to see all The seeds grow but some did not. I saw The plants grow here in our class and we got to measure The plants I would like to do more experiments in class. (*Eduardo*)

Eduardo recognizes that he has learned new English vocabulary and at the same time has learned concepts about plant growth.

> I like the experiments and I like doing like we did in are classroom. I like haveing another one because we learn alot over plants. (*Laura*)

Laura recognizes that she too has learned a lot about plants. She likes doing science investigations, particularly *like we did* in a cooperative learning context.

> I really lean for the report we did class it was very interesting and I would really like to lean more about sicence. (*Sunita*)

Sunita found the science investigation so interesting that she would like more. She too sees the importance of working together. *I really lean for the report* tells how she values the experience of learning in a group, talking about a science investigation, and writing a report together about the findings.

REFERENCES

American Association for the Advancement of Science (AAAS). 1989. *Science for All Americans.* Washington, D.C.

BROWN, H.D. 1987. *Principles of Language Learning and Teaching,* 2nd ed. Englewood Cliffs, NJ: Prentice Hall.

BYBEE, R.W. 1989. *Science and Technology Education for the Elementary Years: Frameworks for Curriculum and Instruction.* Andover, MA: The National Center for Improving Science Education, The Network, Inc.

CELCE-MURCIA, M., and D. LARSEN-FREEMAN. 1983. *The Grammar Book.* Rowley, MA: Newbury House.

CLEMSON, A. 1990. Establishing an epistemological base for science teaching in the light of contemporary notions of the nature of science and how children learn science. *Journal of Research in Science Teaching,* 27: 429–445.

COOK, V. 1989. Universal grammar theory and the classroom. *System,* 17, no. 2: 169–82.

ELLIS, R. 1985. *Understanding Second Language Acquisition.* Oxford: Oxford University Press.

FATHMAN, A.K., and M.E. QUINN. 1989. *Science for Language Learners.* Englewood Cliffs, NJ: Prentice Hall Regents.

GARDNER, P.L. 1980. The identification of specific difficulties with logical connectives in science among secondary school students. *Journal of Research in Science Teaching,* 17: 223–29.

HAZEN, R., and J. TREFIL. 1991. Science literacy: The enemy in us. *Science,* 251: 266–267.

HOROWITZ, R. 1985. Text patterns: Part 1. *Journal of Reading,* 28: 448–54.

KESSLER, C., and M.E. QUINN. 1987a. ESL and science learning. In J. Crandall (ed.), *ESL Through Content-Area Instruction.* Englewood Cliffs, NJ: Prentice Hall.

———. 1987b. Second-language writing acquisition through science inquiry. Paper presented at the 8th World Congress of Applied Linguists, Sydney, Australia.

KRASHEN, S.D. 1987. *Principles and Practice in Second Language Acquisition.* Englewood Cliffs, NJ: Prentice Hall Regents.

LAWSON, A., D.I. LAWSON, and C.A. LAWSON. 1984. Proportional reasoning and the linguistic abilities required for hypothetico-deductive reasoning. *Journal of Research in Science Teaching,* 21: 119–31.

LESSOW-HURLEY, J. 1990. *The Foundations of Dual Language Instruction.* New York: Longman.

LONG, M.H., and P.A. PORTER. 1985. Group work, interlanguage talk, and second-language acquisition. *TESOL Quarterly,* 19, no. 2: 207–28.

LYNCH, P.O., H.H. CHIPMAN, and A.C. PACHAURY. 1985. The language of science and the high school student: The recognition of concept definitions: A comparison between

Hindi speaking students in India and English speaking students in Australia. *Journal of Research in Science Teaching,* 22: 675–86.

MCGROARTY, M. 1989. The benefits of cooperative learning arrangements in second language instruction. *NABE Journal,* 13, no. 2: 127–44.

MOHAN, B. 1986. *Language and Content.* Reading, MA: Addison-Wesley.

National Science Teachers Association. 1991. Taking note: Hot off the presses. *The Science Teacher,* 58: 54.

RICHARD-AMATO, P.A. 1988. *Making It Happen: Interaction in the Second Language Classroom.* New York: Longman.

SACHSE, T.P. 1989. Making science happen. *Educational Leadership,* 47, no. 3: 18–21.

SAVILLE-TROIKE, M. 1984. What really matters in second language learning for academic achievement. *TESOL Quarterly,* 18: 199–219.

CHAPTER 5

COOPERATIVE LEARNING AND SOCIAL STUDIES

Roger E. W-B Olsen

Language development and academic achievement are important goals for students who are limited English proficient (LEP); that is, students who speak English as a second language (ESL) and who are unable to benefit from traditional English-only instruction. Approximately 2 million or about 5 percent of all K–12 public school students in the United States are reported to be LEP (Olsen, 1989, 1991). In addition to those who are limited English *proficient,* others may be limited English *functioning* (LEF); that is, they are unable to obtain full benefit from traditional English-only instruction. Of all U.S. public school students, 22.5 percent may be limited English *functioning* (Olsen, 1989). LEF students include those learning English as a second language who test above minimal levels, so they are not severely or profoundly limited, and native English-speaking students who are unable or who are limited in their ability to succeed with traditional English-only instruction.

Social studies topics in particular may present difficulties for LEP and LEF students because the topics are generally abstract, cognitively varied, and generally highly language dependent. Social studies topics are abstract when they do not refer to things or events directly available in the classroom or, in the case of many students acquiring English as a second language, the concepts may not be part of the students' personal experience or culture. For example, Kutrakun (1989: 2) describes a Hmong student learning in English as a second language:

> I remember watching one Hmong student in a history class one day. This student was doing quite well in her English class and could speak English quite fluently, but was experiencing difficulty in many of her content area classes. On this day, the teacher was explaining some geographic terms, such as peninsula, sound, harbor, and bay. The teacher was showing a map of Washington state and pointing to the Olympic Peninsula and Puget Sound as examples. Mao Xiong, the Hmong student, stared at the map with a very blank look on her face. It seemed she had no idea what the map represented until the teacher said that Puget Sound was like a pocket of water from the Pacific Ocean that sat between the Olympic Peninsula and the mainland. Mao Xiong's face lit up as she understood, but immediately she looked confused again. Without thinking she called out to the teacher, "Oh, but how does the water keep from falling out of the pocket?" Mao Xiong's question showed clearly that she understood the word, but was struggling with the concept.

Social studies topics vary in cognitive complexity, or types of knowledge. They range from discrete information items, such as things, dates, or places (knowledge), to complex relationships about people, places, and events (metaknowledge). Moreover, metaknowledge, such as relationships, cause and effect, and similarities, may be open to interpretation; so there may be no single discrete answer to many social studies questions.

Modifications may be made to focus on specialized vocabulary, grammar, or other discourse features of specific content areas such as social studies (see, for example, Addison, 1988, or Crandall, 1987). However, emphasis only on language register may result in postponed concept learning. This presents difficulties for LEP students, especially those who may enter schooling as non-English speaking adolescents (Collier, 1989; O'Malley and Chamot, 1988, 1990; Chamot and O'Malley, 1987).

Traditional ways to make language-dependent curriculum accessible to low-achieving students include using visuals, props and manipulatives, hands-on activities, such as making timelines, and research projects, such as term papers. For instance, the teacher in the example above used a map to supplement the lesson. But these kinds of activities do not fully address the needs of students acquiring English, and, moreover, they may be presented to students in a step-by-step fashion that "waters down" or decreases the available information rather than increasing the accessibility—the comprehensibility—of the curriculum content. In particular, LEP students may need increased opportunities to verify comprehension, to receive varied explanations, and to relate what they are learning to what they have already learned. And, LEP and LEF students may require more practice with language and with the content they are learning.

Cooperative learning (CL) offers ways to structure the classroom so students engage in instruction that ensures comprehension. For a number of reasons

CL appears to be a superior method of instruction. Not only does it allow students to receive instruction that is "tuned" to them individually but it also increases the variety of ways information can be presented and related to what is already known. In addition, this increased *quality* of instruction occurs in increased *quantity*, because one fourth to one half of the class is actively producing language for specific listeners in small groups or pairs rather than having a single source of input (the teacher) for the whole class. Finally, active listening and speaking in structured groups provide opportunities for language practice that LEP and LEF students cannot get in a more traditional classroom situation.

CL procedures may be used selectively to provide specific kinds of practice with language while emphasizing certain lesson material. For example, an activity in which students ask for clarification and give explanations develops language strategies for clarification and recycles lesson concepts. CL procedures that require students to exchange information, then, may simultaneously draw on clarifications while emphasizing the selected content.

CL activities that involve short answers or manipulating objects can reinforce lesson vocabulary and develop familiarity with lesson content, clarify what has been learned and establish what needs to be learned.

The purpose of this chapter is to show different ways to use CL procedures, structures, and related frameworks. The sample lesson material has been designed to emphasize specific kinds of content that must be exchanged by students. It is assumed that team formation, teambuilding, and classbuilding activities have already occurred, that teams and the teacher are comfortable with CL procedures, and that forms of group and individual accountability have been selected.

Structures are content-free ways to organize social (student–student) interactions (Kagan, 1989; Olsen and Kagan, this volume). CL structures are characterized by positive interdependence and frequently include informal or off-the-record kinds of exchanges between students. Traditional structures such as Whole-Class Question and Answer, Take the Test, or Give Your Oral Report to the Class usually do not formally allow student–student interaction and rarely allow student–student interaction on an off-the-record basis. CL structures such as Three-Step Interview, Roundtable, and Numbered Heads, on the other hand, call for student–student collaboration to prepare answers, to clarify instructions, to understand the material, or to develop appropriate responses. Off-the-record collaboration allows students to try out a way of explaining and then to modify—restate, expand, clarify, or elaborate—as necessary to complete the assignment. Informal comprehension collaboration is important for LEP and LEF students because (a) they receive important additional practice comprehending and producing language; (b) they have additional opportunities to relate what they are learning to what they already know, clarifying what they have learned and what they have yet to learn; and (c) they are provided more than one avenue of access to content by processes of restating, modification, and so forth.

The following interaction structures are used in this chapter:

STRUCTURE	PROCEDURE
Three-Step Interview:	(1) Students are in pairs; one is interviewer and the other is interviewee. (2) Students reverse roles. (3) Each shares with team member what was learned during the two interviews.
Roundtable:	There is one piece of paper and one pen for each team. (1) One student makes a contribution and (2) passes the paper and pen to the student on his or her left. (3) Each student makes contributions in turn. If done orally, this structure is called Round Robin.
Think-Pair-Share:	(1) Teacher poses a question (usually a low-consensus question). (2) Students think of a response. (3) Students use Interview procedure to share answers.
Solve-Pair-Share:	(1) Teacher poses a problem (a low- or high-consensus item that may be resolved with different strategies). (2) Students work out solutions individually (a checker may be needed to ensure everyone stays on task). (3) Students explain how they solved the problem in Interview or Round Robin structures.
Numbered Heads:	(1) Students number off in teams. (2) Teacher asks a question (usually high-consensus). (3) Heads Together—students literally put their heads together and make sure everyone knows the answer. (4) Teacher calls a number and students with that number raise their hands to be called on, as in traditional classrooms.

In addition to the above interaction structures, this chapter also uses jigsawed student activity sheets that provide different kinds of information to different students or may direct them to different activities. This in turn leads to students having different information to share using one or more of the above interaction structures.

Jigsawed information sheets may be referred to in the literature as "A/B" activity sheets, such as "A/B Maps" (Olsen, 1977: 39–45).

Examples with High-Consensus Information

High-consensus information is generally discrete, known or knowable and generally lends itself to true/false or multiple-choice objective testing (see Chapter 1.) For example, historical dates or mathematical sums are discrete and known or knowable. High-consensus information may be associated with the fundamental levels of Bloom's (1956) hierarchy of cognitive knowledge. Low-consensus information, on the other hand, is not described uniformly. It can concern abstract concepts or relationships and could be associated with the "higher" levels of Bloom's taxonomy or with the hierarchy of affective knowledge. The examples in this section emphasize high-consensus information.

High-consensus information is often reviewed through quizzes, worksheets, or tests. These traditional tools may be combined with CL structures such as Interview or Roundtable, for example, so that students take turns answering one another's questions, obtaining necessary explanations or clarifications from group members before taking a test for a group grade. Or, Numbered Heads might be used for a whole-class activity. With these CL structures, students have several opportunities to encounter, to comprehend, and to learn high-consensus information.

Discrete data lends itself to tasks that are not highly language dependent; that is, tasks that may involve drawing, pointing, moving objects, yes/no, *wh*-questions[1], or other short-answer questions. For example, maps can be designed to elicit short answers or nonverbal responses (drawing, pointing). Figure 1[*] maps are jigsawed; that is, they provide different details to different students so no one student has all the information initially. Figure 1 shows a two-part (A and B), three-step (Interview, Roundtable, Numbered Heads) lesson developed from a map of the United States.

Students obtain missing information using Interview, with general directions (as shown) or perhaps with guided interview sheets. Student A first interviews Student B, then Student B asks questions of Student A. The teacher might introduce this lesson with a review of basic map-reading skills such as the points of the compass, left-right, over-under, next to, between (content emphasis), a review of ways to ask for help (language emphasis), or a review of ways to acknowledge help (social-skills emphasis).

---

[1]Wh- questions are Who, What, Where, When and Why.

[*]All figures referred to in Chapter Five appear at the end of the chapter beginning on page 100.

Student A: I need the name of a state. Can you help me?

Student B: (Okay. What do you need?)

Student A: Well, what's the name of the state between Oregon and Wyoming?

Student B: (Idaho.) or (Where's Oregon?)

Student A: How do you spell that?

Student B: I-D-A-H-O. Now it's may turn. What's the state south of Idaho and Oregon?

Student A: Next to both? Nevada. N-E-V-A-D-A.

Student B: Thanks.

And so on.

After Interview, students complete a worksheet similar to Figure 2, using Roundtable. Each group has only one answer sheet and uses only one pen or pencil. They must all agree on the answers before writing on the worksheet, and they take turns writing the answers.

After Roundtable, the teacher uses Numbered Heads to call for answers.

Charts, tables and diagrams can also be used to create jigsawed student data sheets. Figure 3 on pages 103 and 104 is a two-part (A and B), one-step (Interview) jigsaw developed from a text designed for native-English speakers. Figure 3 student sheets contain general directions including how to ask for different kinds of information. A follow-up activity could use Roundtable or Numbered Heads with questions such as, "Which is the biggest?" and "Which has the most people?"

Picture Pairs such as Figure 4 are designed so differences between the pictures have to be identified and described. Think-Pair-Share may be chosen, and the response-task can be appropriate to students' language abilities. For example, beginning students might point to differences, circle changed details, or give a short verbal response such as, "The arrow (is missing)."

Discrete data that are more language dependent, such as timelines or diagrams of relationships, might be chosen to introduce a unit or as part of review rather than as the central component of a lesson.

Jigsawed timelines with every *n*-th event or date blanked out can be used in information-exchange tasks, similar to maps or charts. They may also be appropriate for classifying, cause-and-effect, analysis, or synthesis types of tasks. Figure 5 shows a two-part (A and B), four-step (Interview, Solve-Pair-Share, Roundtable, and Numbered Heads) jigsawed activity based on a timeline. Fifteen to thirty minutes may be required for each step. The timeline provides central organization for the chapter that follows. The activity sheet questions guide students to (a) complete their copies of the timeline, (b) relate the events to history topics already covered, and (c) develop hypotheses about how the events may be related to one another.

Discrete, high-consensus information ensures unambiguous reference for student–student interactions, and allows increased language practice—both producing and comprehending language—important for students acquiring English.

Examples with Low-Consensus Information

In the preceding section, students exchanged or manipulated discrete, high-consensus information. Low-consensus information is not described discretely or is not easily described at all. It generally lends itself to essay or open-ended questions. Low-consensus information includes both concrete and abstract concepts. Low-consensus information also includes unfamiliar knowledge, experienced-based knowledge that may not be readily articulated (such as experience that has not yet been organized and reported), and hypotheses that are being developed. Students frequently describe the same experience differently for a variety of reasons, such as attending to different elements, relating to different interests, different prior experiences, different purposes, and different active vocabularies. It is important to consider that low-consensus information may require more clarifying, explaining, and elaborating than high-consensus, discrete information. We recognize that native-English speakers frequently have difficulty describing low-consensus knowledge; and so LEP and many LEF students, especially, may need help with abstract, difficult, and language-dependent topics—moreso when information that is high consensus for certain cultures may in fact be low consensus for students acquiring English.

Other topics where low consensus may occur include controversies, human values clarification, and situations where different points of view are developed. One way to create low consensus is through "creative controversy," providing conflicting information to different students.

Figure 6 shows two maps and two readings that give different answers to the question "Who Discovered America?" Depending on ability levels (language and knowledge), students might master their parts individually, in pairs, or in temporary "expert" groups. Expert groups could use Interview (I), Solve-Pair-Share (SPS), or Roundtable (RT) to learn and review select vocabulary, events, and geography.

Returning to "home teams," students enter I, SPS or RT to explain—or fight it out—who "discovered" America. A final worksheet is completed with RT or Numbered Heads (NH), which emphasizes the major lesson objectives (Figure 7).

The maps provide tangible references, so that some information is available in nonverbal and semiverbal forms. If the expert groups are heterogeneous for language ability, the more proficient teammates can explain and clarify for the less fluent. Using RT to review ensures that all "experts" will actively listen to each other and request any necessary explanations from their expert teammates. Using RT for the home-team review ensures that each student will contribute, thereby using the new information and providing explanations as necessary.

Activity sheets can emphasize language or social skills rather than content. For example, interview sheets might focus on the concept "discover" (Figure 8). Each student receives the same interview sheet, and students take turns interviewing each other.

Suggestions to Enhance Language Development

Teachers planning CL lessons for language learners may wish to provide language-centered support without distracting from a desired emphasis on content. Three suggestions for such an approach are discussed in this section: to address language functions as part of a social-skills strand, to use processing sheets to emphasize language functions, and to consider student–response tasks that are not highly language dependent.

Language Functions and Social Skills

Many CL researchers and trainers emphasize prosocial behaviors, ways students cooperate with each other, such as encouraging others when they ask for clarification or giving explanations and different ways to request (or give) clarification. Prosocial behaviors are introduced by direct teaching, reinforced by group interdependence, and may be integrated into student worksheets. Coehlo (1988) observed that many social skills thus emphasized resemble language *notions* and *functions* important for students acquiring English (Table 1). *Language notions* are concepts which may be expressed in different ways within and across languages. Synonyms such as ''salt'' and ''sodium chloride'' and expressions such as ''Please pass the salt'' and ''Pass the salt, please'' are different ways to express the same basic notions within English. Students acquiring English may need practice with different ways to convey similar concepts. The restating, explaining, and clarifying that can occur during CL interactions help develop familiarity with comprehending and producing language notions. Emphasizing ways to restate meanings, then, can help students develop competence with language notions.

Language functions refer to ways we can use language to achieve a communicative purpose. Variations in language forms can carry out the same function. For example, ''Ahem,'' ''Well,'' and ''Ah,'' can all function as attention holders during conversation or as ways to break into someone else's speech. ''What is _____?'' ''I don't understand _____'' and ''Is _____ a _____?'' can function to elicit clarification, explanation, or elaboration. When students are taught prosocial skills such as asking for and giving explanations, they are also learning important language functions that can be used in situations outside class. One way to help students acquiring English is to teach gambits that support the prosocial skills being emphasized. Gambits are formulas used in conversation to convey certain communicative purposes. Special gambits might be introduced or reviewed before students begin working with a particular CL task; they could be integrated into student worksheets as reminders of ways to ask for information; and, they could be emphasized with ''process sheets'' (see Tables 2 and 3).

Language notions and functions may be particularly important for students

Table 1
Gambits to Support Social-Skills Language Functions
(see Keller & Warner [1988] for more on gambits and activities)

Social Skill	Function	Gambits
Obtaining Information	Asking for Information	I'd like to know . . . I'm interested in . . . Would you tell me . . . ? Do you know . . . ? Could you find out . . . ? What is . . . ? Could I ask (May I ask). . . ?
	Requesting Clarification	Help! I don't understand . . . Sorry, I didn't get the last part. You've lost me. I don't follow you. What was that?
	Requesting Explanations	Can you explain why . . . ? Please explain . . . Do you mean to say . . . ? I don't understand why . . . Why is it that . . . ? How come . . . ?
	Requesting Elaboration	Would you expand on that? Tell me more about . . . Build up that idea more. I need to hear more about . . .
	Requesting Confirmation	So what you're saying is . . . What you're really saying is . . . In other words . . . If I understand you correctly, . . . So you mean that. . . Does this mean . . . ?
	Requesting Restating	Please say that again. Please restate that. Come again? What?
	Expressing Disbelief	I'm afraid . . . I don't see how . . . But the problem is . . . Yes, but . . . But don't forget . . . That's good, but . . . I doubt . . . Possibly, but . . . What bothers me is . . .

continued

Table 1 (cont.)

Social Skill	Function	Gambits
	Verifying Communication	Would you mind repeating that?
		Would you spell that, please?
		What did you say?
	Interrupting	Excuse me.
		Sorry . . . (Sorry, but . . .)
		Well,
		Can I ask a question?
		I'd like to add . . .
	Returning to the Topic	Anyway, . . .
		In any case, . . .
		As you were saying, . . .
		Where was I?
	Guessing	I'd say . . .
		Could it be . . . ?
		Perhaps it's . . .
		I think it's . . .
		It looks like . . .
		It's hard to say, but I think . . .
Giving Information	Explaining	What it is . . .
	Restating	Another way to say that is . . .
		Or, in other words, . . .
		Using this graph, . . .
		From another perspective, . . .
	Illustrating	For example, . . .
		For instance, . . .
		Take for example . . .
		For one thing, . . .
		To give you an idea . . .
		Look at the way . . .
		Consider that . . .
	Generalizing	As a rule, . . .
		Generally, . . .
		In general, . . .
		By and large, . . .
		In most cases, . . .
		Usually, . . .
		Most of the time . . .
		Again and again . . .
		Time and again . . .
		Every so often . . .
		From time to time . . .
		Every now and then . . .

continued

Table 1 (cont.)

Social Skill	Function	Gambits
	Exceptions	One exception is . . . But what about . . . ? Don't forget . . .
	Presenting Opinion or Interpretation	I think that . . . I'm convinced that . . . Without a doubt . . . I'm positive . . . I'm certain . . . In my opinion . . . I personally feel . . . I personally believe . . . In my experience . . . From what I've read, . . .
	Making Suggestions	What don't you . . . ? Why not . . . ? Perhaps you could . . . Have you thought about . . . ? Here's an idea . . . Let's . . .
	Adding Thoughts	To start with . . . And another thing . . . What's more, . . . Just a small point . . . Maybe I should mention . . . Oh, I almost forgot . . .
	Giving Reasons	And besides, . . . Also, . . . In addition, . . . What's more, . . . Another thing is that . . . Plus the fact that . . . Because of that, . . . That's why . . . That's the reason why . . . For this reason, . . .
	Adding Considerations	Bearing in mind . . . Considering . . . If you recall . . . When you consider that . . .

continued

Table 1 (cont.)

Social Skill	Function	Gambits
	Thinking Ahead	If . . . When . . . Whenever . . . After . . . As soon as . . . By the time . . . Unless . . .
	Correcting Yourself	What I mean is . . . What I meant is . . . Let me put it another way. . . . What I'm saying is . . . Don't misunderstand me. . . . If I said that, I didn't mean to . Let me rephrase that. . . .
	Summarizing	To cut it short, . . . To make a long story short, . . . So, . . . To sum up, . . . In sum, . . . All in all, . . . In a nutshell, . . .
	Checking Comprehension	Are you with me? Do you understand? Got that? Have you got that? Is that clear? Okay so far?
	Verifying Understanding	That's right. Correct. Right. Okay. Yes. Exactly!

acquiring English with social studies topics that involve abstract, complex, unfamiliar or low-consensus lesson material.

CL structures can be used to teach and to build awareness of language functions. For example, Solve-Pair-Share could be used to increase awareness about a function and to identify some appropriate gambits. Students think of different ways to say things that could accomplish the purpose (getting an explanation, for example) and share those ideas with partners. Partners then report to their team groups what they learned, restating or summarizing their partner's ideas. Or, Roundtable could be used to create lists of gambits to support functions, for review or for teambuilding. Teams list as many gambits as possible within a certain time limit (e.g. five minutes). Teams report their scores (total number of gambits listed) to the class. Each team discusses how it might improve the team score. Teams then enter Round table a second time, and report the new scores. Improvement scoring (increase or percentage increase) emphasizes teambuilding. Each team (and the class!) now has its own "menu" of gambits to support the stated function.

Table 2
Sample "Processing Sheet"

Student Summary Sheet

Clarification

	Always				*Never*	
I gave explanations	5	4	3	2	1	0
I rephrased	5	4	3	2	1	0
I used examples	5	4	3	2	1	0
I summarized	5	4	3	2	1	0
I gave applications	5	4	3	2	1	0
I asked for re-stating	5	4	3	2	1	0
I asked for examples	5	4	3	2	1	0
I asked for explanations	5	4	3	2	1	0
I asked for summarizing	5	4	3	2	1	0

The next time we work in groups, I will work on:

_____,

_____, and

_____.

Processing sheets are used after students have completed a lesson to review how they individually cooperated. Table 2 shows a processing sheet focused on giving clarification that might be used with older students. Younger children might be asked to think about only two or three social skills, language functions, or gambits, and their rating sheet could have happy faces instead of a numbered Likert scale (Table 3).

Table 3
Sample "Processing Sheet"

Student Summary Sheet

Explaining

Always   *Never*

I explained
I said things more than one way
I used examples
The next time we work in groups, I will work on:

_____,

_____, and

_____.

Response Task Alternatives

In heterogeneous CL groups, students can teach one another, such as when higher-achieving students provide necessary explanations and clarifications for lower-achieving teammates. English proficient students may help limited English functioning students, and students with greater experience or familiarity with a certain topic may provide explanations necessary to complete a group task. It can be useful, however, to vary the language demands of the student-response tasks, so that not all responses solicited by student worksheets are highly language dependent. Terrell described four stages of language development that are observed with students acquiring English: "preproduction," "early speech," "speech emergence," and "fluency emergence" (Krashen and Terrell, 1983). An awareness of which kinds of tasks are more appropriate for specific stages (Table 4) can be helpful when designing student activity sheets. For example, kinesthetic, one-word or two-word responses might be selected for students whose command of English is largely receptive. Students whose production skills are beginning to develop can be given stage-three tasks, and students who are fluent can handle stage-four assignments. Stage-three tasks can also be used to challenge stage-two students or for easy review for stage-four students.

Table 4
Taxonomy and Student Response Task Types
(adapted from Krashen and Terrell, 1983)

Stage	Performance Indicator(s)	Ask Students to:		
Stage One: Preproduction	Kinesthetic	point watch use arrange or sort out visuals	act out listen match number manipulate	choose draw follow directions gesture
Stage Two: Early Speech	Kinesthetic; *and* one- or two-word utterances	name tell categorize manipulate	label use group or sort words or phrases	number list answer
Stage Three: Speech Emergence	Kinesthetic; one or two words; *and* phrases and simple sentences	describe explain compare write	define retell contrast read	recall summarize follow directions give or list steps
Stage Four: Fluency Emergence	Kinesthetic; words, phrases, simple sentences; *and* complex sentences	justify debate describe in detail	create defend examine evaluate	give opinion analyze complete

Summary

This chapter explored some ways to use cooperative learning to meet needs of limited English proficient and limited English functioning students. Traditional worksheets, tests, and quizzes were adapted as jigsawed activity and information sheets for use with structures such as Interview, Roundtable, and Numbered Heads. Examples using high-consensus and low-consensus information were presented. An advantage of discrete or high-consensus information is that it (a) can ensure unambiguous reference for student–student interactions and (b) allows increased language practice—both producing and comprehending language—focused on basic content vocabulary, concepts, and relationships. In addition, when students are responsible for checking each other's comprehension, then teachers are freed to some degree from correcting as many quizzes and worksheets.

Figure 1 (A) (Developed by Judy Winn-Bell Olsen)

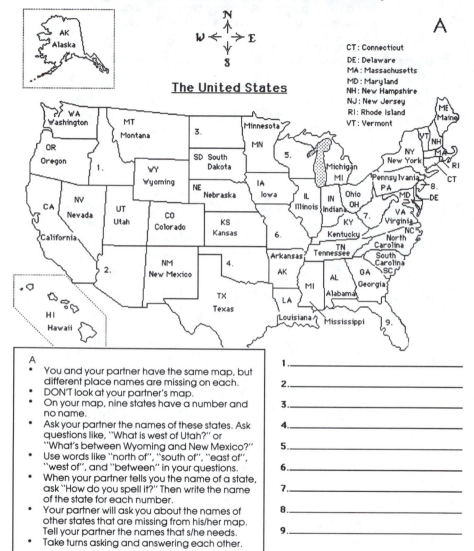

A
- You and your partner have the same map, but different place names are missing on each.
- DON'T look at your partner's map.
- On your map, nine states have a number and no name.
- Ask your partner the names of these states. Ask questions like, "What is west of Utah?" or "What's between Wyoming and New Mexico?"
- Use words like "north of", "south of", "east of", "west of", and "between" in your questions.
- When your partner tells you the name of a state, ask "How do you spell it?" Then write the name of the state for each number.
- Your partner will ask you about the names of other states that are missing from his/her map. Tell your partner the names that s/he needs.
- Take turns asking and answering each other.

1. _____
2. _____
3. _____
4. _____
5. _____
6. _____
7. _____
8. _____
9. _____

Figure 1 (B) (Developed by Judy Winn-Bell Olsen)

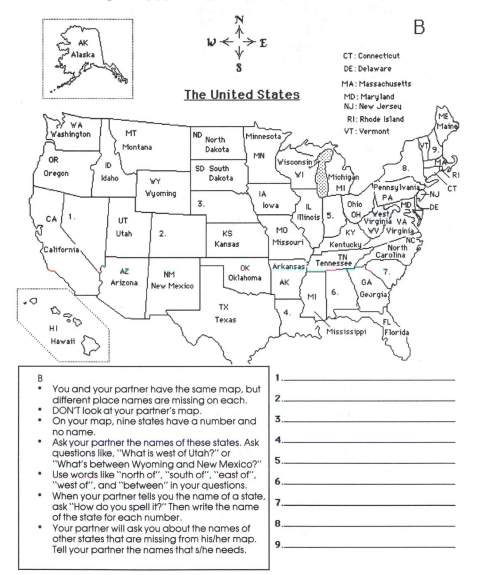

B

CT : Connecticut
DE : Delaware
MA : Massachusetts
MD : Maryland
NJ : New Jersey
RI : Rhode Island
VT : Vermont

The United States

B
- You and your partner have the same map, but different place names are missing on each.
- DON'T look at your partner's map.
- On your map, nine states have a number and no name.
- Ask your partner the names of these states. Ask questions like, "What is west of Utah?" or "What's between Wyoming and New Mexico?"
- Use words like "north of", "south of", "east of", "west of", and "between" in your questions.
- When your partner tells you the name of a state, ask "How do you spell it?" Then write the name of the state for each number.
- Your partner will ask you about the names of other states that are missing from his/her map. Tell your partner the names that s/he needs.

1. _____
2. _____
3. _____
4. _____
5. _____
6. _____
7. _____
8. _____
9. _____

Figure 2
Discrete, High-Consensus Information Review Quiz,
Based on A/B Maps

DIRECTIONS: Each team is to use only one pen or pencil and has only one copy of the quiz. Teams are to agree on the answers to this quiz before writing them down. Take turns writing the answers, using Roundtable.

True or False: Mark + for true and − for false.

———— 1. Idaho is north of Utah.

———— 2. Nevada is north of Idaho.

———— 3. Arizona is west of Utah.

———— 4. Utah is west of Colorado.

Multiple Choice: Write the letter of the correct answer.

———— 5. The state farthest east is
    a. Nevada   b. Nebraska   c. New York

———— 6. The state farthest west is
    a. Nevada   b. Nebraska   c. New York

———— 7. The state farthest north is
    a. North Dakota   b. Kansas   c. Texas

———— 8. The state farthest south is
    a. North Dakota   b. Kansas   c. Texas

———— 9. The states next to Florida are
    a. AL and MS   b. AL and GA   c. GA and SC

———— 10. The states next to Washington are
    a. ID and MT   b. ID and OR   c. OR and CA

———— 11. States next to New Hampshire are
    a. ME, MA, and VT   b. ME, MY, and WY   c. MA, NY and VT

———— 12. The state *farthest* west is
    a. Alaska   b. California   c. Hawaii

Figure 3 (A)
(developed by Judy Winn-Bell Olsen)
A/B Activities: Getting Information from Your Partner

- You and your partner have the same chart, but different information is missing on each chart.
- Find the blanks on your chart, and ask your partner for the information to put in the blanks.
- For *location*, ask "where" questions; for *size*, ask "how big" questions; for *population*, ask "how many" questions; for *acquired*, ask "when" questions; for *present status*, ask "what" questions.
- When you get information from your partner, write it in the blank on your paper.
- Your partner will ask you different questions about your chart. Take turns asking questions and writing down information.
- Don't look at each other's papers!

United States Overseas Territories and Possessions

Name	Location	Size	Population	Acquired	Present Status
Alaska	Pacific	586,400 sq. mi. (1,518,766 sq. km.)	412,000	———	State (1959)
Midway Islands	Pacific	2 sq. mi. (5 sq. km.)	2,300	1867	Possession
Hawaii	Pacific	———	981,000	1898	———
Guam	Pacific	212 sq. mi. (549 sq. km.)	106,000	1898	Territory
Philippines	Pacific	115,707 sq. mi. (300,000 sq. km.)	———	1898	Independent (1946)
Puerto Rico	Caribbean	3,435 sq. mi. (8,897 sq. km.)	3,197,000	———	Commonwealth
Wake Island	———	3 sq. mi. (8 sq. km.)	300	1899	———
American Samoa	Pacific	76 sq. mi. (197 sq. km.)	———	1899	Territory
Canal Zone	Panama	647 sq. mi. (1676 sq. km.)	42,000	1903	U.S./Panama Control
Virgin Islands	———	133 sq. mi. (344 sq. km.)	96,000	1916	Territory
Northern Mariana Islands	Pacific	———	16,680	1947	Commonwealth (1982)
Marshall & Caroline Islands	Pacific	533 sq. mi. (1380 sq. km.)	116,555	1947	U.S. Trust Territory of the Pacific Islands (UN)

Figure 3 (B)
(developed by Judy Winn-Bell Olsen)
A/B Activities: Getting Information from Your Partner

- You and your partner have the same chart, but different information is missing on each chart.
- Find the blanks on your chart, and ask your partner for the information to put in the blanks.
- For *location*, ask "where" questions; for *size*, ask "how big" questions; for *population*, ask "how many" questions; for *acquired*, ask "when" questions; for *present status*, ask "what" questions.
- When you get information from your partner, write it in the blank on your paper.
- Your partner will ask you different questions about your chart. Take turns asking questions and writing down information.
- Don't look at each other's papers!

United States Overseas Territories and Possessions

Name	Location	Size	Population	Acquired	Present Status
Alaska	Pacific	———	412,000	1867	State (1959)
Midway Islands	———	2 sq. mi. (5 sq. km.)	2,300	1867	Possession
Hawaii	Pacific	6,424 sq. mi. (16,638 sq. km.)	———	1898	State (1959)
Guam	Pacific	212 sq. mi. (549 sq. km.)	106,000	1898	———
Philippines	Pacific	115,707 sq. mi. (300,000 sq. km.)	50,310,000	1898	Independent (1946)
Puerto Rico	———	3,435 sq. mi. (8,897 sq. km.)	3,197,000	1898	———
Wake Island	Pacific	———	300	1899	Possession
American Samoa	Pacific	76 sq. mi. (197 sq. km.)	32,000	———	Territory
Canal Zone	Panama	647 sq. mi. (1676 sq. km.)	42,000	1903	U.S./Panama Control
Virgin Islands	Caribbean	133 sq. mi. (344 sq. km.)	———	1916	Territory
Northern Mariana Islands	Pacific	184 sq. mi. (477 sq. km.)	16,680	———	Commonwealth (1982)
Marshall & Caroline Islands	Pacific	533 sq. mi. (1380 sq. km.)	116,555	1947	U.S. Trust Territory of the Pacific Islands (UN)

Figure 4[2]

Motor Vehicle Registration

Can you find EIGHT differences between these pictures?

[2]From *Look Again Pictures for Language Development and Lifeskills*, Englewood Cliffs, NJ: Alemany Press.

Figure 5 (A)

How Did the United States Become a Leading Industrial Nation?

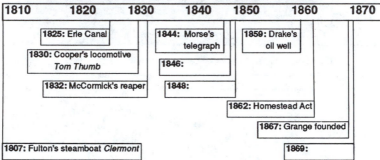

1810	1820	1830	1840	1850	1860	1870

1825: Erie Canal

1830: Cooper's locomotive *Tom Thumb*

1832: McCormick's reaper

1844: Morse's telegraph

1846:

1848:

1859: Drake's oil well

1862: Homestead Act

1867: Grange founded

1807: Fulton's steamboat *Clermont*

1869:

STEP ONE.   Use Interview to complete your timeline. Ask questions such as "What came after?" or "What happened in 1846?"

STEP TWO.   Compare timelines with your partner. Are they the same? You and your partner must agree before you start Step Three.

STEP THREE.   Solve-Pair-Share.

A. (Solve) Answer these questions by yourself.
   1. How are the events in 1807, 1825 and 1830 similar? (How are they like each other?)
   2. How are the events in 1832, 1844 and 1846 similar? What do they have in common?

B. (Pair) Exchange and explain answers with your partner
C. (Share) Take turns reporting answers to your team.

STEP FOUR.   You will use Roundtable to answer some questions about the timeline. Discuss each question and write the answer only after you agree.

ALTERNATE QUESTIONS

1. When was the Civil War?
2. When was the Trail of Tears?
3. When was the last war between the U.S.A. and Great England (England)?
4. When was the Gold Rush in California?
5. When did Texas become a State?
6. Show these on your timeline.

Illustration from M. Schwartz and J. O'Connor, *Exploring American History,* 1986:34b.

Figure 5 (B)

How Did the United States Become a Leading Industrial Nation?

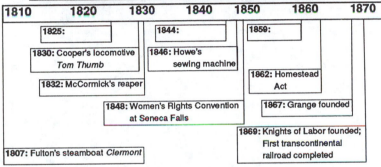

| 1810 | 1820 | 1830 | 1840 | 1850 | 1860 | 1870 |

1825:

1830: Cooper's locomotive
Tom Thumb

1832: McCormick's reaper

1844:

1846: Howe's
sewing machine

1848: Women's Rights Convention
at Seneca Falls

1859:

1862: Homestead
Act

1867: Grange founded

1869: Knights of Labor founded;
First transcontinental
railroad completed

1807: Fulton's steamboat *Clermont*

Teacher Notes

STEP ONE.   (Interview) Students use interview to complete timelines.

STEP TWO.   Students compare timelines.

STEP THREE.   (SPS) Students use Solve-Pair-Share to find similarities among timeline events (transportation, inventions to make work easier). You may also assign the Alternate Questions now, or save them for later. Alternate Questions relate the timeline to earlier lessons.

STEP FOUR.   (Roundtable) Pass out true/false quiz, students discuss and answer 12 item quiz. Interrupt after three minutes and ask how teams might work faster. Give 5 more minutes and review with Numbered Heads.

TRUE/FALSE

1. The Erie Canal was started in 1835.
2. Drake's oil well gave fuel for the first telegraph.
3. The transcontinental railroad was finished after the Civil War.
4. Abraham Lincoln died after Morse invented the telegraph.
5. Cooper's train engine was called the *Clermont*.
6. Cooper's train engine was called the *Tom Thumb*.
7. The Women's Rights Conference was in Souix City.
8. The Women's Rights Conference was before the sewing machine.
9. The *Clermont* was designed to work on the Erie Canal.
10. The California Gold Rush started at Senecca Falls.

Illustration from M. Schwartz and J. O'Connor, *Exploring American History*, 1986:34b.

Figure 6

Jigsaw Activity 5
Who Discovered America?

C

Directions: Look at the map below and discuss it with your group.

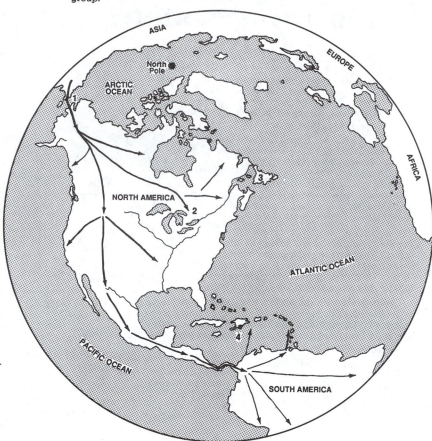

KEY
1. Bering Strait
2. Great Lakes
3. Newfoundland
4. Caribbean Sea

The travels of the native people ➝ ➝

Figure 6 (cont.)

Jigsaw Activity 5

Who Discovered America?

Directions: Look at the map below and discuss it with your group.

KEY

1. Spain
2. Portugal
3. Canary Islands
4. Caribbean Sea

Columbus' voyage

Figure 6 (cont.)

Jigsaw Activity 5: Who Discovered America?

Reading

Directions: Read the story below and discuss it with your group.

1   The first people in the continent of America came before it was called America. They came from Asia, and they came on foot.

2   How was this possible? If you look at the map, you will see that the northeast of Asia and the northwest of North America are very close together. Today, that part of Asia is called Siberia, and that part of North America, in the United States, is called Alaska. Between Siberia and Alaska is only a small body of water called the Bering Strait. A strait is a very narrow body of water that separates two pieces of land. The Bering Strait is only about 50 miles wide.

3   The first people who came to America did not come by boat. Experts think that they came during the last Ice Age, when ice covered large parts of the earth and much of the ocean was frozen. Some of the land was no longer under water. Experts think that the sea bed of the Bering Strait was not covered with water during the Ice Age. The first Americans probably walked across the sea bed of the Bering Strait, not even knowing that it used to be under the sea.

4   They probably did not plan to come here. Twenty thousand years ago, people gathered food and hunted animals. They wandered across the land looking for fruits and vegetables to eat, and following the animals that they hunted. Perhaps the first people in America followed a herd of animals, and crossed to the new continent without knowing it.

5   Twenty thousand years is a long time. During those years, the people moved across the North American continent. Some stayed in the far north, and their descendants live there today. They are the Inuit and Dene peoples, who learned how to live in the very cold climate of the Arctic Circle.

6   Other groups of people moved south. Some reached Central and South America. Some built canoes and travelled across the water to the Caribbean islands, where the Arawak and Carib people lived until the Europeans came. The Caribbean Sea is named for the Carib people.

7   Other groups stayed in Central America. The Aztecs and the Mayans built great civilizations in Mexico. In North America, the people who stayed on the flat prairie land learned how to hunt buffalo and other animals. They lived according to their own laws until the Europeans came to the land. The people on the west and east coasts became great fishers and traders. The people of the woodlands became farmers who lived in permanent villages and had a very organized government.

8   When the Europeans arrived, they found that America was not an empty land. The people they found were not lost. The Europeans were not the first people to come to America; the native people discovered America 20,000 years ago.

All Sides of the Issue, ©1989, Alemany Press, Hayward, CA. Permission granted to reproduce for classroom use.

Figure 6 (cont.)

Jigsaw Activity 5: Who Discovered America?

Reading   D

Directions: Read the story below and discuss it with your group.

1   Christopher Columbus was an Italian from the great port
of Genoa. As a boy, he often talked with sailors in the port
after their long and dangerous voyages across the ocean.

2   He became a sailor, and after one of his voyages he
arrived in Portugal.

3   Lisbon, the capital city of Portugal, was one of the great
centers of learning, exploration, and discovery in Europe.
Columbus studied old maps and read the books of great
geographers and travellers. He began to think that the world
was round like a ball, not flat like a plate as most people then
thought. He decided that it must be possible to sail around the
world and not fall off.

4   At that time, Europeans were trading with China, India,
and Japan. They had to travel overland, going east, to get
there. The journey was long and dangerous, but traders made
the journey because they could get very rich. Europeans
would pay a lot of money for the spices, silks, and jewels of the
East, or "the Indies" as they called it.

5   Columbus decided that he would try to get to the east by
sailing in the opposite direction. If the world was round, he
said, then if he kept sailing west he must eventually arrive in
"the Indies." He estimated that the distance across the Atlantic
would be about 2400 miles and that the voyage would take
about three weeks.

6   Columbus was not a wealthy man. He had to find
someone to sponsor him for the voyage. He needed money for
ships, and he had to pay the crew. For two years Columbus
begged the king of Portugal to sponsor him. However, the
Portuguese finally decided to get to Asia by a different route,
by sailing southeast around Africa. Then Columbus decided
to try the king and queen of Spain. After six years, Queen
Isabella agreed to be his sponsor.

7   After three months of preparation, in August 1492,
Columbus set off with three ships—the Nina, the Pinta, and
the Santa Maria—and a crew of about 90 sailors. They
headed first for the Canary Islands. This first leg of the voyage
took a week, but they had to stay there for three weeks while
they made some repairs and got some final supplies. At last,
on September 6, they set off into the unknown ocean to the
west.

Figure 6 (cont.)

Jigsaw Activity 5: Who Discovered America?

Reading *Continued*

8   Life on board the ship was rough. Only Columbus and the captains of the other two ships had beds; the sailors slept anywhere, in their clothes. They did the cooking on deck. They ate salt meat and fish, and mixed flour with seawater to make a kind of flat bread.

9   Columbus expected the journey to take about three weeks. Unfortunately, his calculations of the circumference of the world were not accurate. Some of the sailors wanted to turn back and go home. On October 12, they finally saw land.

10   Columbus and the other European navigators and geographers of the time did not know that America existed. When Columbus and his crew arrived at a Caribbean island, which they named San Salvador, they thought they were in "the Indies." Because they had reached "the Indies" by sailing west, they called the Caribbean lands "the West Indies," and they have had this name ever since. Columbus then called the people who lived there "Indians." The native people of the Americas are still called "Indians" today, but anthropologists call them "Amerindians" to show the difference from the Indians of India.

11   Until the day he died, Columbus thought he had arrived in "the Indies." He did not know that this was a whole continent that the Europeans would eventually call "America."

12   We know a lot about Columbus' voyage because he kept a journal in which he wrote a record of everything he did and saw. He had to keep accounts for the Spanish king and queen. Spain became very rich and powerful from the land and gold they found in America. They kept records and wrote history books that gave the Spanish point of view. For these reasons, many people think that Columbus discovered America.

Figure 7

Name _____

Jigsaw Activity 5
Who Discovered America? Quiz

Directions: Work alone to answer the questions below.

True or False?

Write **T** if the statement is true, **F** if the statement is false.

1. _____ The Vikings came to North America to search for gold.

2. _____ Leif Ericsson wrote the story of his adventures.

3. _____ The native people came from India.

4. _____ The native people are Amerindians.

5. _____ John the Skillful was hired by the king of England to find new lands.

6. _____ Columbus was working for the king and queen of Spain.

7. _____ The Europeans were looking for a way to get to the East.

8. _____ Columbus made some mistakes.

9. _____ The native people were the first people in America.

10. _____ We can study history only through written records and documents.

Complete the Sentences

Complete each of the sentences with a word from the list below. Use each word only once.

scholar	archeologist	mariner	expert
anthropologist	geographer	navigator	ancestors
settler	climatologist	explorer	descendants
trader	sponsor		

1. A _____ is a sailor.

2. An _____ is someone who knows a lot about something.

3. An _____ travels to new places.

4. Our _____ lived before us.

5. Our _____ will live after us.

6. A _____ is someone who buys and sells things.

Figure 7 (con't)

Jigsaw Activity 5: Who Discovered America?

Quiz

7. An _____ looks for history in the ground.

8. A _____ knows a lot about the world.

9. A _____ goes to live in a new place.

10. A _____ agrees to pay for or support someone else.

11. A _____ studies the weather.

12. An _____ studies the different people of the world.

13. A _____ reads maps and guides ships on a voyage.

14. A _____ spends a lifetime studying.

What Do You Think?

1. Did Columbus discover America? Give reasons for your opinion.

_____

_____

_____

_____

_____

_____

2. Why are the native people called "Indians"?

_____

_____

_____

_____

Figure 8
Interview Sheets to Emphasize the Concept "Discover"

INTERVIEWS: Ask your partner these questions and write down the answers. When you have finished, answer the questions your partner asks you.

1. Have you ever discovered anything?

_____

2. What?

_____

3. Do you remember finding something for the first time?

_____

4. What? (What was it?)

_____

_____

_____

5. Tell me more. That sounds interesting.

_____

_____

_____

REFERENCES

ADDISON, A.A. 1988. Comprehensible textbooks in science for the non-native English speaker: Evidence from discourse analysis. *CATESOL Journal*, 1, no. 1: 49–66.

BLOOM, B.S. 1956. *Taxonomy of Educational Objectives: Cognitive Domain.* New York: Longmans, Green.

CHAMOT, A.U., and J.M. O'MALLEY. 1987. The cognitive academic language learning approach: A bridge to the mainstream. *TESOL Quarterly*, 21: 227–49.

COEHLO, E. 1988. Cooperative group learning: A theoretical and practical overview. Panel presentation at TESOL '88 (Chicago, IL).

COEHLO, E., L. WINER, and J.W-B. OLSEN. 1989. *All Sides of the Issue: Activities for Cooperative Jigsaw Groups.* Englewood Cliffs, NJ: Alemany Press.

COLLIER, V.P. 1989. How Long? A synthesis of research on academic achievement in a second language. *TESOL Quarterly*, 23, no. 3: 509–31.

CRANDALL, J. (ed.). 1987. *ESL Through Content-Area Instruction: Mathematics, Science, Social Studies.* Englewood Cliffs, NJ: Prentice Hall Regents.

KAGAN, S. 1989. *Cooperative Learning Resources for Teachers.* San Juan Capistrano, CA: Resources for Teachers.

KELLER, E., and S.T. WARNER. 1988. *Conversation Gambits.* Hove (UK): Language Teaching Publications (35 Church Road, Hove, BN3 2BE).

KRASHEN, S.D., and T.D. TERRELL. 1983. *The Natural Approach: Language Acquisition in the Classroom.* Englewood Cliffs, NJ: Alemany Press.

KUTRAKUN, S. 1989. The main factors causing LEP students to be at risk in content area classes. *WAESOL Newsletter* (Washington Association for the Education of Speakers of Other Languages), 14, no. 2: 2–3,8.

OLSEN, J.W-B. 1977. *Communication-Starters and Other Activities for the ESL Classroom.* Englewood Cliffs, NJ: Alemany Press.

———. 1984. *Look Again Pictures for Language Development and Lifeskills.* Englewood Cliffs, NJ: Alemany Press.

OLSEN, R.E. W-B. 1989. A Survey of Limited English Proficient (LEP) Student Enrollments and Identification Criteria. *TESOL Quarterly*, 23, no. 3: 469–88.

———. 1991. ESL enrollment update: Survey results (1985–1990). *TESOL Matters*, 1. (in press).

O'MALLEY, J.M., and A.U. CHAMOT. 1988. The cognitive academic language learning approach (CALLA). *Journal of Multilingual and Multicultural Development*, 9: 43–60.

———. 1990. *Learning Strategies in Second Language Acquisition.* Cambridge: Cambridge University Press.

SCHWARTZ, M., and J. O'CONNOR. 1986. *Exploring American History.* Englewood Cliffs, NJ: Globe Book Co.

CHAPTER 6

"I LEARNED TO TALK MATHEMATICS":
USING COOPERATIVE GROUPS WITH COLLEGE MINORITY STUDENTS

Mary Ellen Quinn and Marilyn Molloy

Introduction

I wish I could comprehend a little faster so that I could add more to the discussion.

I believe a longer discussion would help us with the problems we are going to tackle.

This exchange of remarks between two students leaving a calculus class does not sound like what one typically hears from students in college mathematics classes, yet the exchange took place outside the classroom door about midway through the course taught by instructors using a cooperative learning model.

Cooperative learning (CL) takes many forms. It is the purpose of this chapter to describe a model of collaborative learning used in selected mathematics courses for students who are bilingual and whose academic language for mathematics has not been well developed. The model builds heavily upon the research-supported assumptions that attention to language is essential for good mathematics lessons and that

117

the contents of mathematics are extremely useful in creating language lessons for second language learners (Dale and Cuevas, 1987).

Talking Mathematics: A New Approach

Many students entering university level mathematics classes have been taught by teachers who hold the traditional view of mathematics as a language-free discipline (Kessler, Quinn, and Hayes, 1990). They hold a traditional belief, increasingly being denied, that mathematical thought is decontextualized, formal, and abstract (Stigler and Baranes, 1988). But mathematics learning is not language free nor is it immune to the influences of culture and the interactions with the language and culture of its students. Mathematics is as culture bound as is learning in other domains. However, because many teachers hold the traditional culture-free view of mathematics, they do not support the notion that discourse or dialogue plays a vital role in promoting student understanding and reflective awareness in mathematics (Lampert, 1986; Whimbey and Lockhead, 1980). Cazden (1986) observes that conversation in the classroom is generally considered to be a nuisance. She among others concludes that research on the relationship between language and content has not had much influence on teaching to date.

Students are led to believe that mathematics is a universal language needing only symbols to be understood. Teachers think that in the mathematics class, students of limited English proficiency (LEP) will not encounter the language barriers that they do in other more "language-dependent" disciplines. Such false impressions are in direct opposition to what is actually the case. Mathematics demands an extremely precise and controlled use of language. And as Pimm (1987: p 8) notes, mathematical discourse is notorious for involving both specialized terms and different meanings attached to everyday words. He cites the following delightful example of the confusion caused by an everyday word used in the context of an elementary school mathematics class (Pimm, 1987: 8).

> In response to the written question " What is the difference between 24 and 9?", one nine-year old replied, "One's even and the other's odd"; whereas another said, "One has two numbers in it and the other has one."

Of course, the intersection of language and mathematics goes far beyond translating words and symbols or a discipline-specific vocabulary into everyday language. Students need to think about the processes in mathematics and talk about them out loud, thus using language as a tool for grappling with concepts and acquiring a new understanding of the content of mathematics (Crandall et al., 1987). Unfortunately, most talk in mathematics classes has come from the teacher, while students take notes, practice what the teacher has demonstrated, and then work in isolation to perfect the technique (Steen, 1989). Recent studies (Burton, 1984; Dawe, 1984; Connolly and Vilardi, 1989) challenge that position and claim that the interaction between mathematics and language demands that students learn to read, write, and speak about mathematical topics if they are to advance beyond mere rote learners or number jugglers.

The basic ideas at the heart of mathematics are simple and powerful (Bruner, 1960). Those basic or key ideas are more meaningful than the host of details that flow from them. However, those key ideas have only recently been identified in domains such as mathematics (Lampert, 1986; Resnick and Omanson, 1987). Surprizing as this may be, it should make traditional instruction more understandable if it is noted that ''key ideas'' are here intended to involve not only content but also the cognitive structure of the learner (Prawat, 1989). Key ideas enhance the accessibility of the knowledge acquired by the students because they contribute to the development of a coherent cognitive structure. And it is those key ideas that can be brought to light and become clarified if the mathematics class becomes one in which students discuss their own ideas, write about them, and engage in other interactive experiences.

Just as *talking* about the content of mathematics is a new approach for most students, so too is *participating* in small groups as a setting to learn that content. Yet, at least four significant reports (American Association for the Advancement of Science, 1989; National Council of Teachers of Mathematics, 1991; 1989; National Research Council, 1989) have directed teachers to change their methods of instruction in order to have students work in small groups, teaching mathematics to one another, arguing about strategies, and expressing arguments in written form.

In an effort to put the directives of those reports and the findings of current research into practice, we developed a cooperative learning model to meet the needs of our largely Hispanic population. In doing that, we required one section of the precalculus course and one section of the beginning calculus course to spend one fourth of their formal course time working in small groups or study teams. This meant that students attended three lectures per week and one study team session per week. The study team sessions, using a cooperative learning model, were designed to include:

- learning some group techniques
- discussing and writing about key mathematical concepts
- solving specific problems
- developing various approaches to problem solving
- using the specific mathematics register being utilized in the lecture portion of the course both in speaking and in writing.

During discussions, students ''talked'' mathematics and read from their own notes as well as from the mathematics text. In addition to the speaking and reading involved in the discussion, the CL teams wrote mathematics by constructing concept maps and using those maps to develop written concept papers. They also wrote out detailed solutions to word problems and then wrote critiques of one another's solutions. Finally, they created their own original word problems and solutions to those problems. Then they exchanged problems and solutions with one another. In doing this, the students relied heavily upon everyday experiences, making mathematics come alive.

Learning to Talk Mathematics

Because few of our students had engaged in cooperative learning, at least on a formal basis as part of an organized course, they needed some instruction in group techniques. In order to assume various roles within the group, learn how to lead, listen to and encourage one another, and develop a genuine team spirit of cooperation, most students needed instructional guidelines. Helping one another is characteristic of Hispanics in general (DeAvila, 1988; Valverde, 1984); however, for college students to exchange answers freely and assist one another within the mathematics classroom took some "getting used to." For that reason the CL team instructor assigned students to teams within the small groups each week. Team size and membership also varied from week to week. Small groups of between nine and sixteen students were further divided into CL teams whose sizes varied from two to five members. This changing from team to team and from one size team to another size team seemed to help the students become accustomed to working together. Variation helped the students feel comfortable with one another and with the entire small group. Other group techniques that had to be explicitly taught and/or practiced included:

- alternating group roles
- organizing for discussions
- evaluating team and individual efforts
- keeping on task.

The literature concerning cooperative learning (Cohen, 1986; Slavin, 1986, 1987; Fullilove, 1986) was particularily helpful to us as we developed our own versions of their practices. We also found a strong need for frequent positive reinforcement, especially with the Hispanic women.

As our future mathematicians became more comfortable with one another and with the techniques of cooperative learning, the quantity and quality of discussions improved noticeably. They began to become pleased with themselves. Remarks such as: "I feel very comfortable about standing up and explaining our problem" and "Since I live off campus, this is one of the only chances I get to work with others and ask questions" were common. Students even began to regard working within a team setting as a *problem to be solved*. Perhaps this was because we had focused strongly on strategies for mathematical problem solving.

One of the clearest indicators that team learning was a success was the number of students who asked to come to "the other small-group" meeting when they missed their own sessions. That success was also mirrored in words such as:

> I think that this really does help because you can discuss problems carefully and also get to work closely with classmates.

> I can't think of anything that would make our teamwork more helpful except spending more time in class.

Knowing that we needed a period of adjustment to group learning has helped us gradually bring calculus and precalculus students to a realization that mathematics is more exciting and meaningful when learners talk about it among themselves, as opposed to just listening to a teacher explain it. Students also seem to appreciate the fact (Prawat, 1989) that verbalization clarifies thought, that it makes the solution of problems that seemed impossible not only possible but even enjoyable. One student even commented:

> Working within a group environment has given me the opportunity to interact with my classmates on a one-to-one basis; this has helped me to see problems from other perspectives.

The above remark also provides evidence of a feeling of social support from the group experiences. Reflecting the social support experienced from participating in study teams, another student said:

> Discussions on black holes, the space shuttle, etc. were very interesting and enjoyable. More discussions would be nice.

Recognition of the importance of each student taking responsibility for the learning of the other members of the CL team is reflected in the comment:

> I could improve our team spirit if I made sure everyone knows what is going on and if I encouraged them.

Developing Materials

Setting up the small groups from the precalculus and calculus classes and helping the students to become comfortable working in teams is an integral part of the CL team instructor's job. It is also necessary to develop a set of materials uniquely suited to the minority students taking the courses. Basically, we culled three sources for creating meaningful weekly lessons: the course texts, students' daily experiences, and students' readings and writings.

A typical weekly worksheet often included:

1. a list of terms drawn from the section of the course text being studied that week
2. directions for oral discussion or for written work
3. specific problems to explain or work on together
4. directions about what to hand in or what to report orally
5. an assignment.

The terms listed might be newly introduced symbols, such as *the sign for integration;* technical terms specific to mathematics, such as *radian measure;* or everyday words used with a special meaning, such as *degree.* Directions for the students on how to use the list of terms could call on them to ask questions of one another using the terms. Or they might be directed to make a concept map (Jones et al., 1988) using at least six of the terms, or even to use the terms in writing their own problems. To assure precision in the terms, they used their texts as reference books, frequently reading aloud entire passages from the text in order to clarify a point or find a precise definition.

Of course, the mathematics register includes much more than just vocabulary terms. Syntax (sentence structure), semantic properties (meanings such as truth conditions), and discourse features also need to be included for the language of mathematics to come alive. It was the discussion and writing portions of our activities that placed the vocabulary terms in context, allowing students to structure their own mathematical talking. Good discussions require not only topics for discussion but also some well-designed questions to arouse interest, get the conversation moving, and keep the groups on task. This is where the daily newspapers as well as the current reading and interests of the students played an important part in drawing up a list of key questions. For example, when the newspapers and TV carried multiple articles about an earthquake, the discussion of that topic led into using exponents and logarithms to solve earthquake problems. Matching the topic for discussion with the particular mathematical content being taught in the lecture portions of the courses was always a challenge, but this is an opportunity for teacher–teacher cooperation. Teacher collaboration proved to be very fruitful in helping us solve some of our most difficult program problems. As one of the instructors remarked, "It is working. We have lost so few students from the course."

Another approach to utilizing meaningful vocabulary and to structuring ideas was the constructing of concept maps. These are diagrams of ideas or concepts and how those concepts are related to one another. Powerful teaching tools because they allow students to visualize concepts and the hierarchical relationships between them, concept maps facilitate problem solving and the comprehension of text material (Novak and Gowin, 1984). Our students developed their own maps and then refined them as they worked with one another to clarify their own ideas. In addition, they also used their concept maps as a basis for writing brief papers about mathematical topics.

The literature on "writing and mathematics" (Johnson, 1983; Nahrgang and Petersen, 1986; Mett, 1987; Connolly and Vilardi, 1989) proved helpful for developing materials for the writing phase of our program. Ideas garnered from that literature were modified for use on our weekly worksheets. Students became so used to writing out ideas that, without any request to do so, one student even wrote out the procedures she used to solve a problem using the calculator:

> The way you solve the example by the calculator is:
> 1. Enter the number (y) that you want to raise to a power.
> 2. Press y^x.
> 3. Enter the power (x).
> 4. Press $=$ or any key that completes the operation.

Some of the topics for assigned written reports included: real numbers, calculus, limits, and derivatives. Brief papers on an assigned topic usually followed a class discussion and concept-mapping session.

The strategies learned in concept mapping and in writing brief papers proved to be useful to students when they began writing their own word problems. It sometimes was not until a CL group tried to decide upon the context for their team problem that they developed a genuine team spirit, evidenced by their obvious delight in writing meaningful problems for the other teams to solve. Despite the persistent view, deeply ingrained in school culture (Kilpatrick, 1987), that mathematics is a string of procedures to be memorized, CL team students did experience the joy of seeing their own ideas evolve into mathematical problems for solving. They then had problems to work on that were interesting, significant, or went beyond predetermined rules (AAAS, 1989). The meaningful experiential context of the following student-written problems is an example of the interaction between language and mathematics:

> A woman reaches for a spoon in the kitchen. She is frightened by a bug and reacts by throwing the spoon into the air. If the spoon is on a counter 1 meter high and the woman throws it into the air with a velocity of 5 meters per second, what is the amount of time before the spoon hits the counter?
>
> A salmon jumps 3 ft. out of the water to go upstream. How long does he have before he lands in the stream?
>
> A motorcyclist is about to make a jump over a car which sits at a height of 5.1 ft. What initial velocity must the motorcycle have in order to clear the car? What is the time the motorcycle will be in the air?

Those student problems made use of up-to-date examples, examples related to actual experiences from daily living. They brought classroom mathematics to life for the students who wrote them and for the students who shared in solving them.

Obviously the above problems were written after the students had spent some time in the study of the mathematics of motion; however, the same students were much more adept both in problem-solving skills and in writing their own problems when they studied the next topic in their calculus class. Not only were they writing about mathematics, they were also reading one another's problems, correcting one another's wording of the problems, finding their own ways to clarify thought, listening and speaking to one another in some very precise mathematical terms, and growing in social skills. They were active participants in their own learning. They were learning mathematics, language, and prosocial skills at the same time.

Finding Rewards

Are there any added rewards for CL instructors who attend extra planning sessions, develop team strategies, create collaborative learning worksheets, and learn new methods of evaluating students? Yes! Just seeing the enthusiasm and pride with which students represent their teams is a genuine teacher reward. So are the noticeable student gains in self-confidence as they experience peer support while presenting their own ideas and work to the group. And hearing one's students talk about mathematics is music to the ears of any mathematics teacher. As one instructor enthusiastically said:

> They are talking about calculus. They are setting up their own
> meetings. They are calling up for help. They are really working.
> They ask more questions.

The long-range goal of our use of cooperative groups with college minority students is to retain those students as majors in mathematics or related fields. It is too early in our program to report firm statistical results; however, to date, the pattern emerging from our data is positive. Students involved in CL study teams are more willing than those in control groups to continue the study of mathematics and/or mathematics-related disciplines. Achievement of the CL students has provided access to further study in mathematics and science. Current data indicate that significantly more students from the CL intervention group have continued in these fields than those from the control group.

If teachers are rewarded for their extra work, that is good. But for any professional teacher, the more important question is "How are the students rewarded?" An obvious answer would be measurable test scores or grades. Fullilove (1986) at the University of California, Berkeley, has reported some remarkable test results for minority students participating in a mathematics workshop structured to use collaborative learning/study techniques. He and Treisman, who assisted in designing the workshops, conclude that a carefully designed collaborative learning program results in better final grades in mathematics and better persistence/graduation rates for both African American and Hispanic student populations.

Much of the literature on cooperative learning (especially Slavin, 1990) stresses the importance of rewarding students for their contributions to the team effort, thus the necessity of team grades as well as individual grades. We found it essential to provide our students with frequent positive evaluations. Quizzes at the end of a team session resulted in two grades, one an individual grade and the other a team grade. The latter resulted from averaging the grades for the individual team members. Presentations of problems to the group were also graded, using a set of criteria given to the students early on in the course. Since students rotated around the team in making presentations, team grades again were assigned at the end of class.

Improved grades were not the only student rewards for team work. Requests for more team-work time provided evidence that the students were finding advantages other than just grades for working in a team setting. They gained self confidence from the peer support they experienced. An attitude of "we're in this together" prevailed as the semester wore on. Perhaps the results can be summarized by the student who answered the question "What team activity helped you most?" with the statement below:

> Being able to share the different methods used to find a solution to a problem and learning to "talk" mathematics has helped me most.

REFERENCES

American Association for the Advancement of Science. 1989. *Science for All Americans.* Washington, D.C.

BRUNER, J.S. 1960. *The Process of Education.* New York: Vintage.

BURTON, L. 1984. Mathematical thinking: The struggle for meaning. *Journal of Research in Mathematics Education,* 15: 35–49.

CAZDEN, C.B. 1986. Classroom discourse. In M.C. Wittrock (ed.), *Handbook of Research on Teaching,* 3rd ed. New York: Macmillan.

COHEN, E.G. 1986. *Designing Groupwork.* New York: Teachers College Press.

CONNOLLY, P., and T. VILARDI. 1989. *Writing to Learn Mathematics and Science.* New York: Columbia Teachers College Press.

CRANDALL, J., T.C. DALE, N.C. RHODES, and G. SPANOS. 1987. *English Skills for Algebra.* Englewood Cliffs, NJ: Prentice Hall Regents.

DALE, T.C., and G.J. CUEVAS. 1987. Integrating language and mathematics learning. In J. Crandall (ed.), *ESL Through Content-Area Instruction.* Englewood Cliffs, NJ: Prentice Hall Regents.

DAWE, L. 1984. A theoretical framework for the study of the effects of bilingualism on mathematics teaching and learning. Paper presented at the Fifth International Congress on Mathematical Education, Adelaide, Australia.

DE AVILA, E.A. 1988. Bilingualism, cognitive function, and language minority group membership. In Cocking, R.R. and J.P. Mestre (eds.). *Linguistic and Cultural Influences on Learning Mathematics.* Hillsdale, NJ: Lawrence Erlbaum.

FULLILOVE, R.E. 1986. Sealing the leaks in the pipeline: Improving the performance and persistence of minority students in college. Report on *The Professional Development Program's Mathematics Workshop* (PDP), Berkeley, CA: University of California.

JOHNSON, M.L. 1983. Writing in mathematics classes: a valuable tool for learning. *Mathematics Teacher,* 76: 117–19.

JONES, F.J., J. PIERCE, and B. HUNTER. 1988. Teaching students to construct graphic representations. *Educational Leadership,* 46, no. 3: 20–25.

KESSLER, C., M.E. QUINN, and C. HAYES. 1990. Processing mathematics in a second language: Problems for LEP children. In A. Labarca and L.M. Bailey (eds.), *Issues in L2: Theory as Practice/Practice as Theory.* Norwood, NJ: Ablex.

KILPATRICK, J. 1987. Inquiry in the mathematics classroom. In *Academic Connections,* Summer 1987. New York: College Entrance Examination Board.

LAMPERT, M. 1986. Knowing,doing, and teaching multiplication. *Cognition and Instruction,* 3: 305–42.

METT, C.L. 1987. Writing as a learning device in calculus. *Mathematics Teacher,* 80: 534–37.

National Council of Teachers of Mathematics. 1989. *Curriculum and Evaluation Standards for School Mathematics.* Reston, VA.

National Council of Teachers of Mathematics. 1991. *Professional Standards for Teaching Mathematics.* Reston, VA.

NAHRGANG, C., and B.T. PETERSEN. 1986. Using writing to learn. *Mathematics Teacher,* 79: 461–65.

National Research Council. 1989. *Everybody Counts: A Report to the Nation on the Future of Mathematics Education.* Washington, D.C.: National Academy Press.

NOVAK, J.D., and D. B. GOWIN. 1984. *Learning How to Learn.* Cambridge: Cambridge University Press.

PIMM, D. 1987. *Speaking Mathematically.* New York: Routledge & Kegan Paul.

PRAWAT, R.S. 1989. Promoting access to knowledge, strategy, and disposition in students: A research synthesis. *Review of Educational Research,* 59, no. 1: 1–41.

RESNICK, L.B., and S.F. OMANSON. 1987. Learning to understand arithmetic. In R. Glaser (ed.), *Advances in Instructional Psychology,* Hillsdale, NJ: Erlbaum.

SLAVIN, R.E. 1986. Cooperative learning: Engineering social psychology in the classroom. In R.S. Feldman (ed.), *The Social Psychology of Education,* Cambridge: Cambridge University Press.

———. 1987. *Cooperative Learning: Student Teams,* 2nd ed. Washington, D.C.: National Education Association.

———. 1990. *Cooperative Learning: Theory, Research, and Practice.* Englewood Cliffs, NJ: Prentice Hall.

STEEN, L.A. 1989. Teaching mathematics for tomorrow's world. *Educational Leadership,* 47, no. 3: 18–22.

STIGLER, J.W., and R. BARANES. 1988. Culture and mathematics learning. In E.Z. Rothkopf (ed.), *Review of Research in Education,* 15: 253–306.

VALVERDE, L.A. 1984. Underachievement and underrepresentation of Hispanics in mathematics and mathematics-related careers. *Journal for Research in Mathematics Education,* 15: 123–133.

WHIMBEY, A., and J. LOCHHEAD. 1980. *Problem Solving and Comprehension: A Short Course in Analytical Reasoning,* 2nd ed. Philadelphia: Franklin Institute Press.

CHAPTER 7

JIGSAW: INTEGRATING LANGUAGE AND CONTENT

Elizabeth Coelho

This chapter will first outline the basic principles and techniques of cooperative learning and will discuss the benefits of content-based instruction. The rest of the chapter will focus on Jigsaw, a cooperative method of curriculum and classroom organization, and provide practical suggestions for content-based Jigsaw activities and projects using existing and teacher-prepared materials.

The Cooperative Classroom

What is cooperative learning? What makes it work? What kinds of learning tasks are appropriate? How do you organize and manage the groups? This section will provide an introduction to basic principles and practices in cooperative learning.

Basic Principles of Cooperative Learning

Cooperative learning is not a new phenomenon. Evolving from a humanist view of education propounded by Dewey and others, it is an approach to education based on the philosophy that education should be learner centered and learner directed; that learners can be teachers; and that teachers are guides and facilitators rather than the source of all knowledge and direction.

There has been increased emphasis in North American schools on the use of small-group instruction rather than, or as well as, whole-class instruction; however, many teachers are still reluctant to have students work in groups, partly because most teachers have not themselves experienced successful group work as students. We tend to teach as we were taught, just as we tend to parent as we were parented. Some teachers are uncomfortable with group work because they feel that they are relinquishing control, that the students are no longer directly accountable to the teacher and that some will therefore choose not to do any work at all, preferring to allow someone else in the group to do it. These are legitimate concerns. Fortunately, the cooperative learning approach has developed many techniques for classroom and curriculum organization that make group work effective. Jigsaw, the main focus of this chapter, is one of those techniques.

There are some important criteria that should be applied to classroom tasks in order to make group work effective. This list of five basic principles forms the core of *Together We Learn* (Clarke et al., 1990):

- students work in small heterogeneous groups;
- students work in positive interdependence;
- students are accountable both as individuals and as a group;
- students learn through ample opportunity for purposeful talk;
- students learn and practice cooperative skills as they study and explore the subject matter together.

These principles are explained in more detail below, with a special focus on how they promote effective group learning in a multiracial context—where some or all of the learners are still acquiring the language of instruction—and on how they apply to the Jigsaw technique in particular.

Small Heterogeneous Groups   Groups need to be small in order to provide maximum opportunities for oral interaction. Groups of four are very flexible, because they can easily be regrouped into pairs for some activities. Larger than four reduces the amount of interaction opportunities, and some students may begin to contribute and participate less than others.

The studies on the effects of different kinds of grouping indicate strongly that students should be organized into heterogeneous groups for optimum learning. Depending on the composition of the class, some of the criteria that teachers can apply in sorting students into groups include the following: academic achievement, proficiency in the language of instruction, racial and ethnic background, gender, age, personality type, and learning style. Because each student in a Jigsaw group has a different learning task, it is possible to provide learning materials and experiences to meet students' individual needs, as illustrated later in this chapter.

Positive Interdependence   Competitive and individualistic modes of behavior are not inborn, but they are certainly ingrained. Students will work effectively in groups only if it is clear that it is to their benefit to do so. The task must be structured in such a way that it would be better done by the group than by any individual; each member of the group depends on every other member for some aspect of the task. The learning materials need to be developed and distributed in carefully planned ways to convey to students that work on a task is to be a joint, not individual, effort and that the students are in a ''sink or swim together'' situation (Johnson, Johnson, Holubec, and Roy, 1984). The Jigsaw method of curriculum and materials organization creates strong interdependence. It is impossible for students to complete the assignment unless they share information and ideas with each other.

Individual Accountability   Although students work together, each is individually accountable to the group and the teacher for completion of his/her own assignment or portion of it, and for helping others. The group as a whole is accountable for the group process and product, but each individual student is also evaluated by the teacher and peers. Additionally, students do a self-evaluation. Factors considered are the level and quality of participation and the demonstration of learning (through a quiz, assignment, or portion of a group project). The structure of Jigsaw provides each student with an individual learning assignment. Each student is accountable for knowing his/her material and sharing it effectively with the rest of the group.

Purposeful Talk   It is through language that learners come to understand ideas. Students need opportunities to explore, rehearse, and internalize ideas through oral interaction: through ''thinking aloud'' in a small nonjudgmental forum. Cooperative learning groups offer these opportunities, and the Jigsaw technique applied to problem-solving tasks, as outlined later in this chapter, provides each group member with information to contribute to the ''pool'' of information required for solution of the problem. Higher-level thinking and discussion skills are developed through analysis, evaluation, synthesis, and application of this information to the problem.

Group Skills   Students who have been socialized into a competitive or individualistic mode of learning will need to learn how to work effectively in groups. Included in the instructional objectives for a lesson or unit of lessons will be behavioral objectives such as ''managing disagreement,'' ''taking turns,'' and ''offering help.'' (See Chapter 2 for an analysis of how these skills are realized through specific oral strategies.)

Three Kinds of Cooperative Learning Tasks

This is an overview of the three major types of cooperative learning tasks. Each has many variations, generated by teachers and their students as they adapt the techniques to suit their own classroom. Kagan (1989) describes many of them in more detail in his handbook *Cooperative Learning Resources for Teachers.*

Team practice from common input: → skills development and mastery of facts

- All students work on the same material.
- Practice could follow a traditional teacher-directed presentation of new material and for that reason is a good starting point for teachers and/or students new to group work.
- The task is to make sure that everyone in the group knows the answer to a question or understands the material. Because students want their team to do well, they coach and tutor each other to make sure that any member of the group could answer for all of them.
- When the teacher takes up the question or assignment, anyone in a group may be called on to answer for the team.
- This technique is good for review and for practice tests; the group takes the practice test together, but each student will eventually do an assignment or take a test individually.
- This technique is effective in situations where the composition of the groups is unstable (in adult programs, for example). Students can form new groups every day.

Jigsaw: differentiated but predetermined input → evaluation and synthesis of facts and opinions

- Each group member receives a different piece of the information.
- Students regroup in topic groups (expert groups) to master the material.
- Students return to home groups (Jigsaw groups) to share their information with each other.
- Students synthesize the information through discussion.
- Each student produces an assignment or part of a group project, or takes a test, to demonstrate synthesis of all the information presented by all group members.
- This method of organization requires teambuilding activities for both home groups and topic groups, long-term group involvement, and rehearsal of presentation methods.
- This method is very useful in the multilevel class, allowing for both homogenous and heterogeneous grouping in terms of English proficiency.
- This method of small-group organization and instruction was developed by Elliot Aronson and colleagues (1978) more than a decade ago.

Cooperative projects: topics/resources selected by students → discovery learning

- Topic may be different for each group.
- Students identify topics for each group member.

- Steering committee may coordinate the work of the class as a whole.
- Students research the information using resources such as library reference, interviews, visual media.
- Students synthesize their information for a group presentation: oral and/or written.
- Each group presents to the whole class.
- This method places greater emphasis on individualization and students' interests. Each student's assignment is unique.
- Students need plenty of previous experience with more structured group work for this to be effective.
- Group Investigation, a method developed by the Sharans, has had very positive results in concept and language development (Sharan and Shachar, 1988).

Language and Content

Most ESL programs focus, quite appropriately, on the language of daily survival and social interaction—the kind of language usually learned in beginning and intermediate level programs. But the language learning process extends over several years, and students at middle and secondary school still face the formidable task of learning in a language they have not yet mastered at a level of proficiency commensurate with that of their English-speaking peers. Students who may have acquired some fluency in English and are able to read and write with some facility about familiar topics still have to acquire, very rapidly, a vast corpus of language for academic study. This section examines the nature of that language and the context of the learning.

Language as a Tool for Learning

Language is a primary communication tool through which learners explore and come to understand ideas. It takes five to seven years for children to acquire a new language at a level of proficiency equivalent to that of their age-peers. As students advance into middle and secondary school, the corpus of language they have to acquire becomes much larger; and for those who are still learning the language of instruction, it sometimes appears to be an impossible task. As they struggle to catch up with their age-peers, the peers are also moving ahead. At the same time as the language of instruction becomes increasingly sophisticated and complex, the concept load increases in complexity, depth, and volume.

Most ESL students receive direct ESL support for only the first year or two, and almost all are integrated into mainstream classes for at least some of the day right from the beginning, interacting with peers and teachers on content-based tasks.

Many ESL teachers, and some students, feel that this situation is not supportive of language learning; but others have found that successful participation in classrooms where language is a tool for learning about something else enhances acquisition of the language in the context where the learner really needs to use it.

What kind of content classroom provides learning experiences that help ESL learners comprehend the subject matter and continue to learn and practice English at the same time? A classroom that has many attributes of the good ESL classroom. The language employed to communicate ideas is supported by concrete representation, visual images, showing and demonstrating, "hands-on" experiences, and simulations. There are abundant opportunities for meaningful, purposeful talk. Students are introduced to new content with reference to what they already know; the teacher and the curriculum materials take account of the learners' cultural and conceptual background and help students to make links and connections between their own experience and the new information.

Similarly, the ESL program benefits from adoption of some features of the content classroom. Content that is intrinsically important and intellectually engaging provides the basis for tasks that develop academic skills. Language learners need something to talk and read and write about. Mohan (1986) observes that content is not only the subject matter of the content class but also the topics discussed in the language class. Whenever the language teacher and students communicate, they communicate about something, about some topic or content. One cannot ignore content in the language class, just as one cannot ignore language as a medium of learning in the content class. Every language teacher must systematically organize content material to support language learning.

Selecting Content for the ESL Program

What kind of content is appropriate for the language classroom? Unfortunately, many of the ESL texts, designed for mass markets in North America, the United Kingdom, and overseas, feature content that is not engaging, thought provoking, or particularly relevant to the lives of students using them. The content selected for the ESL program should draw on the students' own experiences, the orientation information they need about their new country and the school system, and the demands of other curriculum areas for background information and experiences that students brought up and educated in other countries and cultures may not have. The ESL program that explores a range of topics—social studies, environmental science, the world of work, government and politics, current issues, literature—provides an appropriate variety of contexts for the acquisition of language for application across the curriculum. The ESL class following a content- and task-based curriculum may look like a civics class, a group counseling session, an assertiveness training session, a science class, or an employee training program. At the end of each class, students should leave knowing something more about the world or themselves than they did before, as well as having acquired some new vocabulary and "chunks" of language functional within that context.

Subject-Specific Language

ESL teachers and subject teachers need to examine the demands of language across the curriculum, with special reference to the students who are still learning the language of instruction. Most teachers recognize the special vocabulary of different subjects, but this may not, in fact, present ESL students with the greatest difficulty. In addition to specialized vocabulary, different subject areas feature certain items of syntax and rhetorical organization that are subject specific or of very high frequency in that subject (Coelho, 1982). Some examples are provided below.

Subject-Specific Vocabulary:

Most subjects have their specialized vocabulary. The most obvious consists of those words that have very limited application outside that subject area. A word such as "photosynthesis," for example, is unlikely to be used at school other than in a biology text or classroom.

The second category of subject-specific vocabulary consists of those words that have a general, nonspecific meaning, or several meanings defined by the context, but also have a very specific meaning within the subject area. Words like "mass" have several meanings. Depending on the context, "mass" could be a crowd, a religious ritual, or a tumor. In physics, however, it has a very specific meaning. "Power" has different meanings in geography, mathematics, politics, and history. For language learners, these words are problematic; the dictionary is a poor resource, listing as it does all the common meanings of a word first. "Balance" is a word with a fixed meaning in the accounting class. That definition is given as the seventh of eight in the *Concise Oxford Dictionary.* In history the student encounters the expression "balance of power;" in environmental studies "balance of nature" describes an ecological concept; in law and civics "balance of mind" refers to a legal notion of criminal responsibility; and there are several other context-defined meanings in different subject areas. Subject-specific vocabulary is best explained and acquired within the context that exemplifies and supports it.

Syntax   In some subject areas there is a very high frequency of specific syntactic patterns or language structures. For example, in history a wide range of verb tenses is used to show temporal and causal relationships between events. Students reading the following sentence must attend to verb tense in order to determine those relationships:

> Columbus *had read* Marco Polo and *studied* ancient maps and charts, and *believed* that he *could reach* Asia by a Western route.

In this sentence, events are listed in chronological sequence, and students might be able to rely on that some of the time. However, it is not uncommon for the result clause to appear first in the sentence, before the cause that chronologically precedes it. In the sentence below, the event described second precedes the first. This ordering is marked by use of the past perfect tense *had fled* in the second clause.

> By the late nineteenth century, there *were* several black communities in southern Ontario whose ancestors *had fled* slavery in the United States.

Another syntactic feature of high frequency in certain types of discourse is the passive voice. Several subject areas require students to describe a process, involving almost exclusive use of passive constructions:

> The experiment *was carried* out (science), the logs *are felled* and *floated* downstream (geography/environmental studies), the ballots *are counted* (history/current affairs).

Passive structures are of low frequency in everyday interaction. These academic contexts provide the best opportunity for focusing on their use in a way that is functional.

Rhetorical Patterns   In some subject areas, there are conventions about how ideas should be organized and linked into a coherent whole. For example, students working with scientific material have a context for the development of language for functions such as classification, describing a sequence in a process, and making quantitative and qualitative comparisons. These functions are often signaled by rhetorical devices. For example, students of history need to be familiar with and able to use a large number of words and phrases related to chronological sequencing:

prior to,	initially,	subsequently,
within two years,	ultimately	

These expressions of temporal relationships are often overlaid with linguistic signals of cause and effect:

because (of),	as a result (of),	therefore,
consequently,	as a consequence of	

Rhetorical signals of organization acquired in one subject area are often transferable to other curriculum areas. For example, in geography students are often required to make quantitative and qualitative comparisons, describe a sequence in the manufacturing or agricultural process, or identify cause and effect relationships in ecological, political, and economic aspects of geography.

The most effective context for students to acquire the language of the content areas is within the content area. Because Jigsaw is a cooperative learning method designed to assist students to master quite large amounts of content through talking and sharing information, it is ideally suited to the content-based ESL classroom.

Implementing Jigsaw
in the Language Classroom

What are the benefits of Jigsaw in the content-based language classroom? How should the groups be structured? What preparation do teacher and students need for Jigsaw activities? How does the teacher direct the work of the groups? This section provides practical advice on implementing Jigsaw in the second language classroom.

Benefits of Jigsaw in the Second Language Classroom

The main intent of Aronson and colleagues (Aronson et al., 1978) in developing Jigsaw was to provide opportunities for students to work in racially and culturally mixed groupings in a way facilitating interracial and intercultural trust and acceptance while promoting the academic achievement of minority students. It was outstandingly successful, and has been adopted and adapted for many curriculum areas. The relevance of the approach to second language learners is that Jigsaw provides an excellent learning environment for the acquisition of language through relevant content, the development of academic skills through carefully structured reading and writing activities, and the exploration of relevant content through use of purposeful talk in the classroom.

Because it offers a highly interactive learning experience, the Jigsaw strategy supports the communicative approach in language teaching. In the Jigsaw classroom, students in small groups are dependent on the others in the group for the information they need in order to learn a topic or complete a task. Each student studies and rehearses material with a specific purpose in mind: to be able to teach or tell the others in the group the main points and important details of his or her own piece of information. The group then works together to evaluate and synthesize the information in order to solve a problem or complete a task. Students develop their cognitive skills of analysis, comparison, evaluation, and synthesis of information. These skills are as important for reading and discussing the daily newspaper as they are for academic success.

Retelling or paraphrasing the main points of what has been read or heard is a very effective teaching/learning strategy for the development of reading and listening comprehension, but in the conventional classroom the teacher is the audience for every student. As a result, only a very limited amount of time is available for each learner. In the Jigsaw classroom the student's Jigsaw group is the student's audience, which is shared with only three to five other people.

Moreover, each member of the group has a vested interest in making sure that the sharing of information is effective because the group has to complete a task based on the complete set of information. Students develop their presentation and questioning techniques as a result of a strong motivation to make sure that everyone in the group gets all the information in order to complete the task or quiz that follows.

A genuine purpose for communication exists. This is the most important prerequisite for the development of communicative activities.

In the Jigsaw classroom, an additional benefit to teacher and students is availability of study materials at different levels of difficulty. In conventional classrooms, the level of reading material is likely to be inappropriate for more than half the students in the class. The multilevel nature of most ESL classrooms demands a more student-centered approach. The Jigsaw technique allows the teacher to use several texts or information sources at different levels of linguistic or conceptual difficulty, in one class.

How to Prepare the Class for Jigsaw

Students usually need to learn cooperative group skills over a period of time, through a series of activities of increasing complexity. When groups are first formed, students need to get to know and trust one another. The following activities have been effective in many cooperative classrooms.

Group Formation   In most classrooms, if the teacher instructs students to organize themselves into groups, choosing their own group partners, students will group together with their friends. Most students choose their friends according to perceived similarity; and the result is often that students of the same racial background group together, or the high achievers seek each other out, or boys and girls end up in separate groups, and so on. As a result, the teacher needs to organize the groups, but it is important to be overt about this. Students need an explanation that in this classroom they are expected to learn to get along, communicate effectively, and work with people whom they might consider different from themselves; that everyone deserves opportunities to make more than one or two friends in the class; that these opportunities will better equip them for interaction in the wider society; and that heterogeneous groups have proved to contribute more to everyone's level of academic achievement than other kinds of groups. Parents may need to hear this information, too.

Because students will be assigned to work with others whom they would never voluntarily select as partners, there is need for a number of introductory group activities to help students "break the ice," find areas of common ground, and begin to feel part of a team.

Exploring Commonalities   Quick brainstorming sessions that help to establish areas of common interest or experience are very helpful. For example, the teacher instructs the students to: "Find out what you all have in common," "Make a list of everyone's favorite sport/food/color/book/school subject. . . . " Brainstorming is timed (two or three minutes is usually enough) and the results shared with the class. The teacher will not take volunteers to report for the groups, so it is necessary for each member of a group to be ready to report for the group. The teacher calls on individuals to report, sometimes calling on "the student whose first name is nearest the beginning of the alphabet,'' or ''the person whose birthday is nearest to the end of the year,'' or by having students number off according to the number of students in each group and calling on, for example, ''all the number three's'' to identify themselves and respond for their groups. When students report, coaching by other group members is definitely allowed. This is what fosters cooperation and supports learning. To encourage other groups to listen rather than continue to rehearse their own reports, the teacher tells students they are all expected to be able to parapahrase the report in progress. The teacher may select students or groups randomly or by number to do so. Students are encouraged to refer to the originating group to check that they have included everything, gotten details right, and so on: ''Did I miss anything?'', ''Was that right?''

Identifying the Group   Students of all ages enjoy finding a name for their group. The name can be used in a logo or banner and hung above the group's table to identify their work space. It can identify a section of the bulletin board where group members display pieces of writing, pictures, photographs, newspaper stories—anything that is by, about, or of interest to the members of their group.

Word Puzzles   Acrostic, crossword, and other word puzzles can be used to introduce students to the idea that they may be able to learn more effectively together than alone. This is a radical notion for most of them. The example below was developed for students new to Canada who had been working on some orientation information about their new country (Coelho, 1991:28). Working in groups of four, each student received the same puzzle grid:

Each student in a group of four receives one of the following sets of clues:

Student A	Student B	Student C	Student D
1. It ends with R.	It begins with V.	It's a city.	It's on the West Coast.
2. It's in Ontario.	It begins with O.	It ends with the letter A.	It's a city.
3. It begins with M.	It's big.	It's an animal.	It has double O.
4. It ends with Y.	It's small.	It's round.	It's not worth much.
5. It begins with S.	It doesn't grow.	It's a food.	It came here from Italy.
6. Laws are made there.	It's a place for talking.	It begins with P.	It's in Ottawa.
7. It's golden-yellow.	Canada is famous for it.	It ends with T.	We make flour and bread with it.
8. It's delicious.	It's big.	It's a bird.	It begins with T.
9. It's a winter sport.	It begins with S.	It's not skating.	It's very popular in Canada.
10. People can get hurt.	It's very fast.	It's a sport.	It begins with H.
11. It begins with M.	It ends with A.	It's in the West of Canada.	It's a province.

All students have the following:

12. The hidden word is "_____."

   It means " _____."

The clues include information of the following kinds: spelling/form of word (beginning/ending letter, affixes, part of speech, etc.); category; attributes (size, shape, color, location, etc.); definition. The answers, for readers who lack Canadian cultural background, are as follows:

1. Vancouver
2. Ottawa
3. Moose
4. Penny
5. Spaghetti
6. Parliament
7. Wheat
8. Turkey

9. Skiing
10. Hockey
11. Manitoba
12. Co-operation
    (British and
    Canadian spelling)

The teacher instructs students initially to work independently of each other. The task is to complete the word puzzle. After about a minute, students will be showing signs of frustration with the task. The teacher asks the students to explain why the task is so frustrating; students respond that *they do not have enough information*. The teacher agrees: they do not have enough information *if they are trying to work alone*. However, as a group they do have enough information, and they should share it. The puzzle can be completed only if students share the information each has. Students are instructed to tell each other their clues. They do not exchange papers or show their papers to each other.

When the puzzle has been completed, the focus of the activity shifts to analysis of the process of information sharing. The class discusses the idea of interdependence, that some activities can be done only with the full participation of everyone in the group.

After two or three puzzles of this type, groups of students are usually able to start creating their own and circulating them to other groups for completion. This is a very useful technique for reviewing content and vocabulary. It reinforces reference skills as students search through their material to find words and concepts to include in their puzzles.

Other Activities It takes time and practice to develop group skills and create a cooperative atmosphere. The activity "Whose Suitcase?" described in Chapter 2, with its focus on clarification strategies, is a useful introduction to the kind of language required to facilitate group interaction. Kagan (1989) has some excellent suggestions for teambuilding activities. Some fine cooperative board games for large and small groups of all ages are available from Family Pastimes (see references).

How to Organize Jigsaw Activities

Grouping and Division of the Task In the ESL classroom, the two primary criteria to be applied in sorting the groups are the students' first languages and proficiency levels in English. The diagram below illustrates the dynamics of Jigsaw groups:

```
      A                 A                 A

   B     C           B     C           B     C

      D                 D                 D
```

These are three Jigsaw groups. Each letter represents a different topic or sub-topic. All students identified by the same letter will receive the same material. (The letters do not indicate proficiency level, but the order in which students will present their information to each other.)

Let us suppose that students are to study material on "pioneer life in Canada" (or "early settlers in the United States"). The class will receive some common input: a movie, a field trip, examination of a set of pictures, or other source of background information. The topic then can be divided into four subtopics: homes and furniture, farming methods, food and cooking, and social life.

In the average ESL class, each Jigsaw group of four students probably has one proficient language learner, two average, and one of limited proficiency in English. The tasks or topics are assigned to students according to their language level, and the students who are assigned the same topics regroup into expert groups based on their topic. To accommodate the different levels in the class, materials of different levels of reading and/or conceptual difficulty can be assigned for different topics. For example, one group with less proficient language skills in English might be given a captioned filmstrip with an accompanying cassette tape, while another might get a social studies textbook, and another group of advanced proficiency might be referred to the library to use reference materials. The expert groups look like this:

A A	B B	C C	D D
A	B	C	D
Homes and Furniture	Farming Methods	Food and Cooking	Social Life
(*textbook chapter*)	(*filmstrip and tape*)	(*textbook chapter*)	(*library reference*)

Working in the Expert Groups   These are new groups for the students. At this point it will be necessary to do some new teambuilding activities in order to introduce students to new team members. The activities need not be the same in all the groups. Because these groups are far more homogeneous than the Jigsaw groups in terms of proficiency in English, diversified activities would be appropriate.

In the expert groups, students work on their section of the material, complete some comprehension exercises, perhaps take a quiz on their section of the material, and rehearse the material for presentation in their original Jigsaw groups. The teacher circulates from group to group, discussing and checking responses to the questions, and assisting students to help each other prepare for the oral presentation. They should actually try out the oral presentation in the expert group. The teacher can assist group members in making helpful comments and suggestions: on important information that was omitted, on irrelevant information that was included, on pace and audibility of delivery, on pronunciation problems, on body language, and on the use of specific presentation techniques (such as writing key words on the blackboard).

Working in the Jigsaw Groups When all groups feel that they really know their material and are ready to share the information, the students regroup into their Jigsaw groups. Each student tells the other members of the team about the topic. This can include information (e.g., opinions) that did not come from the source assigned. Students are encouraged to make use of all the knowledge they have.

After students have shared information with each other in the Jigsaw groups, they need direction and motivation for discussion. In this instance, the teacher can provide a set of questions to guide the discussion. At least some of the questions should involve inferences and opinions. There will be some differences of opinion. This makes for better discussion:

Would you like to have lived this kind of life? Why/why not?

What do you think medical facilities were like at that time?

Was life harder in those days?

After information sharing and discussion in the Jigsaw groups, the groups have an opportunity to review the material before taking a quiz. The quiz is the same for all students and is based on the content and vocabulary of all the readings and the discussion in the Jigsaw groups. It is a powerful motivator for students to share information and discuss it effectively. This is its main function. Students may be assigned additional written tasks that can be performed at several levels. (See the follow-up activities for "Industrial Accident," described in the next section of this chapter.)

How to Create and Use Materials for Jigsaw

The preceding outline is for a unit using existing materials. Many teachers who get involved in Jigsaw group techniques find that in the time it takes to research materials at different levels of difficulty, they could have written their own. Moreover, materials written for an ESL class have a linguistic focus that is lacking in most "found" materials, unless they are carefully adapted. In addition, most available materials lack relevance to the lives of immigrants. ESL teachers have always been resourceful in adapting or creating their own classroom materials.

The rest of this chapter provides a detailed, sequenced outline of the steps in creating Jigsaw units and using them with an ESL class.

Choosing a Topic

Topics relevant to the orientation and survival information required by recently arrived students, other subject areas, current affairs, or topics relating to the world of work are excellent sources of ideas for Jigsaw units. Here are some possibilities for topics and subtopics:

Orientation: How our school works

- The credit system: what a credit is, how many you need, levels of instruction and where they lead, compulsory/optional courses, prerequisites.
- Roles of support and administrative personnel and services and how to access them: guidance counselor, principal, librarian, translators, social worker.
- The culture of the school: how students and teachers relate to one another in class and outside, expectations, discipline.
- Extracurricular activities: what's available, how to get involved, how to start new activities.

Sources of information include school calendars and adaptations of material from it; observation and interpretation of student and teacher behavior in a variety of contexts; and contact assignments through visits, interviews, and visiting speakers.

Geography/environmental studies: The pulp and paper industry

- Forestry: regional distribution of forests; logging; transportation to processing centers.
- How paper is made: a sequenced description of the process.
- How paper is used: types of paper and products.
- Environmental issues: replanting; chemical contamination of lakes and rivers; disposable paper products.

Among sources of information are geography and environmental-studies texts, rewritten and/or adapted with language exercises; films and filmstrips; interviews with subject teachers; field trips to paper-processing plants or logging areas; classroom collection of paper products; classroom visits by forestry officials, environmental groups.

Current affairs: How our government works

- What the government does: levels of government/division of responsibility.
- How a government is elected: electoral districts/ridings, selection of candidates, ballots.
- How a law is made: the proposition, the debate, voting, and ratification.
- The head-of-state: rights and responsibilities of head-of-state and his/her delegates or representatives (U.S. state governors, governor general/lieutenant governors in Canada)

- Citizenship: how to become a citizen of the United States or Canada; rights and duties of citizens.

Sources include rewritten segments from American and Canadian history texts; visits to institutions of local/state or provincial/federal government; films and filmstrips; classroom visits by citizenship instructors and history teachers; peer tutors from history or civics classes; visit to a citizenship court or ceremony; materials prepared for newcomers and future citizens by state or provincial and federal agencies.

Topics with an element of controversy generate more discussion, and very stimulating Jigsaw units can be created from newspaper stories. Most newspaper reports provide several different perspectives on a story. (Not to do so would be flagrantly biased!).

Industrial Accident: A Model Jigsaw Unit

Outlined below is a step-by-step description of *"Industrial Accident."* This unit for adolescent and adult learners is based on details from a newspaper report of an industrial accident (Coelho, 1991; Coelho, Winer, and Olsen, 1989). This description is provided as a model for the development and effective use of Jigsaw materials for the second-language classroom.

Four statements are written about the accident. The four statements are given by the victim, his supervisor, the union official, and the safety engineer. The statements are different in perspective and purpose. For example, the safety engineer is anxious to exonerate the company and herself, whereas the union official is very critical of working conditions and safety standards at the plant. The statements are written at different levels of linguistic complexity to accommodate different proficiency levels in the class. Visual support is provided in two diagrams, showing the scene before and after the accident. (See prereading activities that follow.)

Group Structure　The class is organized into four expert groups before the four texts are distributed. If a class is very large (more than five or six in each expert group), these groups are subdivided into smaller groups. If this is the first time these groups have met, the teacher needs to first provide some introductory teambuilding activities. These can be related to the topic: Find out what jobs everyone has, has had or would like to have. Share some of the problems you or your friends and relatives have had at work. What do you know about accident insurance on the job? How is work here different from work in your country?

Directed Reading in the Expert Groups　In the homogeneous (more or less!) expert or topic groups, students deal with comprehension and mastery of their section of the material. ESL students are often inefficient readers in English, even those who have advanced reading skills in their first language. They are anxious about comprehension at the word level and are most likely dictionary-dependent.

They are often frustrated because, in their efforts to understand every word, they become very slow and may fail to grasp main points. ESL students are faced with reading material that is too difficult for them throughout the five to seven years it takes to become fully proficient in English. They need to develop effective strategies to help them get meaning from this material. A program of directed reading, as outlined below, can help students to understand their purpose in reading and to develop a variety of reading strategies for specific purposes.

Jigsaw Activity 3 *
Industrial Accident

D

Directions: Look at the diagrams below and discuss them with your group.

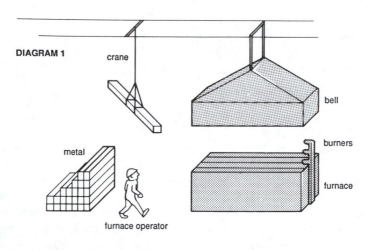

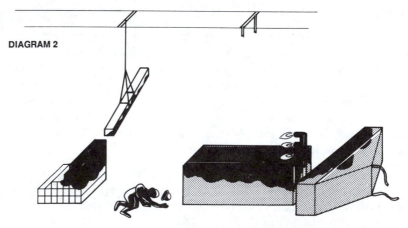

*A Canadian version of this material is available in *Jigsaw* (Coelho, 1991).

Prereading activities:

- Before the texts are distributed, the title "Industrial Accident" is written on the board, and students are asked: *What do you think this Jigsaw unit is going to be about?*
- All guesses should be accepted, without commenting on their accuracy. Accuracy is unimportant. What is important is that students approach a reading task with some prior expectation, which they will confirm or revise as they read the text.
- The texts are distributed to the expert groups, with the instruction: *Look at the diagrams. What do you think happened?*
- The expert groups discuss this question for a minute or two; then individual students report their groups' ideas.

Reading the text:

- The next instruction is: *Read only as far as necessary to find out if your guess was right or not.* Students need to know that the really effective reader reads no more than necessary to fulfill a specific purpose. Those who continue reading further than the introduction are no better able to answer the prereading question than those who stop when they have found what they were instructed to look for. The four introductory paragraphs give almost the same information:

    > TEXT A: A month ago there was an accident at the Adams Metal Company plant in Steeltown, Illinois. The furnace operator, Daniel Vretanos, was hurt in the accident. This is his statement about what happened on the day of the accident.
    >
    > TEXT B: A month ago there was an accident at the Adams Metal Company plant in Steeltown, Illinois. The furnace operator was seriously injured. The workers' union sent an investigator to find out what happened; this is his statement.
    >
    > TEXT C: A month ago there was an accident at the Adams Metal Company in Steeltown, Illinois. The furnace operator was seriously injured. The company's safety engineer investigated the cause of the accident. This is her report.
    >
    > TEXT D: A month ago there was an accident at the Adams Metal company in Steeltown, Illinois. The furnace operator, Daniel Vretanos, was seriously injured. This is the statement by his supervisor about what happened on the day of the accident.

- Students are encouraged to make some guesses about the meanings of unfamiliar words (e.g., "investigated"), and they will confirm or revise their guesses as they read the rest of the text.
- Skimming for the Main Idea: Students now make some guesses about the

cause of the accident. Then they skim their texts to find out if their predictions were accurate. The teacher circulates to check that the students in each group are skimming: reading quickly for the main idea, not stopping over difficult vocabulary, or trying to memorize details.

- Reading for Details: This question is on the blackboard to direct the second reading of the text: *Can you decide from the information in your text who is to blame for the accident?* Students check the details in their texts and discover that they need more information in order to decide this. Already they are motivated to get information from others in the Jigsaw group.

- Students work on reading and vocabulary exercises designed to encourage students to refer back to the text, to locate specific information, to make guesses about word meanings, to develop inferences, and to evaluate the information in the text.

The following examples are based on the furnace operator's statement:

Example A: True, False, or ?

_____	He came late for work.
_____	He lit the furnace before it was full.
_____	All the burners lit up.
_____	There was gas in the air.
_____	Nobody else was hurt.

These questions are both factual and inferential. Some are on the main points, and some are on details. The ? option is for students to choose when they feel that they don't yet have enough information. It is part of the design that none of the texts provides enough information to answer all of the questions. These questions will resurface in the information-sharing session in the Jigsaw groups, where students can get the answers from those who have different pieces of information, different pieces of the Jigsaw puzzle.

Example B: Find the Words

Find the words that have these meanings:

paragraph 7: *the cover of the furnace* _____
             a sudden bright light _____

These questions refer students to the context so that they can infer the meaning of specific words. Some may be known words that have a different meaning in this context. For example, the furnace cover is a bell. Students learn to rely on context rather than on dictionary translations for reliable clues to meaning.

Example C: Think About It

Is this a good place to work? How do you know?

What questions would you like to ask about this story before deciding who is to blame for the accident?

These are open-ended questions that require students to evaluate the information and decide where the gaps are in the story.

Postreading:

By now, the students have good comprehension of their material. The teacher has been able to circulate from group to group helping and guiding them through the exercises.

- When the exercises have been checked and corrected, each expert group makes up four or five comprehension questions on their text.
- They will use these questions later in the Jigsaw group to check that the group members have understood the main points in the presentation.
- In their expert groups, students have an opportunity to prepare an oral presentation of the main points. The teacher visits each group to make sure that they have selected the main points and can speak about them without reference to the text.
- The teacher encourages students to rehearse aloud to each other and indicates how they can help each other. A strong sense of cooperation and a lot of peer-tutoring on language use occurs in the expert groups at this point. Students are eager for their group members to perform well in the Jigsaw group.

Synthesizing the Information in the Jigsaw Groups   When all the expert groups feel ready to share the information, the class regroups into the Jigsaw groups.

- Students now take turns telling each other about their texts.
- The teacher circulates from group to group, emphasizing that students should ask one another questions to make sure all understand the content of each text.
- As each student finishes a presentation, comprehension questions developed in the expert group are administered to members of the Jigsaw group.
- The presenter collects the answers as soon as they are completed, and problems are clarified before the next person makes a presentation.
- Directed discussion: Students compare the information in the four statements to decide on the probable cause of the accident, and who (if anyone) is to blame. Students report back to the class on their group findings and on

the reasoning behind their conclusions. In this unit, there is a strong emphasis on cause-and-result statements. To help learners with them, a list of useful expressions is posted: "because/because of," "as a result/as a result of," "so," "that," . . . .

- Each group also makes some recommendations on what the company and its workers should do to prevent accidents in future. This involves the use of "should," "ought to," "it would be a good idea to," as well as other ways of making suggestions and recommendations.

- Vocabulary development: Students are given a list of words that appear in some of the texts. Each student in the Jigsaw group has some of the words in the text, and has practiced them in the expert group. Now the students are instructed to explain the words to each other in the Jigsaw group, using contextually-based examples from their texts. This is taken up with the whole class, and a vocabulary exercise may follow of the cloze type in which every n^{th} word, usually between seven to twelve words, is deleted.

Evaluation:

- Quiz: There is a content quiz that is taken independently, and is based on the content of the texts and the Jigsaw group discussion. It tests comprehension of the main points in each presentation and some vocabulary items. There is an open-ended question based on the group discussion. It should be marked only for comprehension and reasoning.

- Debriefing: If this is the first Jigsaw unit for the class, there should be a discussion and evaluation of the group process. After receiving their individual evaluation marks for the quiz, the Jigsaw groups brainstorm these questions in order to report back to the class:

  How could we improve our group mark on the quiz?

  How could we make sure that everyone in our group understands each other?

  What do our best teachers do to explain something or help us to understand?

  What responsibility do we have as listeners?

  The responses are posted on a chart in the classroom as a reminder to students that these are strategies and attitudes which will be effective in class, and which are valued by the teacher.

- The focus now turns to the oral strategies that help to make group work effective. (See Chapter 2.)

- After finishing their first Jigsaw unit, students write an informal evaluation of the Jigsaw activities. Students respond to these questions as honestly as they can:

  How do you feel about this method of working in class?

  What did you like about it?

What didn't you like?

Complete this statement: I think it would be better if . . .

The responses show who is still uncomfortable with the group activity or the oral aspects of the work. If there is resistance to working in groups, it should not be ignored. Students should be allowed to work individually if they wish, but they still have to take the same quiz as everyone else. This means that they have to work on four times as much material. Most of the resistance disappears at this point!

The evaluation will help to indicate which groups (if any) need to be changed because of personality conflicts, or because observation of the students working on this material has changed the teacher's evaluation of their relative language levels.

Follow-up Activities   So that this unit can be applied to real-life situations, such useful materials as forms and information booklets for Workers' Compensation and Unemployment Insurance benefits can be brought in. Students scan the booklets to find specific information that could apply to the case of the injured worker in this Jigsaw unit. They can also practice filling in some of the forms for this worker. In order to do this effectively, they must invent some details about the worker's family life and financial situation: number of dependents, normal weekly wage, and other relevant information.

Other writing tasks may include a letter from the employer to the worker, wishing him a speedy recovery (but admitting no responsibility); a letter from his wife to the children's teachers, explaining their absence from school for a few days; a list of safety rules for the factory (using "must," "may not," etc.); or a letter from a fellow employee to the injured work mate, describing events at the factory since the accident (using present perfect tense: "things have changed around here," "they have closed the furnace room," "they have repaired the burners"; or, for a more advanced group, some passive constructions: "some changes have been made around here," "the furnace room has been closed," etc.)

Conclusion

Is it really worth the extra effort to organize students into such carefully structured groups? Is it worth spending so much time researching, adapting, and creating material? At first glance, this does look like a lot of work. However, there is no need to write a whole year's curriculum at once; try one or two units first, and see how your students respond. If it goes well, you might be able to enlist other teachers to form a cooperative writing team. You can start by using existing materials that can be divided into Jigsaw pieces for your class. If you want to start creating your own materials, the cooperating teachers can divide the labor and write one text each or be responsible for developing one set of a particular kind of exercise.

A compensating factor is that the role of the teacher changes significantly, from agent of control and disseminator of all knowledge to that of catalyst and advisor. Contrary to many teachers' fears, the students become more task oriented in a cooperative learning situation, in which they have more control over the material and their learning of it. In a well-organized cooperative classroom, students take on a lot of the responsibility for the classroom activities, freeing the teacher to give individual attention where needed. (See Chapter 9 for more on the role of the teacher in the cooperative classroom.)

More significant, perhaps, is the fact that students learn better this way, in all kinds of subject disciplines. According to Kagan (1986), active oral involvement of students in cooperative learning classrooms is critical for academic achievement gains. Engagement with task-related information and explanation has been found to correlate with such gains. This is no less true for the medium of communication than for the content. For the ESL teacher, the real reward lies in the knowledge that Jigsaw units integrating language and content provide genuine communication in a structured environment that assists ESL students to make sense of the language and to acquire valuable information at the same time.

REFERENCES

ARONSON, E., N. BLANEY, C. STEPHAN, J. SIKES, and M. SNAP. 1978. *The Jigsaw Classroom.* Beverly Hills, CA: Sage.

CLARKE, J., R. WIDEMAN, and S. EADIE. 1990. *Together We Learn: Cooperative Small-Group Learning.* Toronto: Prentice Hall Canada.

COELHO, E. 1991. *Jigsaw,* Revised ed. Markham, Ontario: Pippin Publishing Ltd.

————. 1982. Language across the curriculum. *TESL Talk,* 13: 56–70.

COELHO, E., L. WINER, J.W-B OLSEN. 1989. *All Sides of the Issue.* Hayward, CA: Alemany Press.

Family Pastimes. *Catalogue of Cooperative Games.* Perth, Ontario: Family Pastimes annual catalogue. (Catalogue of Cooperative Games. R.R. 4, Perth, Ontario, K7H 3C6.)

JOHNSON, D., R. JOHNSON, E. HOLUBEC, and P. ROY. 1984. *Circles of Learning.* Alexandria, VA: Association for Supervision and Curriculum Development.

KAGAN, SPENCER. 1986. Cooperative learning and sociocultural factors in schooling. *Beyond Language: Social and Cultural Factors in Schooling Language Minority Students.* Los Angeles, CA: Evaluation, Dissemination, and Assessment Center, California State University.

————. 1989. *Cooperative Learning Resources for Teachers,* San Juan Capistrano, CA: Resources for Teachers.

MOHAN, B. 1986. *Language and Content.* Reading, MA: Addison-Wesley.

SHARAN, S., and H. SHACHAR. 1988. *Language and Learning in the Cooperative Classroom.* New York: Springer-Verlag.

CHAPTER 8

TEACHER TALK
IN THE COOPERATIVE
LEARNING CLASSROOM

Yael Harel

Introduction

A crucial aspect of teaching English as a second language is the nature of teacher talk. Although many studies point to the positive effect of small-group interaction, little research attention has been given to examining teacher talk in classrooms that use differing types of classroom management for second language instruction. This chapter contrasts styles of teacher talk in teacher-fronted classrooms—those in which the teacher stands in the front of the room with all students facing forward—with styles found in cooperative learning classrooms.

Findings from a large-scale study conducted in an English as a second language setting in Israel focus specifically on how teachers, trained in the Communicative Approach to language teaching, shift speech styles when they move from facing a whole class to working with small interactive groups. This chapter, then, explores the question of how teacher talk, the style of language the teacher uses for instruction, differs when the classroom management situation changes for a given teacher even though the basic assumptions about second language teaching remain constant for that teacher. The aim of examining the teachers' utterances in both situations, frontal and CL, is to clarify which one allows for more application of the Communicative Approach current today in teaching English as a second language. Along with this, the study examines the differences in speech patterns of the teachers when they go from frontal classes to cooperative groups.

Hypotheses forming the basis of the study are:

1. ESL teachers trained to use the Communicative Approach (CA) switch to non-CA verbal communication patterns in frontal lessons but utilize them in small-group lessons.
2. The quantity of teacher utterances differs between frontal and small-group lessons, with teachers speaking more in frontal situations.
3. Frontal verbal behavior patterns do not enable communicative learning among the students, but teachers' verbal behavior in cooperative small groups does facilitate learning in the spirit of the Communicative Approach.

Five ninth-grade ESL teachers in two junior high schools participated in the study. Each was recorded in both teacher-fronted and cooperative learning situations. Language used was then analyzed to determine the specific features of teacher talk characterizing the two teaching situations. Differences in speech patterns as teachers go from frontal classes to cooperative groups provide insights into the type of teacher talk that supports the positive effects of cooperative learning in small groups.

Few studies have examined verbal communication patterns characterizing different kinds of lessons. Changing the class organization has a greater influence on student verbal behavior than does personality or any other variable. Bossert (1977), for example, found that in small-group teaching the connection between teacher and student is more informal, more individual. This study, however, did not investigate classes for teaching English to nonnative speakers.

For ESL, Long and Porter (1985) reviewed studies dealing with small cooperative groups. They found that the linguistic and pedagogic advantages of this type of classroom management enabled acquisition of English under optimal conditions. In addition, they found an increase in the quantity and quality of the student utterances. Students could express themselves in authentic communicative environments, making use of all of the speaking activities reserved to the teacher in a frontal lesson. Furthermore, the absence of a native speaker in the small group does not cause learners to make more errors.

Exploring linguistic tasks carried out in small groups, Doughty and Pica (1986) and Pica and Doughty (1985a; 1985b) point to a positive influence of interactive tasks. Such tasks can provide optimal conditions to create an authentic need to use the second language, which in turn facilitates acquisition of the language.

In a study conducted by Bejarano (1987) comparing the effects of two different cooperative learning groupings (Discussion Group, Student Teams-Achievement Divisions or STAD) with a whole-class method on language achievement for middle-school students acquiring English, results revealed that both CL approaches led to significantly greater success than the whole-class method. Students in CL classes outperformed those in teacher-fronted classes on the overall score of a language achievement test.

Summarizing some of the advantages offered by CL in second language settings, McGroarty (1989) identifies linguistic, curricular, and social benefits. However, she points out the need for more research directed at identifying the types of cooperative tasks and group structures that best serve teachers and their students in attaining full communicative competence in academic settings.

Teaching Contrasts in Frontal and CL Classrooms

Teacher-Fronted Classrooms

A teacher-fronted classroom is intended to present information to all students in a uniform manner. A basic idea behind a frontal approach is equality. The frontal classroom management approach is also efficient and economical for transmitting material, enabling the "covering of more ground" than interactive situations. The teacher has the power of control. The teacher also has the information to ensure correct explanations, leaving nothing to chance. Long and Porter (1985) describe the frontal lesson as administered like a wedding ceremony with predetermined functions, in which the teacher asks the questions, initiates, reinforces, and summarizes.

Among conspicuous drawbacks to this teaching situation is that, in facing the teacher, students have their backs to one another. As the central figure in the class, the teacher transfers, channels, and controls the flow of information. Personal discussions among students are considered disruptive. Student silence and discipline become essential elements in conducting a frontal lesson.

Furthermore, status relationships among students determine the right to speak. Those with a higher educational standing make use of that right to a greater extent than those of lower standing, with the result that the latter are prevented from active participation. Competition for the teacher's attention also works against strengthening personal bonds in the class and often leads to student isolation (Hunter, 1972; Flanders, 1970; Sommer, 1967). Moreover, teaching in the frontal class is directed at the average student, failing to meet the needs of those above and below.

The content in teacher-fronted classrooms is frequently based on following the textbook, often reading sections aloud and completing exercises. Discussions led by the teacher generally take the form of questions and answers. Posing questions in a teacher-fronted class is primarily intended to check knowledge, not to search for answers. Students understand that the teacher is familiar with the answers and that the goal of the questions is merely to check student knowledge. This is the teaching situation widespread in the schools in Israel and around the world (Gage and Berliner, 1979).

In regard to the quantity of verbal behavior in the teacher-fronted classroom,

Flanders (1970), found that teachers speak up to 75 percent of the time, leaving little time for student expressions.

Cooperative Learning Classrooms

As demonstrated in the various chapters of this text, cooperative learning is based on interactions among group members. The teacher acts as a facilitator of learning, approaching the group when necessary. Cooperation, rather than competition, is the operative dynamic. (See Coelho, Chapter 2, in this volume.)

Tasks that can be used in teaching English cooperatively are many, including role-play, scenarios, group discussions, solving mysteries, reading together, peer teaching as preparation for tests, researching a subject, and preparing a study project from varied sources of information.

Since the work of Dewey (1916), who provided the inspiration for the Group Investigation Method, small-group learning has been accepted as a socializing agent. It offers an opportunity for advancing interethnic integration in a group in which students are expected to work cooperatively as equal partners. An ethnic mix is a required condition for improving the social relations and learning achievements of students, but it is not a sufficient condition to advance the learning achievements of students with low socioeconomic status. It is necessary to intervene in planning the instruction. Ethnic mixture is not a remedy but rather an opportunity for creating conditions suitable for fulfilling learner's goals. In a study reported by Sharan and Hertz-Lazarowitz (1980) using group methods for teaching Arabic as a second language, an improvement in achievement among students of Eastern ethnicity was found. Another study (Sharan et al., 1984), using CL for teaching English to both Eastern and Western students, found that cooperative learning appeared to have a positive influence on the achievements of all students in the group.

In addition to social advantages, CL results in greater academic achievement when compared with frontal teaching (Slavin, 1991; Johnson et al., 1981; Sharan and Sharan, 1976). Little, however, has been studied about the verbal behavior of teachers, the teacher talk, in this setting.

Like the teacher-fronted classroom, cooperative learning can be viewed as a form of classroom management (Richard-Amato, 1988). In this study CL was used for implementing a Communicative Approach to teaching English to nonnative speakers.

The Communicative Approach to Second Language Teaching

Some years ago Hymes (1972) claimed that the acquisition of grammatical competence, in the Chomskyan (1965) sense, is insufficient. It must be accompanied by sociolinguistic competence, competence in everything touching on acceptability of the language in a given context. Others went on to reiterate that it is not enough to know the form of language or even its vocabulary. The Communicative Approach stresses the importance of integration between the functional and structural aspects of language (Stern, 1983; Littlewood, 1981; Breen and Candlin, 1980; Brumfit and Johnson, 1979; Widdowson, 1978). Knowledge of the appropriate use of language and the ability to structure discourse interactions (Canale and Swain, 1980) must be taken into account in any discussion of communicative competence.

In an approach based on genuine communication, communicative needs—that is, the specific language needs characterizing various communication situations—form the basis for designing a curriculum and the communicative tasks for its implementation (Nunan, 1989; Nunan, 1988). Communicative competence develops with the acquisition of communicative strategies during the process of communicating within the immediate social framework. A framework, then, for acquiring a second language is one in which students are involved in the process of reciprocal activity, communication with others in which the focus is on the content or meaning of the message rather than on the form.

An efficient way to get students actively involved in communication situations is through learning tasks designed as "information gaps." These are created when certain information is supplied to some learners and kept from others, or when some receive a certain part of the information and others a different part. These situations create an instrumental need for reciprocal verbal activity in order to complete the missing information. Tasks are taken from daily life within the experience of the learners and are designed to respond to the communicative needs of the individual student. (Doughty and Pica, 1986; Breen and Candlin, 1980).

Teacher Talk Contrasts in Frontal and CL Classrooms

Do ESL teachers whose training is exclusively oriented toward the Communicative Approach use different verbal behaviors as they move back and forth from frontal to cooperative lessons? If so, what are the stylistic differences? This is the basic question of this research.

Five experienced ESL teachers working with ninth graders in two junior high schools in Tel-Aviv provide the data for answering this question. Their students represented a mixed population of both high and low socioeconomic status in a desegregated school. During a semester's study, all of the teachers participated in a course teaching how to use in cooperative learning in ESL classes. There they learned to impart discussion skills by means of experiential exercises. Additionally, they were also enrolled in a course on principles of the Communicative Approach applied to teaching English and another course on the preparation of learning tasks for group study. The program was sponsored by the Tel-Aviv Municipality and the Supervision of English in the Ministry of Education and Culture.

At the end of the semester, each teacher provided data by teaching one class using frontal teaching and one using cooperative learning. The total time recorded was 204 minutes for teacher-fronted classes and 186 minutes for small group classes. Data were then classified according to categories of teachers' verbal behavior developed from ethnographic studies and then integrated with a quantitative approach. The three groups of categories in which a distinct difference between the two methods was found were: (1) lecture and short questions, (2) corrections, rather than assistance at the time of performing a task, and (3) instruction and discipline.

Teacher-Talk Style in Teacher-Fronted Classrooms

Five major features characterized teacher talk in frontal situations: (1) teachers speak a lot, (2) teachers lecture, (3) teachers ask short questions, (4) teachers use correction extensively, and (5) teachers give instructions and commands frequently.

In the frontal approach, the teacher makes an average of four utterances per minute, lecturing and asking short questions. In other words, the teacher reserves the right to initiate interactions. Under these conditions there is not much opportunity for interpersonal communication among the students. Students adjust to the requirements, answering the short questions in a "ping-pong" style, or they simply listen passively. Opportunity for students to try out their new language system, or interlanguage, is minimal.

The unauthentic character of the short questions asked for the sake of checking negates any genuine communication in the class discussion. In addition, students are aware that failure to give a rapid and precise answer is a failure in front of friends. Only the most self-confident students willingly participate. Furthermore, the low level of the "ping-pong" questions does not encourage higher cognitive thinking and results in an educational loss.

One of the paradoxes of posing broader questions is that often the anticipated answer, intended to advance the lesson as planned in the syllabus, is not obtained (French and MacLure, 1981). Teachers then ask short questions to prevent this, using strategies such as inserting part of the answer in rephrasing the questions. As Heap (1980) argues, nothing in this interaction teaches nor does it serve in evaluating students.

Corrections used in the teacher-fronted classroom can cause students to lose self-confidence when "an audience" waits for a slip and the teacher "snares" a mistake. Intellectual functioning decreases in such an atmosphere. Threatened students quickly drop out of the race and remain silent. Immediate error correction also interrupts the fluency of speaking and breaks down communication.

With regard to giving instructions and imposing discipline, the teacher holds the reins in both hands in a frontal lesson, giving instructions and commands, making disciplinary comments. This authoritative atmosphere threatens students generally, imposing considerable anxiety.

Teacher-Talk Style in Cooperative Learning Classrooms

In cooperative learning classrooms, the style of teacher talk has four major characteristics: (1) teachers speak little, (2) teachers provide broad questions to challenge thinking, (3) teachers assist students with the learning task rather than providing error correction, (4) teachers give few commands, imposing less disciplinary control.

Analysis of the data for this study reveals that the quantity of teacher talk in CL classrooms was only 25 percent of that in teacher-fronted situations. Statistical analysis of the data showed the difference to be significant. The difference was not found between more or less "talkative" teachers but rather in the way that each teacher reduced the quantity of utterances in the group organization or classroom management situation.

Central to the group tasks are broad questions challenging thinking and providing a source of student motivation. Although the process of defining questions according to taxonomies is not that simple (Bloom, 1956), posing broad questions does offer educational advantages. Apart from research issues surrounding the nature of open and broad questions, the freedom to engage interactively in discussion and to negotiate meaning in small groups sets communicative conditions that facilitate second language acquisition. Such is the case with CL groups.

In second language acquisition theory, it is widely held that errors can reveal something of the internal process of learning the language (Ellis, 1985). No longer viewed as transgressions, they are seen as an essential part of learning a second language. Attention, however, must be paid to the manner of handling errors. Feedback can advance the student's learning of the language, but it should not interfere with trying to communicate through the target language. In small group interactions, the teacher learns to rely more on the student's natural process of language acquisition (Krashen, 1987), learning to listen to the errors in an effort to decipher their meaning. The teacher responds to errors in a positive manner, often without correcting them directly. Effective feedback is necessary, however, for the continued existence of communication. When the request for assistance comes at the student's initiative, the effect of feedback remains positive and can advance learning. The small-group pattern of instruction allows for a student to ask for help whenever needed. The teacher can immediately approach to assist without disrupting overall comprehension and the fluency of speaking observed for the group. The remainder of the time allows for communicative interactions using "comprehensible output" (Swain, 1985) and letting the natural process of acquisition take place (Long and Porter, 1985; Krashen, 1987; Brumfit, 1984).

In the group environment, a further opportunity for error correction exists through receiving corrections from peers. According to Long and Porter (1985), such corrections are very willingly accepted by students.

The pattern of control in the cooperative learning situation is informal and nonauthoritative. As part of this study, students were interviewed about their preferences in regard to frontal vs. CL situations. Student responses strongly expressed preference for cooperative learning with comments such as "It's more pleasant for me to work with my friends in a group." or "In general, I'm more comfortable in a group without a teacher over me." Other students noted "My friends help me." and "It's fun in a group." In effect, a student sums up the Communicative Approach in a cooperative learning setting by noting, "I speak, too, and learn more English."

Conclusions

Hypotheses for this study were all confirmed. Despite training in the Communicative Approach given to experienced ESL teachers in advanced studies and teacher training, there was a significant difference in the verbal communication patterns of teacher-centered lessons contrasted with CL lessons. A difference was found in the quantity of the teachers' utterances, with many more in the frontal lessons than in the CL lessons. The frontal transmission model behavior patterns discouraged communicative learning. Even though trained to use a Communicative Approach, teachers changed style in their teacher talk when they changed the teaching situation. As a result of the lecture, the short questions, the many instructions, the disciplinary comments and corrections characterizing the style of teacher talk in a transmission lesson, the Communicative Approach fails.

In contrast, optimal conditions for the Communicative Approach occur in the cooperative learning classroom. Shifts in the style of teacher talk result in the teacher speaking much less, assisting in performance of tasks only when asked to do so, and facilitating conditions for students to work among themselves, cooperatively, in an authentic communicative atmosphere. The verbal behavior patterns of teacher talk in the CL setting encourage and support communicative activities.

As predicted at the start of this research, the five English teachers broke the communicative pattern of instruction in the teacher-centered lesson and returned to it in the small CL lesson. Of importance in the findings for this study is that the teacher's pattern of verbal behavior appears to be determined by the classroom organization rather than by formal training in a particular methodology. Basically, the teaching style remains noncommunicative in frontal, teacher-centered classes and communicative in cooperative learning classes regardless of teacher training and second language teaching trends. In other words, teacher talk in the cooperative classroom has all the characteristics needed to facilitate second language acquisition.

REFERENCES

BEJARANO, Y. 1987. *TESOL Quarterly*, 21, no. 3: 483–504.

BLOOM, B.S. 1956. *Taxonomy of Educational Objectives: Cognitive Domain.* New York: Longmans, Green.

BOSSERT, S.T. 1977. Tasks, group management, and teacher control behavior: A study of classroom organization and teachers' style. *School Review*, 85: 552–63.

BREEN, M.P., and C.N CANDLIN. 1980. The essentials of a communicative curriculum. *Applied Linguistics*, 1, no. 2: 89–112.

BRUMFIT, C. 1984. *Communicative Methodology in Language Teaching: The Roles of Fluency and Accuracy.* Cambridge: Cambridge University Press.

BRUMFIT, C.J., and K. JOHNSON. 1979. *The Communicative Approach to Language Teaching.* Oxford: Oxford University Press.

CANALE, M., and M. SWAIN. 1980. Theoretical bases of communicative approaches to second language teaching and testing. *Applied Linguistics*, 1, no. 1: 1–47.

CHOMSKY, N. 1965. *Aspects of a Theory of Syntax.* Cambridge, MA: M.I.T. Press.

DEWEY, J. 1916. *Democracy and Education.* New York: Macmillan.

DOUGHTY, C., and T. PICA. 1986. 'Information Gap' tasks: Do they facilitate CL acquisition? *TESOL Quarterly*, 20, no. 2: 305–25.

ELLIS, R. 1985. *Understanding Second Language Acquisition.* Oxford: Oxford University Press.

FLANDERS, N. 1970. *Analyzing Teacher Behavior.* Reading, MA: Addison-Wesley.

FRENCH, P., and M. MACLURE. 1981. Teachers' questions, pupils' answers: An investigation of questions and answers in the infant classroom. *First Language*, 2: 31–45.

GAGE, N.L., and D.C. BERLINER. 1979. *Educational Psychology.* Chicago: Rand McNally.

HEAP, J.L. 1980. What counts as reading: Limits to certainty in assessment. *Curriculum Inquiry*, 10: 265–92.

HUNTER, E. 1972. *Encounter in the Classroom: New Ways of Teaching.* New York: Holt, Rinehart and Winston.

HYMES, DELL. 1972. On communicative competence. In J.B. Pride and J. Holmes (eds.), *Sociolinguistics: Selected Readings.* Harmondsworth, England: Penguin.

JOHNSON, D.W., G. MARUYAMA, R. JOHNSON, D. NELSON, and L. SKON. 1981. The effects of cooperative, competitive, and individualistic goal structure on achievement: A meta-analysis. *Psychological Bulletin*, 89: 47–62.

KRASHEN, S.D. 1987. *Principles and Practice in Second Language Acquisition.* Englewood Cliffs, NJ: Prentice Hall International.

LITTLEWOOD, W. 1981. *Communicative Language Teaching.* Cambridge: Cambridge University Press.

LONG, M.H., and P.A. PORTER. 1985. Group work, interlanguage talk, and second language acquisition. *TESOL Quarterly*, 19: 207–28.

McGROARTY, M. 1989. The benefits of cooperative learning arrangements in second language instruction. *NABE Journal*, 13, no. 2: 127–43.

NUNAN, D. 1988. *The Learner-Centred Curriculum.* Cambridge: Cambridge University Press.

————. 1989. *Designing Tasks for the Communicative Classroom*. Cambridge: Cambridge University Press.

PICA, T., and C. DOUGHTY.1985a. The role of group work in classroom second language acquisition. *Studies in Second Language Acquisition,* 7, no. 2: 233–48.

————. 1985b. Input and interaction in the communicative language classroom: A comparison of teacher-fronted and group activities. In S. Gass and C. Madden (eds.), *Input and Second Language Acquisition.* Rowley, MA: Newbury House.

RICHARD-AMATO, P.A. 1988. *Making It Happen: Interaction in the Second Language Classroom.* New York: Longman.

SHARAN, S., and R. HERTZ-LAZAROWITZ. 1980. A group investigation method of cooperative learning in the classroom. In S. Sharan, P. Hare, C.D. Webb, and R. Hertz-Lazarowitz (eds.), *Cooperation in Education.* Provo, UT: Brigham Young University Press.

SHARAN, S., P. KUSSELL, R. HERTZ-LAZAROWITZ, Y. BEJARANO, S. RAVIV, and Y. SHARAN. 1984. *Cooperative Learning in the Classroom: Research in Desegregated Schools.* Hillsdale, NJ: Lawrence Erlbaum.

SHARAN, S., and Y. SHARAN. 1976. *Small Group Teaching.* Englewood Cliffs, NJ: Educational Technology Publications.

SLAVIN, R.E. 1991. Synthesis of research on cooperative learning. *Educational Leadership,* 48: 71–82.

SOMMER, R. 1967. Classroom ecology. *Journal of Applied Behavioral Sciences,* 3: 489–503.

STERN, H.H. 1983. *Fundamental Concepts of Language Teaching.* Oxford: Oxford University Press.

SWAIN, M. 1985. Communicative competence: Some roles of comprehensible input and comprehensible output in its development. In S. Gass and C. Madden (eds.), *Input in Second Language Acquisition.* Rowley, MA: Newbury House.

WIDDOWSON, H.G. 1978. *Teaching Language as Communication.* Oxford: Oxford University Press.

CHAPTER 9

THE ROLE OF THE TEACHER IN THE COOPERATIVE LEARNING CLASSROOM

Wendy McDonell

Introduction

"But if this is your class, Mom, why aren't the students looking at you?" These words were spoken while my young child was looking at photographs that were laying on my desk. This observation is appropriate for introducing a chapter on the role of the teacher. It says a lot about the changing role of the teacher in the second language classroom. Why aren't students looking at us and why aren't we standing at the front of the room teaching anymore?

It is the intent of this chapter to examine the rich and diverse roles of the cooperative learning (CL) teacher who is working effectively in a second language classroom. This chapter will identify key elements of the role of the CL teacher, clarify the process the teacher needs to follow, and demonstrate the benefits for the second language learner.

Key Elements of the Cooperative Learning Teacher's Role

The Teacher as Inquirer

From research on effective teaching, we know that a successful teacher understands children, their language, and how they can learn (Goodman, 1986). This knowledge, going beyond intuitive and emotional thinking, is rooted in sound research and theory. It is this knowledge that allows teachers to make informed decisions. Teachers know that their competency rests on exploring the underlying processes of how teachers teach and students learn. Teachers knowing why they are doing something is more lasting than simply knowing what they are doing. The process of knowing enables educators to develop a personal philosophy. From this vantage point, teachers can begin to provide sensitive and sound programming and can articulate this to students, colleagues, and parents.

Cooperative learning teachers are continually examining and questioning their beliefs, values, and assumptions. Examining attitudes and values held about the culturally diverse learner, race, class, and minority languages is particularly important in the context of teaching in a multilingual, multiracial classroom. These beliefs, values, and assumptions strongly affect teachers' educational philosophy and their instructional practice.

In order to plan for the learner, the CL teacher needs to know the learner. The teacher must ask the following questions: What is the age of the learner? What is the language proficiency level? What are previous learning experiences, interests, abilities, and needs? Other considerations often overlooked are the culturally absorbed ways of learning and displaying knowledge (Rivers, 1987).

Effective language teachers working with minority children are cognizant of the importance of language and the part that it plays in enabling access to the mainstream culture. They know that the focus of language is on communication of meaning and that one learns language through its use in purposeful contexts. They know that activities involving real communication carry out meaningful tasks. Using language meaningful to the learner promotes learning (Nunan, 1989; Enright and McCloskey, 1988).

In terms of attitudes and expectations, CL teachers believe that the second-language learner has the ability to learn. They acknowledge learner potential, expecting learners to be successful. In no way do they perceive second language learners as deficient. These positive expectations, similar to those held by most minority parents, are communicated to the learner implicitly and explicitly. However, CL teachers believe that not only the learner can learn but also that the teacher can learn as well. This mind-set affects the learning process and has an empowering effect on all involved. With this kind of teacher orientation, there are no inhibiting factors to prevent success.

Lastly, the cooperative educator believes in an interactive/experiential model of pedagogy that liberates students from dependence on instruction. This encourages learners to become active generators of their own knowledge. These educators are redefining the role of the teacher and examining the structure of the classroom. They are committed to educational equity and are the first to admit that the transmission model of program delivery confined our at-risk students to a passive role that induced a form of "learned helplessness" (Cummins, 1989).

To sum up then, CL educators are informed about the issues of teaching and learning. They know how children learn and how they acquire a first and second language. They value the language and culture that second language learners bring to the classroom. They have adopted, in Cummins terms, an "additive orientation" to students' culture and language. They are prepared to examine their response to diversity, their tolerance for ambiguity, their ability to be flexible, and their commitment to educating the minority student. They are aware of the cultural and linguistic differences of their students, viewing these individual differences positively. They know the implications of culture and race on learning and seek ways to make the curriculum more culturally relevant. Finally, they believe that teacher-directed and dominated classroom structures need to be replaced by an approach that organizes the classroom into a language-rich environment, so that learners can interact with and learn from one another as well as from the teacher and the world around them (Clarke et al., 1990.) In other words, CL teachers value collaboration and encourage cooperation among the students within their classroom.

The Teacher as Creator

Since the cooperative classroom is process oriented, teachers interested in effective group work must realize that the learning environment is highly structured and well organized. Keys for structuring a successful CL classroom are found in creating the social climate, setting goals, planning and structuring the task, establishing the physical arrangement of the classroom, assigning students to groups and roles, and selecting materials and time (Johnson et al., 1984).

Let's begin with the creation of the social climate. The learning environment is positive, caring, supportive, secure, tolerant of errors, and trusting. Individuals are valued and mutually respected. Learners are encouraged to take risks and learn from their mistakes. The classroom atmosphere is active and interactive. It nudges the learner to be productive.

Another important element in creating this positive learning environment is the equal partnership. Teachers and learners negotiate and shape the learning together. The tasks planned in the cooperative classroom reduce the teacher's power and control. Shared power, ownership, and decision-making take over. Learners gain confidence, becoming responsible for their learning.

While planning and programming for the learner, teachers reflect on what they know about the students and what would be appropriate in terms of approach and resource. The learning experiences that are planned are structured so that learners have the opportunity to build on what they already know, have a clear sense of direction, and have enough time to develop their understandings (Reid, Forrestal, Cook, 1984). The teacher needs to take time to learn about students' previous background before deciding on objectives for the instructional situation.

Before each learning experience, the teacher needs to specify what academic/ language objective and collaborative skill objective will be emphasized in order to help learners set goals. There may also be some negotiation about the set of intentions that students and teachers hold. Also learners are made aware of these intentions and know what is expected.

Once this decision has been made, the teacher creates learning experiences structured for positive interdependence, individual accountability, intergroup cooperation, and opportunities for the second language learner to use language purposefully and meaningfully in the context of experiencing specific cooperative skills.

In order to facilitate a group learning approach, the classroom should be arranged so that the group can sit close enough to each other to talk quietly, maintain eye contact, and share materials. Circles are usually best because they communicate equality. There should also be a clear access lane to every group. In addition, groups should be far enough apart not to interfere with one another (Johnson and Johnson, 1987).

Student access to relevant material must also be considered. As students seek more information for their problem-solving experiences, they will need reference books, dictionaries, and books on related subjects. These should be nearby. It is also important to include at the learning centers relevant books with visuals, maps, posters, and manipulatives. To facilitate arrangements, students can help move furniture, set out, and put away materials. This creating together enhances responsibility.

The next consideration is assigning students to groups. Groups are basic to the classroom organization. Students are grouped on the factors that the teacher knows about the learner, such as language proficiency level. For young learners, I believe it is important to let them sometimes select their own group members. At other times, the teacher forms the groups. For older learners, it is more appropriate to structure heterogeneous groups. It is important to share reasons for doing so with the learners. However, I must quickly add that repeated use of teacher-assigned groups sends the message that only the teacher's choice of group will succeed. This is not a helpful message to communicate in an "Our Classroom Environment" (Moorman and Dishon, 1983).

How long a group works together depends on a number of variables, including the length of the unit. It is hoped that in the long run every student will work with every classmate (Johnson and Johnson, 1986). The size of the group generally varies from two to six. On rare occasions there may be eight. It has been my experience that groups of three or four allow for maximum participation.

Time is crucial in implementing successful group work. Reid and her colleagues (1989) note that if students do not have enough time, they cannot engage in necessary explorations. Too much pressure impedes effective learning. When students feel that they do not have enough time and are worried about completing a task in the given time frame, the effectiveness of the small group suffers. Equally destructive to the group is too much time. When both teachers and learners gain more experience with group work, they will strike a balance for using time more efficiently.

Among the most important resources available to learners are their group members. In addition to these resources, teachers select materials that are authentic, purposeful, culturally relevant, and promote interaction in a language-rich environment. They are prepared for the multilevel classroom and invite learners to draw on their own experiences to learn.

The Teacher as Observer

> I used to teach children and evaluate their progress. But now I kid-watch, facilitate the learning of children, and try to discover why learners do what they do. I have learned to celebrate children's strengths as language users (Lorraine Krause, St. Telephore, Quebec, Canada, Lakeshore Board of Education).

Watching and listening to students are natural activities in every teacher's day. Such activities can be formal and informal, planned or unplanned. Observation is the basis of decision making about each learner's progress. It also provides the rationale for specific programming. Observation is an integral part of the teaching process. Cooperative small-group learning provides the teacher with the opportunity to observe, reflect, and intervene in supportive ways.

When we listen and observe, we find out learner interests, strengths, needs, and feelings. We find out what the learner brings to or takes from the learning experience. We discover what learners' surprises or questions are and how they are solving problems. We are able to assess what second language learners know about language and culture. We are given the opportunity to assess group interaction and to monitor how learners are practicing social skills. Finally, observing groups at work gives us the basis to reflect on our own teaching and learning practices. It gives us reasons for supportive intervention.

As mentioned above, observations can be informal and formal. One type of informal method is *global observation* while a more formal type is typically referred to as *systematic observation*. In global observation, the teacher stands back, listening to the groups. The teacher then records observations,. e.g. body language, degree of involvement, gestures, or tone of the talk. Once these are noted, the teacher may reflect on them in an attempt to interpret the observations in a nonjudgmental way.

Systematic observations focus the teacher's observations. Often the teacher prepares a checklist in order to identify essential skills for cooperative interaction. In the Metro Toronto School Board document *Together We Learn* (Clarke et al., 1990), it is suggested that in order to use checklists effectively, the teacher is encouraged to do the following (see Appendix A for sample observation sheet.):

1. Be unobtrusive, not taking the students' attention away from the work they are doing.
2. Plan the observation. Decide how many groups to observe and the length of time for observation.
3. Use one observation sheet for each group.
4. Make a tally mark each time you observe a cooperative skill.
5. Observe nonverbal communication, such as facial expressions and body posture.
6. Avoid trying to observe everything.
7. Take a few minutes between groups to make notes on general impressions and important observations that fit into the categories on your observation sheet.
8. Keep observation sheets to assess growth over time. You could use one observation sheet per group per week, using a different colored marker for each day's observation.

Initially, CL principles recommend that the teacher be the observer. The teacher demonstrates the role of the observer. By the time students are ready to assume the role, they will know what to do. Johnson and Johnson (1987) suggest that the learner be given adequate instructions and practice on gathering the observation data and sharing it with the group. Having students monitor their own group process is part of handing back to the learner ownership and responsibility. That is not to suggest that the teacher does not continue to observe. Teachers need to let learners know about the observations. Student anxiety is reduced when learners are told what teachers are looking for and how they will collect and report the data (Moorman and Dishon, 1983).

Having made these observations, the teacher now asks the question,"What does it all mean?" The teacher needs to reflect on what has been observed in order to make assessements. These reflections lead to more goal setting for collaborative skills, and for planning appropriate learning experiences. The teacher can choose to reflect on the situations: (1) by asking questions such as "What am I doing to encourage this dependence?"; (2) by talking about results of the observations with colleagues in order to get a different opinion, or (3) by keeping notes of the observations and questions. Over a period of time, a pattern emerges that will inform the teacher.

In North York School Board's document *Look! Hear!* (1983), the process for effective observations is described as follows:

- recording observations
- being objective and nonjudgmental
- considering the whole child

- observing on a regular, systematic, and frequent basis
- including spontaneous and on-going observations
- using efficient recording techniques
- planning to observe for a specific purpose
- monitoring product and process before, during, and after a task
- observing the learner from many points of view
- using spectator and participant modes
- considering a framework of child development

Having observed the group, the teacher then processes these observations with the group, although it need not be an in-depth process. However, some attention is given to how the groups worked together. Group members are invited to talk about how the group work was done and what things went well. The areas to be worked on could also be identified. The teacher can share observations made during the whole-class sharing time.

There are two very important purposes for group work: (1) completing the task, (2) building and maintaining constructive relationships (Johnson and Johnson, 1986). While students are working together, often the focus is solely on the task. It is during processing time that attention focuses on how learners worked together (see Appendix B for processing considerations). The recognition that the teacher and learner contributed to one another's learning and maintained a constructive working relationship is what makes cooperative learning so different from traditional approaches. Group processing sessions are opportunities to evaluate the learning and give feedback to group members; they also have the potential to be enjoyable and validating.

The Teacher as Facilitator

The role of facilitator means that the teacher is prepared to step aside to give the learner a more meaningful role. Effective facilitators are prepared to intervene and to assist in the problem-solving process. They support and encourage the learner's desire to learn.

The teacher-facilitator can be seen roving about the room, helping students and groups as needs arise. During this time the teacher interacts, teaches, refocuses, questions, clarifies, supports, expands, celebrates, and empathizes. Depending on what problems evolve, the following supportive behaviors are utilized. Facilitators are giving feedback, redirecting the group with questions, encouraging the group to solve its own problems, extending activity, encouraging thinking, managing conflict, observing students, and supplying resources (Cohen, 1986). Once again, learners receive the message that the teacher has faith in their ability to solve problems. The control of the task is being shifted from the teacher to the learner. The learner is being nudged continually toward the goal of successful problem solving.

While the teacher is facilitating the academic and the social learning, there are many demonstrations in the classroom. When the teacher intervenes, there are demonstrations of problem-solving language and behaviors. When students are encouraged to go back over a discussion to pursue a new strategy, there are demonstrations of negotiation. When students are asked to reflect on how the group worked together, there are demonstrations of cooperative skills. Last but not least, is the fact that the facilitator demonstrates effective leadership. And if what Frank Smith (1988) says is true—that children learn that which is demonstrated to them—then we can assume that demonstrations and collaboration have an empowering effect on second language learners.

The Teacher as Change Agent

In a plenary speech entitled "How Schools Must Change" given to the Ontario Reading Association in October, 1989, Frank Smith noted that the only changes that make profound differences in schools are changes made in the social structure. In other words, changes that affect the way teachers and students perceive one another and themselves ultimately affect the social climate for learning.

If that be the case, then the basis for effective change in schools rests on the interpersonal relationships found within the schools. Should we not then examine these relationships in order to change schools? Smith suggests that we begin with collaborative inquiries by teachers and students. Classroom inquiry becomes a natural agent for change.

The work of Glenda Bissex (Bissex and Bullock, 1987) and Ann Berthoff (in Goswani and Stillman, 1987) supports the view that the teacher has a key role in reforming the classroom. These researchers state that when teachers allow the classroom to become a place of inquiry, where questions are explored in meaningful contexts and teachers and students collaborate to seek answers, then teachers have a redefined role as teacher-researcher. By becoming researchers, teachers take over control of their classrooms and become experts themselves. They trust their intuitions, take risks, and believe in themselves as part of the decision-making process. The result is that they are claiming autonomy and liberating themselves from outside forces. They are generating active professionalism and are being respected as professionals. The teacher is the most important factor in the transformed classroom.

Bissex (Bissex and Bullock, 1987) defines the teacher-researcher as one who observes, questions, learns, and becomes a more complete teacher. As stated earlier in this chapter, the CL teacher observes the learner and the learning process in the small-group setting. This looking again and again with an informed eye at what is happening in the classroom is part of the teacher-as-researcher process.

From these observations comes a desire to know more. Problems become questions to investigate and opportunities to learn. Teachers continue to grow in their role as researcher when they ask questions such as: What is the group learning?

How do the learners interact? What are the learners valuing? or What have I learned from this experience?

This process of questioning results in teachers becoming learners. Attention is now focused on what teachers have learned rather than simply what they have taught. In this cooperative community all are learning. Teachers are asking questions of the students and of themselves in order to learn.

As a result of this observing, questioning, and learning, we find a more complete teacher. We find a teacher who knows and does. More importantly, as a result of having studied learners and the classroom environment, teachers have begun to examine themselves as part of the context and the way they teach. Such teacher inquiry lends itself to educational reform from within.

Knowledge and sound practice enables the teacher to be a communicator. The teacher can now articulate reasons for teaching a certain way and explain why cooperative learning for second language learners works. The teacher can become an advocate for the second language learner, communicating initiatives and programs to students, staff, parents, and the community at large.

Beyond informing, teachers need to collaborate with community resource persons who can provide insight to students and educators about different cultural, religious, and linguistic traditions characterizing the student population (Cummins, 1989). Schools act as change agents when they take on a more collaborative dimension. As Cummins argues, we empower minority students in the school contexts to the extent that communities themselves are empowered through their interactions with the school. This is an urgent call for parents and teachers to be partners in the education of minority children.

Before I conclude this section on the teacher as change agent, I need to make explicit the point that the degree of change at the teacher level is strongly related to the extent teachers interact with one another (Fullan, 1982). Success at the school level relies on the collegiality among teachers. In this light, I am advocating that CL be encouraged among teachers. The process would be the same as the one used for encouraging cooperation among students (Johnson and Johnson, 1987). Sufficient trust and openness needs to be present so that teachers will be able to share ideas, ask one another for help, come to value collegial support and interdependence, and be willing to learn and develop on the job. Demonstrations of teachers working collaboratively is the best encouragement for cooperation among students.

Conclusion

The message that lies within this chapter is that the teacher is the key. Teachers make the difference. Christa McAuliffe, the teacher astronaut, once said, ''I touch the future, I teach.'' We do make a lifelong impact. Whether we like it or not, teachers demonstrate what learners learn. How the learners experience our presence is what is remembered. If this memory is to be significant, then we as teachers must live the great values that we invite our learners to hold (Van Manen, 1986). Only then will we be teachers worth remembering.

Appendix A

Observation Form[1]

Record examples of what group members do and say.

Group: _____   Date: _____

Names	Encouraging	Checking for Understanding	Sharing Ideas and Information

[1]*Source:* J. Clarke, R. Wideman and S. Eadie, *Together We Learn: Cooperative Small-Group Learning,* Toronto: Prentice Hall Canada.

Appendix B

Key Ingredients to Successful Processing[2]

- allowing sufficient time for it to take place
- making feedback specific
- maintaining student involvement
- reminding students to use their collaborative skills while they process
- ensuring that clear expectations as to the purpose of processing have been communicated

REFERENCES

BISSEX, G., and R. BULLOCK, eds. 1987. *Seeing for Ourselves*. Portsmouth, NH: Heinemann Educational Books, Inc.

CLARKE, J., R. WIDEMAN, and S. EADIE, 1990. *Together We Learn: Cooperative Small-Group Learning*. Toronto: Prentice Hall Canada.

COHEN, E.G. 1986. *Designing Group Work*. New York: Teachers College Press.

CUMMINS, J. 1989. *Empowering Minority Students*. Sacramento, CA: California Association for Bilingual Education.

ENRIGHT, S., and M.L. MCCLOSKEY. 1988. *Integrating English: Developing English Language and Literacy in the Multicultural Classroom*. Reading, MA: Addison-Wesley.

FULLAN, M. 1982. *The Meaning of Educational Change*. Toronto: OISE Press.

GOODMAN, K. 1986. *What's Whole in Whole Language?* Richmond Hill, Ont: Scholastic-TAB Publications Ltd.

GOSWANI, D., and P. STILLMAN, eds. 1987. *Reclaiming the Classroom*. Portsmouth, NH: Heinemann Educational Books, Inc.

JOHNSON, D., and R. Johnson. 1987. *Learning Together and Alone*. Englewood Cliffs, NJ: Prentice Hall.

————. 1986. Mainstreaming and cooperative learning strategies. *Exceptional Children*, 52, no. 6: 553–61.

JOHNSON, D., R. JOHNSON, E. HOLUBEC, and P. ROY. 1984. *Circles of Learning*. Alexandria, VA: Association for Supervision and Curriculum Development.

MOORMAN, C., and D. DISHON. 1983. *Our Classroom*. Portage, MI: Personal Power Press.

North York Board of Education Curriculum and Staff Development Services. 1983. *Look! Hear!* North York, Ont: North York Board of Education.

NUNAN, D. 1989. *Designing Tasks for the Communicative Classroom*. Cambridge, England: Cambridge University Press.

[2]*Source:* David Johnson and Roger Johnson, "Mainstreaming and Cooperative Learning Strategies," Exceptional Children, 52, no. 6: 553–61.

REID, J., P. FORRESTAL, and J. COOK. 1989. *Small-Group Learning in the Classroom*. Scarborough, WA: Australia Chalkface Press.

RIVERS, W., ed. 1987. *Interactive Language Teaching*. Cambridge, England: Cambridge University Press

SMITH, F. 1988. *Joining the Literacy Club*. Portsmouth, NH: Heinemann Educational Books, Inc.

VAN MANEN, M. 1986. *The Tone of Teaching*. Richmond Hill, Ont: Scholastic-TAB Publications Ltd.

CHAPTER 10

COOPERATIVE LEARNING IN GRADUATE PROGRAMS FOR LANGUAGE TEACHER PREPARATION

Peter A. Shaw

Introduction

This chapter argues for cooperative learning (CL) as a significant component in the graduate-level preparation of language teachers, specifically in MA programs in TESOL (henceforth MATESOL) and Teaching Foreign Languages (henceforth MATFL). The case is built from the following statement of belief: that, in any teacher education program, even at the graduate level, the greater the congruence between what is said and what is done, the more greatly enhanced is the effectiveness of the program; that CL must be demonstrated and experienced as well as explained. The end point of the case is the benefits: an enhanced and more enjoyable learning experience during the program; students better prepared to teach; and students better prepared to work with other teachers. First, however, the background.

Background

Consider the following scene: It is a class in second language acquisition (SLA), a required course in a MATESOL/MATFL program. The instructor, having placed on reserve in the library five journal articles dealing with the issue of age and SLA, begins the class by asking for a volunteer to summarize the first study (a scene not unlike the Professor Kingsfield class in *The Paper Chase* when the hero's day is ruined when he is called upon to summarize the first case, which he has not read; our hypothetical TESOL professor, being more kindly, uses a general solicit). Of the fifteen students, the five who have not read the article at all initiate diligent and prolonged gaze-avoidance behavior, staring at their fingernails or the view outside the window. Five more, who only skimmed it, search ferociously through their notes. The five who read it locate their notes and pore over them but are not inspired to volunteer. The instructor changes her strategy and begins to elicit details:

I: Who were the subjects in this study? Nancy?

S1: Er . . . Dutch people . . . or Germans . . . learning English, I think . . . and some of them were kids and some teenagers and some–er–adults . . .

I: Ken, can you help?

S2: I'm sorry. I didn't get to this one.

I: Mutsuo, can *you* help?

S3: Subjects were Americans living in Holland acquiring Dutch.

I: Okay.

Consider a second scene: It is a class in syntax, part of an Introduction to Linguistics, a required course in a MATESOL/MATFL program. The professor distributes a handout containing a formal statement of the transformational rule known as "particle movement" and a list of sample sentences. She then gives a less formal account of the rule and goes through the derivation of the first two sentences, drawing trees on the blackboard and writing up each step. Next, the instructor reads sentence 3 and asks the students to apply the rule. She stands at the blackboard, chalk ready. There is an awkward pause and then three or four students who have figured out the rule the first time dictate the correct solution. Okay, says the professor, any questions? There are none, so she proceeds to an exposition in which particle movement is related to two other transformations: dative movement and heavy NP movement. About five minutes into this, however, students (not those who previously participated) begin to interrupt with questions that reveal that they have not grasped either the principle or workings of particle movement. The instructor flinches inwardly, asking herself: This is graduate school—why can't they all understand? She then regroups and begins a derivation of sentence 4, causing the four students to sink back in their seat, stifling yawns of boredom.

A final scenario: The instructor of a class in curriculum design sits at his desk with a pile of group projects, reviewing the semester. He had intended to alleviate students' problems with the bulky and complex course project (Perform a needs analysis for a particular language learning situation and develop from the results a curriculum, sample syllabus outlines, a unit, a lesson, and materials.) by organizing them into teams. However, numerous problems arose: Of five teams, only two made it intact to the end of the semester. The others broke up into pairs, with some students insisting on finishing up alone. Valuable office hours were consumed with students complaining about group members and seeking resolution of seemingly petty squabbles; some groups could never finish anything, others met deadlines early, but with sketchy, inadequate products. And the final projects were larded with little messages such as "Sue and I wanted you to know that we wrote nearly all of this" or "Tracy was supposed to do section 6 but forgot."

While these accounts may seem exaggerated, even unreal, I believe they represent significant difficulties for students and teachers at the graduate level. These obstacles directly parallel problems identified in K–12 education addressed by CL. Thus, the SLA teacher's frustration with the students' erratic reading habits and unwillingness to volunteer, S2's embarrassment at having to admit that he has not done the reading, S1's inadequate response that is then underlined by S3, whose satisfaction from knowing may be diminished by being put in the position of showing up her colleagues; the syntax teacher's difficulty in dealing appropriately either with the quickest or the slowest segments of the class, boredom of the former and frustration of the latter; and the mistaken assumption of the curriculum professor who thought that putting his students in groups would facilitate their work. All these phenomena are reflected in the CL literature in various forms according to grade level. For example, let us compare the difficulties encountered by the curriculum instructor above with the comments of Schultz who, when events compelled him to examine why his early attempts with CL were not successful, explains (Schultz, 1989: 43):

> First, I had not adequately prepared my students for cooperative learning. They had eleven years of independent and competitive lessons to unlearn; they and I both needed to be trained in cooperative methods. Second, I needed to focus on the differences between group work and cooperative work; the latter requires positive interdependence, face-to-face interaction, individual accountability, group processing, and interpersonal skills.

We may then pursue the parallel like this: The SLA professor might explore a Jigsaw (Aronson et al., 1978) approach to reading the literature and exploring issues in collaboration; the syntax instructor can learn Student Team Learning (STL) procedures like STAD, TGT, or TAI (see Chapter One of this volume or Slavin, 1986, for details) to complement presentations with student-team problem solving; and by deploying team building and other aspects of Co-op Co-op (Kagan, 1985), the curriculum teacher might improve team performance as well as enrich the experience for all concerned.

This then is the first claim underlying the case for CL in a MATESOL/MATFL program: better teaching and learning. This is clearly an empirical issue; however, it can be offered here only as a hypothesis, not as a proven fact. The same applies to those following below. As Slavin (1990) points out, the case for CL in grades 2 through 9 is made by an impressive and coherent body of research; that for grades 10 through 12 is much scantier; evidence from the tertiary level is virtually nonexistent.[1] This said, here are the premises on which the case for CL is built:

1. *That learning is facilitated and improved when collaborative team activities of various kinds are used to complement other forms of instruction.* I am not suggesting that the syntax teacher stop presenting new material or that the SLA teacher should not lead a whole-class discussion, but those instructional features will be all the more effective when accompanied by CL procedures.

2. *That team learning renders the overall experience more enjoyable and develops self-esteem and a higher appreciation for others.* Reducing the isolation and competitiveness of graduate school will produce effects comparable with those documented by DeVries et al., 1979; Madden and Slavin, 1983; Slavin et al., 1984; Fraser et al., 1977.

3. *That CL experiences better prepare students for key aspects of their future professional life.* Kagan (1989) and Johnson and Johnson (1983, 1984), among others, have stressed the importance of collaborative skills in the workplace and noted the alarming rate with which otherwise qualified individuals lose their jobs because of their inability to get along with colleagues; they then demonstrate the significant role played by CL in nurturing these skills. In the past, teaching might have seemed an exception to this need. However, the spread of phenomena such as team teaching, integrated curricula, coaching, mentorship programs, resource teachers, school improvement programs, and teacher support groups have brought teachers into increasing contact with one another. Further, I would argue that, beyond certain aspects of pedagogy, there is nothing in our profession—be it curriculum integration, syllabus creation or modification, materials preparation, test writing, school plans, textbook adaptation, or teacher development—that is not done better by teams than by individuals. In my own experience, however, teachers do not necessarily always work well together.

4. *That, as claimed at the outset, aspects of methodology or pedagogy are best inculcated in teachers-in-training by direct experience as well as demonstration and explanation.* The limitations of a typical MA-level methodology class are such that students may experience no more than an hour or so of Total Physical Response (TPR), Natural Approach, Silent Way, and so on. They are seen, briefly experienced, discussed, assessed, and then dropped. In the case of CL, students can have a detailed and lengthy exposure incorporating various kinds of experience (see Table 2). These experiences

[1]See Fraser et al., 1977, for a glowing exception.

are *learning* experiences rather than direct *language* experiences, but I suggest that several weeks of personal learning through TGT or Jigsaw or Co-op Co-op provide just as useful a basis for discussing their use in language teaching as a twenty-minute demonstration of TPR in a foreign language.

5. *That, as an aspect of language teacher preparation, CL has much wider application than many recent methodological proposals.* Unlike TPR or the Natural Approach, it has diverse application to all levels of proficiency; unlike Community Language Learning, it can be used with large groups of learners; unlike Grammar Translation or the Communicative Approach, it is not committed to a particular view of language learning or a particular type of syllabus.

6. *That language education in general has treated both the concept and the particulars of group work much too loosely and inexactly.* The pioneering work represented in a survey such as Slavin et al. (1986) enables us to approach group activities in a much more detailed and precise fashion. Students who are very familiar with the mechanics of various procedures are in a good position to effect this detailed application in their language instruction.

On these premises, then, is constructed the detailed proposal that follows.

Cooperative Learning in a MATESOL/MATFL Curriculum

This section is a brief commentary on three diagrammatic summaries: Table 1 shows CL components in a sample curriculum; Table 2 sketches the relationships among different deployments of various forms of CL; Table 3 is similar to 2, but more specific, detailing CL ''structures'' (as the term is used by Kagan, 1989).

Table 1 exhibits eight possible components of a curriculum for training ESL and foreign-language teachers and systematically incorporating cooperative learning. These components are briefly described here and two of them are further elaborated later.

Initial Orientation and Learner Training

At the outset of the program, a three-to-five day workshop apprises students of the basic nature of CL and its use in the program, and it begins the process of enhanced awareness and skills required for successful participation. Students experience basic structures and receive initial training for team learning.

Literature Review

In an early (first semester) course, probably in Methodology, students examine the CL literature and become familiar with its various forms and the research findings associated with each. This would be a good opportunity to deploy the Jigsaw procedure, with each team becoming expert in a given CL type.

Critical Analaysis

The presentation of the principles of CL in the literature is analyzed, again in the methods class, in terms of learning theories and pedagogic axioms encountered in the language teaching field. In particular, the relationship between CL and com-

Table 1
The Place of Cooperative Learning in a TESOL/MATFL Program: A Proposal

Cooperative Learning

	Theory	Practice
Orientation	Theory and research findings outlined	First experience of basic structures (e.g. Jigsaw, Roundtable)
Semester 1	Methodology: Read literature and discuss	Linguistics: Experience teambuilding, STAD, TGT, TAI Methodology: Observe groupwork
Semester 2	Sociolinguistics: Critically discuss social/linguistic aspects of groupwork	Sociolinguistics: Experience Jigsaw Curriculum Design: Experience Co-op Co-op
Semester 3	Second Language Acquisition: Critically discuss groupwork literature	Research Seminar: Experience Group Investigation
Semester 4	Practicum: Review theory and research	Practicum: Coaching (Cooperative teaching); use in own teaching: discuss techniques
Exit Mechanism	Discuss, evaluate	Describe/develop ideas (Do in a team?)

municative principles is assessed: CL serves to expand the notion of communicativeness in language teaching. The most traditional grammar exercises, for example, take on a new tone when worked in teams. Concepts that are somewhat vague or loose in language teaching can be fleshed out in great detail in CL terms: The notion of the information gap, for example, is exploited in depth in Jigsaw and Co-op Co-op procedures.

Observation

To the extent possible, students are given the opportunity to view CL in action (either live or on videotape) in various situations. Ideally, these observations would cover both language classes and subject-matter classes at various grade levels. Data from these observations serve as further input to critical discussions and, in my experience, it does not much matter where the data are collected.

Meaningful Exposure

At the same time as students are becoming familiar with the literature, observing CL in action, and beginning critical discussions of its principles and practices, they may also be assembling experiences of its different forms. Thus, for example, a segment on syntax is taught using STAD; a series of classes on phonology incorporates TGT; a sociolinguistics class uses a Jigsaw approach to the extensive literature to be covered; a curriculum design class uses Co-op Co-op to structure the semester-long team project. The anticipated result is not only a deeper understanding of CL, but a better and more enjoyable learning experience. Three of these possibilities are explored further later on in the chapter: STAD in a syntax class, Jigsaw in sociolinguistics, and Co-op Co-op in curriculum design.

Practical Experience and Coaching

MATESOL/MATFL programs normally include a practicum, often late in the course sequence as the culmination of the practical strand. Working with a coaching partner (see Kagan, 1989, on cooperative coaching), students have the opportunity to try out CL techniques in practice-teaching situations. Feedback is received from the coaching partner, the supervising teacher, and the practicum instructor.

Review and Summary

As close to the end of the program as possible (preferably as part of the practicum), students review their entire experience, especially (1) meaningful exposure and (2) practical experience and coaching. Points from the original critical analysis should be reviewed and reexamined in the light of subsequent experience. Students may also begin to anticipate which aspects of CL will be most appropriate for the particular career in language teaching they intend to pursue.

Assessment

As graduate programs move away from formal written examinations as an exit mechanism and begin to explore the use of projects and other potentially collaborative devices, CL may play more and more key roles. Certainly, whatever the nature of the final hurdle, an assessment of CL in language teaching would be a pertinent topic for students to address. Finally, the paucity of evidence from graduate level situations in education would dictate that a program incorporating CL should make every effort to assess its effectiveness.

To understand better the possibilities for using CL in a graduate program, Table 2 lists various cooperative procedures, their application in grades 2–9, their presentation in short workshops, their possible role in graduate classes, and their possibilities for language teaching. These notes address the final two columns only; the rest is richly described in the CL literature.

The items listed in Table 2 may be broken down even further. Three approaches (see Chapter One for explanation)—STAD, TGT and TAI—are particularly appropriate for working problems; that is, applying a principle or formula to different data. The general procedure is:

1. instructor teaches the new concept or principle;
2. student teams achieve mastery by working problems together;
3. some form of individual assessment is done;
4. teacher-led debriefing takes place.

This may be effectively applied to the teaching of formal linguistics, as in our earlier example of the particle movement in Section 2:

1. instructor teaches the particle movement transformation;
2. student teams derive sentences using the new rule;
3. individuals derive a final sentence by themselves;
4. teacher answers any final questions, goes on to relate new rule to others similar in function.

Another possible application would be in a course covering educational research methods:

1. instructor teaches the concept of standard deviation (SD);
2. student teams calculate means and SD for different data and explain significance;
3. students work alone on a further data sample;
4. instructor answers final questions, reviews importance of SD.

There is, of course, a crucial difference between K–12 and graduate education. Scores and grades for individual students in the latter case often need not be regularly recorded. Step 3, the individual assessment, is therefore routinely dropped in the MATESOL/MATFL courses; in its place, two or three tests may be given on an individual basis. In a language analysis class, for example, the syllabus comprises three blocks: phonetics and phonology; morphology and syntax; and discourse analysis. Student teams work on data-based problems throughout each segment and then take a closed-book test as individuals.

A second grouping is Jigsaw and Cooperative Integrated Reading and Composition (CIRC). These both apply to dealing with reading material. Jigsaw uses extensive reading dealing with a number of sources on the same topic, with each student reading a subset of the overall corpus. CIRC, emphasizing intensive reading, uses a single text that everyone reads. The application of Jigsaw to courses such as Sociolinguistics, Second Language Acquisition, or Methodology—all cases where students must become familiar with an extensive literature—requires a reappraisal of an often basic principle of graduate education: that all students read all the source material.

This is too complex an issue to debate here. I will simply offer the following position based on experience and common sense (and again, at least by analogy from research in the K–12 arena). Graduate students will: read more when faced with a realistic rather than an overwhelming reading load; read more effectively when given a clearly defined responsibility for a realistic amount of material; read more effectively when given a clear task; understand and retain material at least as well when a colleague explains it to them as when they read it themselves. (My guess is that understanding and retention are actually improved when peers teach each other material they have read in a team setting, but it is enough that the results are equal to the old system.)

To put Jigsaw into effect, the sociolinguistics teacher, let's say, has to work harder outside class. The readings must be divided up between the teams and work sheets developed to guide both the reading and the team discussions, both expert and regular, in class. In return, the instructor works at least differently, perhaps more enjoyably, in class: circulating among expert groups as they grapple with the significance of a particular study; eavesdropping on teams as the experts report; leading the discussion that pulls everything together.

In contrast, CIRC provides a means of closely examining a single text, particularly early in a course when a typical kind of written discourse is encountered for the first time. The reading aspect of CIRC develops specific aspects of the reading

Table 2: Seven Approaches to Cooperative Learning and Their Applications

Approach	Application in Grades 2–9	3-Hour Work-shop	MATESOL/MATFL Application	Language Learning Application
STAD	Language arts Physical science Mathematics (Slavin 1980, 1983, 1986)	Quibblean spelling (see Kagan, 1985)	Formal linguistics, e.g. syntax	Spelling
TGT	Life science Language arts Mathematics (Slavin 1980, 1983, 1986)	Photosynthesis unit in Slavin, 1986	Formal linguistics, e.g. phonology	Vocabulary
TAI	Mathematics: self-instruction units (Slavin, Leavey & Madden, 1986) (Slavin, Madden & Stevens, 1990)	See Appendix 9 in Slavin, 1986	Educational research methods	Grammar
Jigsaw	Science Social studies Literature (Aronson et al., 1978)	"How to succeed without even vying" (Kohn, 1986)	Sociolinguistics, second language acquisition	Extensive reading Reading about a topic + discussion
CIRC	Language Arts (Madden et al., 1986)	Sample short text, split in halves	Research seminar	Literature Intensive reading
Group Investigation	Science (Hannigan, 1990) Social Studies (Sharan & Sharan, 1990)	NA	Research project	Data-based project in a content course
Co-op Co-op	Social studies team project (Kagan, 1989)	NA	Curriculum design project	Team project in a content course

skill, especially prediction. When transferred to a typical TESOL research study, for example, students might:

- read only the introduction and then predict the methodology of the study;
- read the methodology and predict the results;
- read the results and predict the conclusions.

In similar fashion, it may not always be assumed that students are in a position to readily write research papers and other forms typical of the field. CIRC has useful suggestions for collaborative approaches to these tasks.

Finally, Group Investigation and Co-op Co-op provide approaches to team projects and research. They are available for structuring projects that are too large for individual students to undertake. This means that projects in curriculum design, test development, second language acquisition, or sociolinguistic research can be more substantial, more detailed, and hence more meaningful; and it is in these projects that students begin to develop and deploy the collaborative professional skills that are a significant by-product of the experience.

The next four sections give details of CL elements in the curriculum of a TESOL/MATL curriculum: first, the Orientation segment and then three CL approaches: STAD in syntax, Jigsaw, and Co-op Co-op.

Example 1: Cooperative Learning, Orientation, and Learner Training

As Table 1 indicates, the first step in incorporating CL into an MATESOL/MATFL curriculum is in an initial period of orientation and learner training. Components together with the number of hours given to each as indicated in brackets include:

- Introduction to the program [1]
- Introduction and profiles of faculty [0.5]
- Detailed description of required courses and electives available in the coming semester [3]
- Account of the TESOL/FL professions, including career opportunities, professional organizations, publications [3]
- Academic skills: training in effective reading, listening/notetaking, class participation, writing and research skills in applied linguistics [3]
- Setting the questions: student and faculty discussions, from their collective experience, of issues in ESL, EFL, and FLT that need to be addressed; a role-play exercise [4]
- Cooperative learning: an initial CL experience; a brief account of CL, in language teaching and in education generally; the use of CL in the program [6]

This initial CL training is included at this stage for the following reasons:

1. In line with the general principles of learner training, full disclosure is intended, so that students understand
   a. that CL will be used,
   b. why CL is used,
   c. what benefit they will reap as graduate students,
   d. what benefit they will reap as future teachers.
2. Students, in the light of 1b and 1c, are given initial training in prosocial aspects of group work, problems to anticipate, and how to solve them.
3. CL activities provide an excellent means for students to get to know one another and the faculty so that they can start to work together.
4. CL activities can be great fun: Their inclusion will enhance the overall enjoyment of the orientation and begin the students' graduate-school experience in a very positive fashion.

The CL component[2] consists of the following:

1. A one-hour session consisting of an introduction to the notion of CL and a team exercise in which students get to know each other by exchanging personal information, in particular their reasons for joining the program.
2. A three-hour session, the following day, with this agenda:
   I. *Plumb Consensus Exercise (1)*[3]: *Individual Values Clarification:* The worksheet (see Appendix A) presents certain fundamental issues in CL. Students record their initial, personal responses by circling the numbers on the first line opposite each item.
   II. *Neighbor Roundtable*[4]: Student teams are formed to brainstorm, on the qualities of a good neighbor. Each team's list is edited, prioritized, and then combined with those of other teams. Next, teams put their heads together to compare these qualities with those desirable in a co-worker. Teams are then asked to list and share any aspects of their education that helped to develop these qualities.
   III. *Jigsaw Reading:* A five-page article from *Psychology Today* ("How to Succeed Without Really Vying" by Alfie Kohn) is distributed, one page per student. Students read and gather in expert groups (all who

---

[2] I would stress the implication of the title in Table 1: that much of this is a proposal, a possible model rather than current practice in any actual program. However, the details of this orientation reflect what has been offered in the MATESOL/MATFL program at the Monterey Institute of International Studies.

[3] This activity was introduced to me by the late Walter Plumb, who said he took it from an IBM Corporation idea for generating discussion and consensus in executive meetings. I have chosen, however, to name it after him.

[4] This activity was devised by Kathleen Kitch, whose ideas have influenced me throughout this chapter.

have read the same page) to prepare a brief summary by completing a work sheet. The teams then reassemble to brief each other, thus reassembling the information in the article.

IV. *Research Summary:* Based on the outline given in Appendix B, the findings from studies in CL are presented.

V. *CL in the MATESOL/MATFL Program:* A diagram similar to Table 1 is presented and discussed so that students understand what to expect from the program from CL perspectives.

VI. *Problems in Teamwork:* A set of some possible problems in the use of CL at the graduate level is distributed (i.e. see Appendix C). Teams put their heads together to suggest solutions and then role play the specific form of words they would use to put the solution into effect.

VII. *Plumb Consensus Exercise (2): Team Values Clarification:* In the light of activities II–VI, students now affirm or reassess their original individual response by circling numbers on the second line. The teams then attempt to reach consensus in the following manner, for each item in turn:

    a. team members give their response number; these are summed and a team mean is calculated;

    b. team members each calculate their own distance from the mean and note it in the space provided;

    c. the team member who is farthest from the mean speaks first; all others speak in descending order of distance from the mean, so that the last to speak is closest to consensus; members may pass if they have nothing to add;

    d. when discussion is complete (by agreement or by time limit), team members circle a final reaction on the third row and the team means and individual differences are recalculated.

A brief discussion follows, along two lines. The first is for teams to announce their final positions (means) for each item and to assess the degree of consensus (variation from the means). They describe the influence of new information on their views (line one to line two) versus the influence of the arguments of their team colleagues (line two to line three). This permits the instructor to underline the value of both these processes in a graduate program, and to encourage students to be open to both. Secondly, the groups assess the usefulness of an exercise of this kind as a framework for organizing discussion and encouraging consensus. Application to upper intermediate and advanced levels of language instruction may also be mentioned.

The session ends with a final Roundtable activity. Teams are asked to list the characteristics of effective group work and to derive behaviors that they intend to manifest when called upon to work in teams.

3. A two-hour simulation, in which students prepare and role play a scene based on a typically problematic situation in contemporary language education: for example, the best way to meet the needs of LEP students at the high-school level. Documents (newspaper articles, school-board minutes and directives, school memos, letters from parents, etc.) give a detailed background to the simulation; role cards (principal, ESL teacher, counselor, parent, school-board member, etc.) give specific profiles of the participants. Students examine the documents and are then each given a role card. Expert groups (all the parents, all the principals, etc.) then meet to discuss the details of the character and rehearse behavior for the coming encounter. Finally, the scene is played out and a decision reached. Debriefing can include expert groups reassembling to compare performances and outcomes. Finally, the whole class discusses the experience.

Example 2: STAD in a MATESOL/MATFL Syntax Class

STAD (Student Teams-Achievement Divisions) is based on subject matter that may be divided into discrete units of work. Each unit has four components: teaching or presentation to the whole class, teamwork, individual quizzes, and finally a process by which individual progress is charted, team aggregates recorded, and significant progress recognized. Before charting this process in a syntax class, however, two issues must be discussed: team formation and teambuilding.

In K–12 situations, teams represent a cross section of the class in terms of sex, ethnicity, and academic proficiency. (See Slavin, 1986, for a useful discussion of the criteria and their application.) In a graduate linguistics class, the following have been found effective:

Previous study of linguistics
> Students with previous experience in formal linguistics declare themselves and are distributed across groups.

Languages spoken
> Teams are formed to maximize the number of languages known in each group.

Place of birth
> Students with the same regional dialect are placed in different groups; international students are placed one per team.

Gender
> Usually a minority, it seems, the men are distributed one or two per team.

Availability outside class
> This is the crucial factor, as the system requires that student teams meet outside of class.

Thus, appropriate times for team meetings are listed on the chalkboard and students sign up until there are four or five per group. The instructor then tries to enforce the other four criteria by moving people around, as long as the alternate meeting time is appropriate.

Kagan (1989) describes teambuilding as a process for creating trust and mutual support. The result can foster more efficient academic work. Kagan calls for teambuilding in cases of racial or other tensions and wide discrepancies among achievement levels. In my experience with graduate students, however, it is essential even in the absence of such serious considerations. Given their long histories of independence and competition and given the complex and challenging tasks they face, I have found that establishing a strong team identity and developing team communication skills and working processes are essential for effective CL functioning.

On the other hand, when teambuilding activities are divorced from academic work and take time from instruction, their value must be carefully weighed. However, if a teambuilding activity can be used with language learners, it has a benefit above and beyond the present course; plus, graduate students react well to the playfulness and creativity inherent in many activities designed to develop team identity and mutual dependence. Thus, these activities, applicable in any situation, are recommended:

Team name
> Students choose a name for their team, reflecting something positive they have in common;

Team banner
> The name plus other information is worked into a visual design that all members must help to design and draw;

Quality initials
> Teams develop a pair of positive adjectives for each member, corresponding with their initials (Peter Shaw, Profound and Stimulating); these are then incorporated into a rhythmic chant, presented to the rest of the class;

All-time ''goodies'' and ''baddies''
> Teams choose two baseball (or other) teams, one of their heroes, one of people they do not value. (The ''goodies'' might have an infield, for example, of Mozart at first, Woody Allen at second, Tom McGuane at short, and Stephen Krashen at third).

Other activities are designed. Here is my favorite, the least taxing on the instructor:

Heads together on teambuilding
> Teams devise appropriate teambuilding activities for their class. The two or three most popular and creative are then tried and assessed. (Alternatively, teams devise teambuilding activities for language learners in various situations).

A further advantage of working with mature, aware students is that they can reflect on their team experiences as an extension of teambuilding. This may be enhanced by suggesting roles—Recorder, Chairperson, Encourager, Checker, Observer, for example, and using feedback forms (Kagan, 1989).

One final point about teambuilding: in K–12 situations, the groups operate in class under the teacher's supervision. Since, in graduate school, insufficient class time precludes this arrangement with most teamwork taking place outside class, difficulties must be anticipated and discussed as part of teambuilding.

STAD may now be implemented. As described above, material is introduced in a class presentation. Students are then given data sets and worksheets to explore the new concept or rule (such as particle movement). Slavin and his colleagues (1986) emphasize the significance of team members doing their best for the group, and the team in turn helping one another. This peer support is important for its positive effects on academic performance.

Each week a variety of exercises is provided. Teams may do as many or as few as they wish, but must turn in at least one solution upon which they have all agreed. They are aware that they are preparing for a mid-term part of which they will take individually and part which they do as a take-home together. Those less confident with the material use their colleagues to clarify things; the more able, by explaining and teaching, make their own grasp even more secure. Individual mid-term scores are added to the team part, and the team with the highest score is rewarded. The important thing, however, is that through collaboration, each individual has achieved the best possible result.

Example 3: Jigsaw in Second Language Acquisition

We may now step through the scenario from the beginning of the chapter in terms of cooperative learning. After initial teambuilding, students have become used to a team approach to the literature. In preparation for discussing the issue of age and second language acquisition, the instructor has placed five articles on reserve in the library. The fifteen students are assigned, in teams of three, to read one in detail and, as a group, to be familiar with the others. They must negotiate ahead of time how to achieve this. (Professors who are not comfortable with the idea of students not reading a particular study will ask that all students at least skim the other four.) At the outset of class, students sit in groups according to the article they read in detail (students 1, 6, and 11 with article A; 2, 7, and 12 with B; etc.). Guided by worksheets provided by the instructor, each expert group reaches consensus on the main points of the article and its relevance to the overall topic.

When the allotted time has expired, the class re-forms into the three teams. Each student briefly presents the findings, and questions are posed and responded to. When a group expert cannot answer a question, it is noted and passed either to another team or to the instructor. A second worksheet guides the group to integrating the material and reaching justifiable generalizations. These are then presented to the class as a whole and discussed. The instructor, through the worksheets and contributions to the discussion, makes sure that students go beyond facts to the analysis and integration essential at the graduate level.

At some point in the MATESOL/MATFL curriculum, students' attention should be drawn to the possibilities of Jigsaw for language instruction. In a topic-based syllabus, for example, learners can be organized in exactly the same way to read different sources. The practicum should include practice in selecting reading materials, adapting them where necessary, and preparing worksheets.

Example 4: Co-op Co-op and Curriculum Design

The Co-op Co-op model (Kagan, 1989) is intended to provide a collaborative experience that completely lacks the element of competition. While TGT, STAD, or TAI all provide for competition among student teams, Co-op Co-op provides for students first to cooperate in teams and subsequently to share the products of this collaboration with their classmates. Given that graduate students are relatively less interested in and motivated by competition among teams, and given the appropriateness of Co-op Co-op for work in social studies (Slavin et al., 1986), this is an appealing format for teamwork in many MATESOL/MATFL classes: sociolinguistics and curriculum design are good examples.

Table 3 sketches the relationship between a middle-grade social studies project and a team assignment in a curriculum design course. With the exception of Steps 2 and 3, the parallel is exact.

Step 1: The teacher leads a discussion in which students explore their relationship to and potential interest in the general area of possible topics and in specific examples. In the social studies case, students talk about their interests in the events and people of a specific year: politics; foreign affairs; trends in fashion, music, and food; sporting achievements; movies; TV, and so on. The curriculum class discusses the locally available language learning/teaching situations, features of interest and relative ease of access and investigation. Students also examine and discuss previous needs analysis and curriculum projects and list the various tools of investigation and analysis. (These various approaches to needs analysis correspond here to the mini-topics featured in Steps 4–6.)

Step 2: Here there is a significant difference: the social studies teacher assigns students to teams, aiming for heterogeneity in terms of ability, ethnicity, and gender (as above). The curriculum, while keeping the criteria listed above in mind, generally allows students to form teams according to interest: a group interested in a local adult ESL program or foreign languages in high school will work together. The professor has to balance groups by negotiating with overly large teams (more than seven) and isolated individuals or pairs. Teambuilding then follows, although the social studies project may come well into the semester and teams may already be

Table 3
Three Applications of Co-op Co-op

	Social Studies, Grades 6–8	Curriculum Design	ESL Content Class
STEP 1 Student-centered class discussion	Task: Choose 1 year in the period 1950–70 and present major events, trends, etc. Class discusses possibilities.	Task: Do Needs Analysis in language learning situation and base curriculum on results. Discuss possible sites.	U.S. Geography: Choose an area of country and present important features. Discuss features of interest.
STEP 2 Team Formation & teambuilding	Heterogeneous assignment. Teambuilding minimal if Jigsaw and other CL work prior to project.	Students self-select by interest in a site. Teacher works to balance by numbers and other criteria.	Heterogeneous assignment by L1, proficiency level, etc. Teambuilding.
STEP 3 Team topic selection	Teams choose a year.		Teams choose an area.
STEP4 Mini-topic selection	Students each select an aspect of the year chosen.	Students plan various Needs Analysis instruments and divide work.	Teams list aspects (agriculture, cities, climate, etc); each takes one.
STEP 5 Mini-topic preparation	Students research in library, interview older people, etc.	Students interview, give questionnaires, do case studies, etc.	Students do library research, etc.
STEP 6 Mini-topic presentation	Students present findings to team.	Team assembles data.	Students share findings with team.
STEP 7 Preparation of team presentation	Team orders data and and devises varied presentation.	Data organized verbally and visually. Analysis prepared.	Team prepares presentations with maps, etc.
STEP 8 Team presentation	Findings are presented to class. All team members participate.	Data and analysis presented.	Team presents information.
STEP 9 Evaluation	(1) Individual contributions by team; (2) team presentation by class.	(1) Individuals by team; (2) team by class; (3) written version by instructor.	(1) Team by class (2) team by instructor; (3) teacher feedback on language use.

in existence and functioning well. In the curriculum class, teams are formed in the first week of class and teambuilding is again considered essential.

Step 3: At this point, the social studies teams select their topic. The teacher monitors the process to make sure that two teams do not select the same topic. This step is not necessary in the curriculum case, as teams were formed around topics in the first place.

Step 4: Social studies teams return to the aspects they discussed and negotiate for the one (sports, fashion, politics) they want. Curriculum students discuss the overall form of their investigation and then allocate tasks: conduct interviews, observe classes, design a questionnaire, and so forth. In each case, the plan is submitted to the instructor for approval and suggestions.

Step 5: The research is carried out: in the library, off campus, or by telephone. The teacher keeps track, often by allocating short periods of class time for teams to discuss their progress and support one other.

Step 6: The research is complete. Students brief each other as to their findings. They then make final helpful suggestions and send each other scurrying back to sources for final details. At the graduate level, this all takes place out of class.

Step 7: Also out of class, the graduate students formulate their presentation, preparing overhead projector transparencies (OHP slides), hand-outs, and other visuals. The social studies students plan in class and are encouraged to be creative and vary their style of presentation (present a typical meal, a fashion show, a dance style, or a political speech, for example.)

Steps 8 and 9: The findings are delivered. In the graduate case, many questions from other teams are answered, often stimulating much discussion. Individual and team efforts are assessed by colleagues, other teams, and instructors. In the curriculum case, a written report is submitted, with a copy going to the real-world context where the work took place, and an additional reaction is often provided.

Table 3 also provides an application of Co-op Co-op to a project in an ESL content course. Here, the parallel with the social studies class is also very close; teacher assistance with and assessment of language use is also present. Again, the curriculum class should provide opportunities for planning such a project within the context of a content course.

Assessment of CL in Graduate TESOL Programs

It is not possible in small graduate programs to conduct the kind of process–product, control–group/experimental group studies that have so consistently validated the effectiveness of CL in K–12 settings. In particular, the lack of reliable, objective measures of achievement prevents the assessment of learning or retention.

What is possible is to consult the students themselves, using, for example, the kind of assessment instrument shown in Appendix D. I have evaluated two consecutive years of my course language analysis (an introduction to linguistic analysis, including phonetics, phonology, morphology, syntax, and discourse) using CL as a

Table 4
**Mean Scores on Evaluation Items from Two Language Analysis
Classes Using Cooperative Learning**

Items on supplementary evaluation (Appendix D)

	1	2	3	4	5	6	7	8	9
Year 1 class means: n = 26	4.85	4.85	5.36	4.65	4.33	5.33	4.13	3.16	4.2
Year 2 class means: n = 19	5.5	5.61	6.0	5.67	5.93	6.2	3.8	3.87	5.2

significant component. Students completed the supplementary evaluation each time; the results are shown in Table 4. These data may be set against my own impressionistic findings.

Somewhat disappointed with the effectiveness of teamwork in Year 1, I made these changes for the following year:

- more attention to the formation of teams
- more and more varied teambuilding activities
- more regular group work in class
- more choice of activities for out-of-class teamwork
- more rewards and acknowledgment for successful teams
- increased proportion of grade for team activities

I find the results encouraging: The Year 2 class reported a better experience all around (more enjoyment, significant learning, and a better response to teambuilding). For myself, there was a significant challenge in providing appropriate exercises for team work and in making optimal use of class time. The enthusiasm of students deriving from their group work makes them demanding of class time. Therefore, lectures and other teaching presentations must be efficient and to the point.

In summary, both from the language analysis course experience and from use of Co-op Co-op and Jigsaw in other courses, I have witnessed the positive effects predicted at the outset in terms of my students' learning, their satisfaction with the learning experience, and the improvements in assignments and projects. The effects in terms of their language teaching career is yet to be seen. The next stage is to devise ways of objectively measuring and recording these gains and to explore more fully the nature of a cooperative classroom at the graduate level. I approach this task secure in the knowledge that I enjoy my teaching, am a better organizer and facilitator of learning, and can help better prepare the next generation of language teachers.

Appendix A: Values Clarification

MATFL/TESOL Program: Orientation and Student Preparation

Cooperative Learning: Plumb Consensus Exercise

Read each item carefully and circle your reaction on the first line of numbers. Later, you will have an opportunity to reassess your position by circling numbers on the second line. Then enter the group mean as it is calculated, and figure out your distance from that mean. After group discussion, circle on line 3 your final decision.

1   completely disagree
2   strongly disagree
3   disagree
4   neutral
5   agree
6   strongly agree
7   completely agree

							Your Distance from Group Mean	Group Mean

Item 1
The more group work is used in the MATFL/TESOL program, the more I will learn.

1 2 3 4 5 6 7 ____ ____
1 2 3 4 5 6 7 ____ ____
1 2 3 4 5 6 7 ____ ____

Item 2
The more group work is used in the program, the more I will enjoy it.

1 2 3 4 5 6 7 ____ ____
1 2 3 4 5 6 7 ____ ____
1 2 3 4 5 6 7 ____ ____

Item 3
The more group work is used in the MATFL/TESOL program, the better I will be prepared for my future job.

1 2 3 4 5 6 7 ____ ____
1 2 3 4 5 6 7 ____ ____
1 2 3 4 5 6 7 ____ ____

Item 4
The more group work is used in the program, the more I will benefit as a person.

1 2 3 4 5 6 7 ____ ____
1 2 3 4 5 6 7 ____ ____
1 2 3 4 5 6 7 ____ ____

Item 5
The more group work is used in the MATFL/TESOL program, the more effective I will be as a teacher.

1 2 3 4 5 6 7 ____ ____
1 2 3 4 5 6 7 ____ ____
1 2 3 4 5 6 7 ____ ____

Item 6
I am in the MATFL/TESOL program not to learn from the faculty but from my fellow students and from our group's interaction with the material provided.

1 2 3 4 5 6 7 ____ ____
1 2 3 4 5 6 7 ____ ____
1 2 3 4 5 6 7 ____ ____

Appendix B: Research Summary for Orientation

TESOL/MATFL Program: Orientation and Student Preparation

Cooperative Learning Research Summaries

A. GENERAL EMPIRICAL

A1.   Academic Achievement

Cooperative learning increases student achievement: better learning, increased retention, more creativity, better problem solving skills.

A2.   Intergroup Relations

People who cooperate learn to like each other better.

A3.   Self-esteem

Students learning in teams experience enhanced self-esteem, more than those in traditional learning contexts.

A4.   Harder Work

Students working in teams stay on task and are more productive.

A5.   Enjoyment

Students derive greater enjoyment from working in teams than from working by themselves.

A6.   Student Behavior/Class Management

When students work in teams, they behave better and are easier to manage.

A7.   Better Work Performance

Students who have been through cooperative learning programs are more successful in their subsequent employment.

B.   SCHEMATIC

B1.   Learning Occurs in the Presence of

a. inclusion   (teambuilding)
b. affection   (the ''encourager'')
c. influence   (role assignment, ''gatekeeper'')

B2.   Learning Requires Some Type of Emotional Link.

C. SOME BENEFITS OF COOPERATIVE LEARNING ARRANGEMENTS IN SECOND LANGUAGE INSTRUCTION (McGroarty, 1989)

C1. *Linguistic*

 a. Increased frequency and variety of second language practice through interaction

 b. Possibility for development or use of the first language in ways that support second language skills

C2. *Curricular*

 a. Opportunities to integrate language with content instruction

 b. Inclusion of a greater variety of curricular materials to stimulate language use as well as concept learning

C3. *Social*

 a. Freedom for language teachers to master new professional skills, particularly those emphasizing communication

 b. Opportunities for students to act as resources for one another and thus assume a more active role in learning.

Appendix C: Group Work Problems

TESOL/MATFL Program: Orientation and Student Preparation

Cooperative Learning: Some Possible Group Work Problems

1

Student *K* clearly enjoys group work tremendously, but her enthusiasm is sometimes overwhelming. At group meetings to work on the project she talks far more than anyone else, not always on the subject, and then demands extra meetings to make up the time wasted. What might you say to her?

2

Student *W* always produces his part of the work on schedule, but it is never what the team had agreed. He does good work and takes part in the planning and brainstorming. He also volunteers willingly to do his part; but he always changes it without consulting the rest. What might you say to him?

3

Student *D* seems like a great team member: He always offers his house for team meetings, provides excellent food and drink, volunteers to make copies, prepares OHP slides, and so on. But when it comes to generating ideas, planning, brainstorming, or filling in tedious details, he has nothing to contribute. What do you say to him?

4

Student *R* hates group work. He whines constantly at group meetings and complains endlessly about the time they take from his busy schedule. He is occasionally rude to other team members who express enthusiasm about what is going on. However, when the task or material at hand catches his attention, he works well and contributes usefully. What might you say to him?

5

Student *T* has an exaggerated respect for the course instructor. She expresses no confidence in group decisions and is constantly going to see the professor to check things, usually without consulting the group. She also shows the teacher drafts of her part of the project to get early feedback. What might you say to her?

Appendix D: Evaluation of CL Experience in Two Consecutive Years

Linguistics 430
Language Analysis

Supplementary Evaluation

Please take a little time to read and complete the following items by circling the appropriate number for each response. Be frank and thoughtful, but do not agonize. Do not write your name. You may add any comments you wish, but remember the final exercise includes a detailed written assessment from each group of cooperative learning.

The use of the CL (group) approach to learning in this class

1. was
   1. highly detrimental
   2. something of a drawback
   3. a slightly negative feature
   4. of no consequence one way or the other
   5. a positive feature
   6. a distinct plus
   7. highly beneficial
2. made mastering the material
   1. a great deal more difficult
   2. distinctly more difficult
   3. a little more difficult
   4. neither more difficult nor easier
   5. a little easier
   6. distinctly easier
   7. a great deal easier
3. made the experience of doing the out-of-class assignments
   1. a great deal less worthwhile
   2. less worthwhile
   3. slightly less worthwhile
   4. neither more nor less worthwhile
   5. slightly more worthwhile
   6. more worthwhile
   7. much more worthwhile

4. made performing the out-of-class assignments
   1 a distinct pain
   2 more difficult
   3 a little more difficult
   4 the same as always
   5 a tad easier
   6 distinctly easier
   7 a great joy

5. made the in-class group work
   1 pretty much a waste of time
   2 less useful
   3 a little less useful
   4 neither more nor less useful
   5 a little more useful
   6 more useful
   7 much more useful

6. made the overall experience of the course
   1 much less enjoyable
   2 less enjoyable
   3 a little less enjoyable
   4 the same, either way
   5 a little more enjoyable
   6 more enjoyable
   7 much more enjoyable

7. My group was/groups were
   1 way too small
   2 too small
   3 a little too small
   4 just fine
   5 a little too big
   6 too big
   7 way too big

8. The training I received for working in a team was
   1 woefully inadequate
   2 too little
   3 slightly inadequate
   4 enough
   5 a little too much
   6 too much
   7 horribly overdone

9. The training I received for working in a team was
    1 entirely inappropriate for one of my dignity and maturity
    2 largely inappropriate
    3 somewhat inappropriate
    4 okay in parts
    5 largely appropriate
    6 nearly all appropriate
    7 entirely appropriate

REFERENCES

ARONSON, E., N. BLANEY, C. STEPHAN, J. SIKES, and M. SNAPP. 1978. *The Jigsaw Classroom.* Beverly Hills, CA: Sage Publications.

DEVRIES, D.L., P. LUCASSE, and S. SHACKMAN. 1979. Small group versus individualized instruction: A field test of their relative effectiveness. Paper presented at the American Psychological Association, New York.

FRASER, S.C., A.L. BEAMAN, E. DIENER, and R.T. KELEM. 1977. Two, three, or four heads are better than one: Modification of college performance by peer monitoring. *Journal of Educational Psychology,* 69, no. 2: 101–8.

HANNIGAN, M.R. 1990. Cooperative learning in elementary school science. *Educational Leadership,* 47, no. 4: 25.

JOHNSON, D.W., and R.T. JOHNSON. 1983. *Learning Together and Alone: Cooperation, Competition and Individualization.* New Brighton, MN: Interaction Book Company.

JOHNSON, R.T., and D.W. JOHNSON. 1984. *Structuring Cooperative Learning: Lesson Plans for Teachers.* New Brighton, MN: Interaction Book Company.

KAGAN, S. 1985. *Cooperative Learning Workshops for Teachers.* Laguna Niguel, CA: Resources for Teachers.

———. 1989. *Cooperative Learning Resources for Teachers.* San Juan Capistrano, CA: Resources for Teachers.

KOHN, A. 1986. How to succeed without even vying. *Psychology Today,* September 26: 22–29.

MADDEN, N.A., and R. E. SLAVIN. 1983. Cooperative learning and social acceptance of mainstreamed academically handicapped students. *Journal of Special Education,* 17: 171–82.

MADDEN, N.A., R.J. STEPHENS, and R.E. SLAVIN. 1986. *A comprehensive cooperative learning approach to elementary reading and writing: Effects on student achievement.* Baltimore, MD: Johns Hopkins University, Center for Research on Elementary and Middle Schools.

MCGROARTY, M. 1989. The benefits of cooperative learning arrangements in second language instruction. *NABE Journal,* 13: 127–143.

SCHULTZ, J.L. 1989. Cooperative learning: Refining the process. *Educational Leadership,* 47, no. 4: 43–45.

SHARAN, Y., and S. SHARAN. 1990. Group Investigation expands cooperative learning. Educational Leadership, 47, no. 4: 17–21.

SLAVIN, R.E. 1980. Effects of student teams and peer tutoring on academic achievement and time on task. *Journal of Experimental Education,* 48: 252–57.

————. 1983. *Cooperative Learning.* New York: Longman.

————. 1986. *Using Student Team Learning,* 3rd ed. Baltimore: The Johns Hopkins University.

————. 1990. Research on cooperative learning: Consensus and controversy. *Educational Leadership,* 47, no. 4: 52–55.

SLAVIN, R.E., M. LEAVEY, and N.A. MADDEN. 1984. Combining cooperative learning and individualized instruction: Effects on student mathematics achievement, attitudes, and behaviors. *Elementary School Journal,* 84: 409–22.

————. 1986. *Team Accelerated Instruction: Mathematics.* Watertown, MA: Mastery Education.

SLAVIN, R.E., N.A. MADDEN, and R.J. STEVENS. 1990. Cooperative learning models for the 3 R's. *Educational Leadership,* 47, no. 4: 22–28.

CHAPTER 11

COOPERATIVE INSERVICE EDUCATION

Judy Winn-Bell Olsen

In this chapter, we will consider some of the basic issues of staff development (a current term for inservice teacher education) and examine one procedure and some activities for staff development in cooperative learning (CL). The chapter is comprised of three sections: a description of inservice education and how it differs from preservice education; an outline of some basic issues generic to staff development of any kind; and a suggested format for conducting inservice workshops in cooperative learning. The words "trainers," "staff developers," and "presenters" are used interchangeably in this chapter to refer to the people who plan and conduct inservice workshops for working professionals (who in this context are mostly teachers—though administrators, counselors, and other workers in the educational setting may also be included).

Features of Inservice Education

Inservice education—the further professional development of active educators—is very different from the university-based, preservice education required for credentials, which begins most educators' careers. Among characteristics distinguishing preservice from inservice education are the following features.

Focus on Local Needs

Unlike preservice education, inservice can focus on the immediate particular needs of a particular faculty and their students in a particular setting. As a result, it can address local needs in a way that more generalized instruction cannot.

Inservice education for teachers is of special importance in areas with rapid shifts in population such as an influx of new groups of limited English speakers. It can also be important in the case of changes in legal and administrative requirements. Such changes can occur with the passage of a legislative act, development of mandates by a state board of education, or implementation of a new master plan by a particular school district. Inservice education is important, too, in developing and maintaining faculty morale and building a healthy school climate.

Interest Factors

Practicing, experienced teachers are notoriously ''tough customers'' for inservice programs. The burden is on the staff developer to be engaging in presentation, believable in message, and approachable with skeptics. Although educators in a university setting often have all these qualities, there is likely to be a more willing suspension of disbelief (or at least not as loudly voiced) in a preservice university setting than in an inservice staff development context.

Relationships

Often the ongoing, in-charge staff developer is ''one of us'': perhaps a member of the school district or someone not too different from the teachers in the workshop sessions—someone whose experience and persona the participants can identify with. While this makes the good staff developer even more believable, in some ways there is less patience, less margin for error for the ''off-day'' or the activity gone awry when inservices are led by someone with less personal and professional distance from the participants.

Time Factors

Unlike most university classes, inservice sessions may be held only a few times during the school year. They may, however, be of considerable length—from three hours to two days in duration. The short, one-shot workshops are not recommended as being of much lasting value (McREL, 1989). Workshops of greater length may be part of a larger plan for long-range development of a faculty or a district over a period of two to five years. Here the end goal is not likely to be a certificate or degree, but implementation of particular teaching procedures and development of a particular philosophy throughout a school or district.

Financial Responsibility Factors

Usually, inservice staff development is offered by a school district, which must not only pay for staff developers but provide the place and the time for the program. Frequently, participants need released time from teaching, which necessitates paying substitute teachers—often the largest expense in planning any extensive inservice staff development. (This is in sharp contrast to preservice university-based teacher education, which is generally at the prospective teacher's expense.) As a result, the school district has a strong financial interest in an immediate, effective impact on its trainees, as well as in long-range results.

Planning and Development Needs for Local Participation

Education in general and inservice education in particular need strong local participation in certain crucial aspects:

Needs Assessment

The first job of the inservice planner/staff developer is to assess and define the local needs. For an "outside expert" invited to provide workshops, it is particularly important to provide information on local needs as they are perceived by various levels of administration, the faculty in the field, and other involved personnel—such as counselors, aides, parents, and in some cases the students themselves. All relevant groups need to feel that they have been heard (Yedlin and Olsen, forthcoming).

Local Product

It is important that the structure of the staff development proceed in such a way that the participants have an active hand in shaping a final product produced in the inservice sessions—whether that product be actual materials, a plan for implementation, or a set of clearly articulated principles.

Ongoing Growth

It is also important to develop the sense that staff-development sessions are the *beginning* of the development process, and that the process should continue with interaction among all the involved staff after the staff developer's commitment has been fulfilled. The last part of this chapter addresses this issue.

Some Basic Issues

Although the specific focus of this chapter is cooperative learning with application to language teaching while modeling CL techniques, readers should also find useful applications for staff development, procedural and philosophical, in other subjects as well. While emphasizing one particular format for presenting and practicing CL principles and techniques, this chapter raises some issues related to *all* types of inservice staff development:

Issue 1: Who and How

There are interesting differences between willing participants to keep in mind here. Some attendees (let's call them Type A) want only "the nuggets"—the specific activities that they will use in ways that suit them. They are Type A's partly because of experience. They may have had more exposure to procedures and philosophy of what is being presented, or they may already work in ways consistent with that philosophy, and so "pick it up" more quickly. Many resource teachers, regular conference attendees, and voluntary takers of courses tend to be Type A's.

Other willing participants (Type B) want a larger framework, with sufficient time to experience and discuss a step-by-step approach. They may not absorb the new philosophies and procedures as quickly as the A's; but when they have absorbed them, can apply them well. Type B's are less likely to seek out staff development opportunities on their own time, but may well comprise the largest portion of an inservice group.

Planning effective staff development depends in part on getting a sense of what proportion of the audience will be A's and what proportion will be B's. Generally, the proportions should determine pace and emphasis rather than the actual content of the staff development. Even old-timers and fast-trackers need a reminder of how it all fits together and why to do it at all (see issue 3). Part of the art of staff development is determining how much and what kind of reminder—particularly if there are others in the session who are new to the process.

Issue 2: How vs. How Long

As much as possible—unless the audience is a very experienced group of A's—the staff development presentation for CL should model all the steps of a cooperative lesson. However, because of the amount of processing (participant discussion) to be done, not all relevant aspects can be covered in one or two workshops, particularly for beginners. An ongoing dilemma revolves around the questions of balance: How much overview and how much in-depth attention to detail? These questions will be addressed through some of the suggestions in the procedures described on the following pages.

Issue 3: How vs. Why

A major question for any staff developer planning workshops for practicing teachers who can "use this tomorrow" is how much attention to pay to general conceptual information and how much to specific procedures. What is the appropriate balance? Attention only to "how to" and not to "why" does not ultimately lead to effective transfer of staff development (Joyce and Showers, 1980, 1983).

The balance of "how" and "why" was also a relevant question in constructing a format for CL staff development given in the next section. I have tried to address both the conceptual and the procedural. In some cases, I give general commentary. In other cases, I provide specific materials used in staff development, partly as an example of format and partly for the specific CL information contained in the materials.

Most of the procedures and specific activities presented here are models for application to the language classroom. It is intended that trainees first (a) participate in the activities, then (b) discuss the procedures for developing and implementing those activities, and finally (c) use the structure of the activity in their own teaching, changing the specific content to suit student needs.

Getting Started—One Format for Staff Development Workshops in Cooperative Learning

What follows is one suggested format for presenting CL techniques and principles in a cooperative way. Fortunately, CL structures are useful for engaging interest at any level. This makes it possible for adults to learn about principles while participating in the procedures in meaningful ways.

In brief, the suggested steps are as follows:

1. Establish presenter credibility while developing whole-group unity.
2. Form small groups or teams.
3. Build team unity.
4. Explore information processing structures.
5. Investigate other cooperative techniques.
6. Explore social considerations.
7. Plan for ongoing growth.

Details for each step are outlined in this section.

Establish Presenter Credibility While Developing Whole-Group Unity

Two kinds of presenter credibility come to mind: (a) credibility as a staff developer who can respond appropriately to the needs of the audience, and (b) credibility as a knowledgeable information source with a well-formed presentation plan.

Establishing Credibility as a Responsive Staff Developer

Ask participants what they expect from the workshop (Cooper et al., 1990) and affirm their responses by listing them—on large pieces of newsprint, if possible. Tell them what you have planned to do and which of their expectations it will meet. If you have done a needs assessment as suggested in this chapter, you should be able to predict at least some of the responses and plan material that will fit at least some of your participants' expectations. You can use the list of responses as a checklist at the end of your session to remind participants of what they requested and what they did in the workshop. (If responses are quite different from what you planned, on the other hand, you can remove the list quietly when participants are busy with the first exercise. If you will be leading more than one session with such a group, however, you might use such a list at the end of your first session for brainstorming with participants on how to address particular expectations the next time.)

Establishing Credibility as a Knowledgeable Source

This is probably most easily done by some preliminary lecture/overview—a this-is-what-to-expect presentation given by the staff developer(s) to the participants. It may be important to inform attendees that they are expected to engage actively in different kinds of activities and that pedagogical reasons for their activity will be revealed in the course of the workshop.

Some staff developers show a particular preference for (a) or (b); others combine the two; and others choose one or the other to fit the needs of a particular situation.

Starting the Workshop with a Whole-Group Presentation

It may be difficult for some of us as facilitators/presenters who are committed to a particular point of view to remember that not all attendees may be comfortable with group work or know why they are being asked to participate interactively. Although the well-meaning presenter may want to "not waste any time" by jumping into group work immediately, there is the risk that some participants will resist. An introduction in a more traditional format (speaker to full audience) gives participants a chance to see who the presenters are and what they have to offer, which it is hoped will encourage participants to suspend judgment when trying new and potentially risky things. (This approach is also helpful in many adult and high school ESL classes when students have not yet been exposed to CL.)

In responding to the question of how long to remain in the traditional speaker-to-audience mode, two possibilities come to mind:

A. Something not more than twenty minutes or so. Then "group and get on with it."

B. Something really too long—say, over an hour—so that by the time grouping and activities start, the audience is restless and glad for the change. In this case, it should be clearly pointed out that the long lecture experience has a particular purpose: to draw contrasts with the group experience.

Sometimes in staff development it is strategically important to keep the entire group together longer than you would have liked because of unforeseen circumstances: Perhaps a significant part of your audience has not yet arrived, or there are temporary problems with equipment, materials, or location.

Even within the large-group format, the speaker can begin to vary dynamics by periodically using Think-Pair-Share. Participants each turn to one other person and discuss opinions, reactions, or predictions in response to a question from the presenter. (Limit total time to five minutes or less.) If used more than once during the opening, Think-Pair-Share can be varied the second time by a second step. After discussion with the first partner, participants turn to someone else and summarize their discussion with partner 1. This is particularly appropriate for major issues or themes.

Form Small Groups or Teams

Often great interest revolves around the topic: How big can "small groups" be? Literature cited by Kagan (1989,1990) suggests between three and seven persons. Teachers of young children suggest no more than four in a group (Cooper, 1990).

On what principles should staff development participants be grouped? I recommend grouping participants first, then discussing the why's and how-to's of the procedure. Some possibilities are:

A. totally random grouping
B. preplanned heterogeneous groups
C. participant-determined heterogeneous groups

In sessions of more than a few hours, more than one type of grouping should be used.

Totally Random Grouping

Matching cards: best in a session of no more than forty trainees. Decide how large you want your groups—say, four per group. Pre-prepare cards or slips of paper to match in sets of four. Each set of four is different. Sets might include four identical pictures, four parts of a picture to put together, four pictures of a sequence of events, or members of a set such as four pictures or names of vegetables, items of clothing, rivers, states, presidents, or local landmarks. Cards are shuffled and dealt out at random to participants. Participants mill around comparing their cards until they find other participants holding cards that they believe combine to form a card set. Participants then sit down together, introduce themselves, and tell the larger group why they believe their cards form a set for grouping together. (*Note:* Card sets of five or threes are needed when the group does not divide evenly into groups of four.)

A good opening activity for groups of this type is to brainstorm what kinds of card sets members would design for their classes and why.

Counting off: For groups of four, divide four into the total number of participants—say thirty-three. Your number will be eight, with one remainder. Have participants count off by eight as you point to them sequentially: 1,2,3,4,5,6,7,8,1,2,3,4,5,6 . . . etc. The last person will be a #1. You will have seven groups of four and one group of five, for a total of eight groups.

Check to be sure people remember their numbers ("Who's a #1? Raise your hands please. Who's a 2? A 3?" etc.) Then ask participants to group with others who have the same number ("All the #1s, sit over here, please. #2s, sit there. #3s, sit over there" and so on, through the #8s.)

A good opener for participants, once they have found and are seated with their teammates, is to list the steps in the procedure by which they were just grouped. It is not immediately obvious to some that the size of the group (in this case, four) is divided into the total number of participants to get the number of groups to be formed. A classic error of the novice is to have participants count to four—which will produce four groups of eight people.

Preplanned Heterogeneous Groups

If you know names of participants, make posters listing the members of each team. A principle of CL theory is to make the groups as heterogeneous as possible. This is particularly useful if there are any negative personalities to contend with. One way of dealing with such individuals is to group them with strong, positive personalities. In actual classroom practice, however, some teachers of children prefer to put all the most negative children in one group and plan to sit with that group most of the time (Cooper, 1990, personal communication).

A good opening activity for groups of this kind is for participants to figure out the principle on which they are grouped. In so doing, they also learn something about one another if they are not already acquainted.

Participant-Arranged Heterogeneous Groups

A poster with directions for participants is on display when they first arrive at the session. Participants are instructed to mark their name badges with particular colors and symbols to represent relevant criteria. Criteria could include levels taught, disciplines taught, school site, number of years of experience, number of years of staff development, and anything else not immediately obvious to the eye.

When it is time to group, the workshop presenter explains the heterogeneity principle and asks the participants to group themselves accordingly, using information from the badges and any visible characteristics (gender, age, race, etc.) that seem appropriate.

Build Team Unity

This is as important in the staff development context as in the classroom. Adequate time is needed to explain, experience, monitor, and process—particularly for people who are new to CL. Of the many possibilities for team builders, three that may be particularly appropriate linguistically include:

- Extremes and Averages—see Table 1.
- Same and Different—see Table 2.
- Roundtable—see Table 3.

Table 1
Extremes and Averages*

Purpose: to learn about teammates

to build a sense of "team"ness

to practice superlative language forms

to practice averaging

Procedure: Students are in groups of four to six. They answer questions given on a handout or poster. The question should require them to talk to each other to get information and come to consensus on the answer.

Sample questions (for use in teacher staff development sessions):

1.   In your group, who has the longest name? (Count first and last names together.)

2.   Who has lived in the most cities?

3.   Who has the least amount of money with them right now? (Use this as a humorous element in staff development only. It is not suitable for most students)

4.   What is the average height of your group members?

5.   What is the average length of time that your group has worked in education?

6.   Make up your own question and have your group answer it.

Comments: Design items to elicit different kinds of information, as suggested in the sample questions:

*Item One: something that requires people telling group members their names. *Variations:* Who has the most vowels/consonants in his/her name? How many names have you had in your life so far? (Count nicknames, "pet" names, etc.)

*Item Two: something that requires revealing something about your personal life that is not too personal. *Variations:* Who has attended the most schools? Who has the most brothers and sisters? Who has the most pets? Who slept the most/least last night? Who got up the earliest/latest this morning? Who lives farthest from school?

*Item Three: some tangible, visible thing about you right now. *Variations:* longest thumb, shortest hair, most colors in clothing. (*Avoid* attributes that might cause embarrassment: longest nose, biggest ears, etc.)

*Items Four and Five: Use the same kind of variation in designing questions found in items 1,2,3, but complete averages.

*Item Six: It's fun for students to make their own questions, too, but accentuating positive or neutral attributes.

Acknowledgments: Thanks to Paul Nixon and Karen Batchelor de Garcia, from whom I learned the "Extremes and Averages" concept. Permission granted to duplicate this page for staff development, if credit notes are included.

For many ESL classes (as opposed to staff development sessions) you may want to ask just one or two questions for warm-up and then get on with your main lesson, particularly when students are familiar with this cooperative structure and its purpose. In a staff development session, however, novice teachers need time to experience and process the technique. The best processing requires some feedback from groups—Numbered Heads reporting works well here. (See chapters one and nine for description of Numbered Heads.) In staff development, Extremes and Averages with processing may well take 30–40 minutes. In an ongoing ESL class, it should not be structured to take more than 5 minutes most days if its purpose is group warm-up. In a lesson focusing on communication skills, however, it could appropriately be structured to last 20–50 minutes.

Table 2
Same/Different

Comments: This is less complex than Extremes and Averages and takes less time. Use it when you have little time, or in a subsequent staff development session when you need to build a new group with participants already familiar with the principles.

Purpose: to learn about teammates; to build a sense of "team"ness

Procedure: *A.* Members of the group must find one (two or three) attribute *all have in common.* (Some physical attribute, something in their personal history, what they're wearing, or a common interest are examples.)

B. Then they must find one (two or three) ways in which *each is different from every other* (such as different heights, number of people in household, hair length, ages. Male-female, on the other hand, would not be an example of "all different" in a group of three or more, because more than one person would be the same gender.) Avoid prompting unless the group needs or asks for help. Do emphasize that each must differ from every other.

This is a relatively unstructured "getting to know you" for fluent speakers. In staff development sessions, you might want to encourage participants to find the most unusual similarities or differences that they can.

This procedure is appropriate for intermediate and advanced classes. It could also work with advanced-beginners with some guidance.

Table 3
Roundtable

Purpose: to review simple information (if a classroom, not a staff development, exercise); to build interdependence among team members.

Procedure: Participants are in heterogeneous groups, ideally four to six members. They share *one* piece of paper and *one* pencil.

The leader asks participants to make a list of related items. Examples for staff development might include: "List what you encounter in a typical teaching day."

or "What do you need the first week of school?" The task should be relatively easy recall for all group members.

Participants must share the task by passing the paper and pen around with *each writing one item in turn.* They can help one another by making suggestions, spelling words aloud, and so forth; BUT each person must write in turn.

When all have written an item, the paper is passed around again, and continues until "time" is called. Lists are totaled. Groups then report the number of items written.

Note: This is most effective when done more than once. After the first round, groups can compare scores and read some of the lists aloud. Then announce that the groups will do the same activity with a new topic. Give a few minutes to discuss how they might better their score. Point out that the proximity of participants is a factor. A "tight" circle with participants leaning toward each other, involved in the activity, facilitates the activity. Encourage helping one another with ideas as the paper is passed around. The planning, concentration, and race against time—particularly with repeated trials—helps to build excitement, along with a sense of belonging and responsibility to the group.

Idea for Roundtable from Spencer Kagan; staff development materials by J. W-B Olsen.

Explore Information Processing Structures

Joyce and Showers (1980) often cited research indicates that practical inservice staff development is more effective when the underlying theoretical principles are clearly presented. Not all of the theory, however, needs to be covered in the traditional lecture format. Cooperative structures can be used to introduce some or all of this information, combining needed conceptual content with procedural experience. In this section we will look at group tests and variations of Jigsaw.

Using a Group Test as an Opener

A "test," whose items are really intended to stimulate group discussion, can be a good attention focuser on major points and a good illustration of the support and power of a group. After announcing the test and passing it out, the presenter explains that the group can discuss each question and arrive at a consensus answer. Give a time limit. When time is "up," the presenter can elaborate on the major points in going over the answers after individual group discussions. Since points of view on major topics have been developed through discussion, participants may be more ready to listen to what the speaker has to say.

A Group Test as a Staff Development Opener: Example

Discuss these questions with your group. Then choose the answer that the group agrees is best.

Multiple Choice

1. ''Cooperative learning'' means learning through:
   a. positive interactions with the teacher.
   b. positive interactions with the materials to be learned.
   c. positive interactions with other students about the material.
   d. all of the above.

True or False

2. T____F____Cooperative learning is a relatively recent development.
3. T____F____Cooperative learning was developed for language teaching.

Multiple Choice

4. The most important kind of approval for most K–12 (kindergarten through twelfth grade) students is:
   a. approval from teachers
   b. approval from peers
   c. approval from parents

5. What kinds of students benefit from cooperative learning?
   a. high achievers
   b. middle achievers
   c. low achievers
   d. all of the above

6. What kind of group formation is most effective for long-range benefits in classes with stable populations (that is, *not* open-entry, open-exit classes)?
   a. students grouped separately by ability
   b. students in heterogeneous (mixed ability) groups

Short Answer

7. Today, most entry-level jobs in the United States are found in what parts of the economy?

8. According to employers, what is the most common reason for firing a first-time worker?

Bonus Question

9. Who invented the mimeo machine?

* *This quiz was developed by Judy Winn-Bell Olsen (1988) as a "starter" for co-op workshops*
* *Information sources for Questions 1–8 are works by Kagan (1989) and Johnson, and Johnson (1989); for Question 9, the original* Trivial Pursuit © *(1981) game.*

Answers to the Quiz with Comments:
For the Staff Developer

1. d
2. F   The Johnsons (1989) cite over a hundred years of studies comparing cooperative learning with competitive and individualistic modes.
3. F   Although the usefulness of structured interaction currently has great appeal for language teachers, cooperative learning was actually developed for regular subject-matter classes.
4. b   Because of the power of peer pressure, much individual and group behavior can be shaped through particular cooperative activities stressing individual accountability and positive interdependence.
5. d
6. b   Studies of homogeneous vs. heterogeneous groupings show that *all* students gain knowledge and skills in heterogeneous groups.
7.   In service industries and information-processing—where communication skills with a variety of kinds of people are important. Communication skills and social skills with many kinds of personalities can be developed in heterogeneous cooperative groups.
8.   For inability to get along with other people. Social skills can be acquired with CL.
9.   This is a creative "for fun" question. Often someone guesses "Sal Mimeo." Foreign language teachers sometimes suggest "Yvette Mimeo." The real inventor was A.B. Dick.

Using Jigsaw in Staff Development

Jigsaw is a particularly useful structure for staff development workshops, partly for its value in demonstrating cooperative principles and partly for its effectiveness in making dense or lengthy text more manageable. Some of the material on theory or other background information can be divided into jigsaw parts, thus putting responsibility on the participants to "get" the material. The responsibility of the trainer, then, is to choose or design readings of an appropriate length and to craft appropriate discussion questions.

Three particularly useful variations of Jigsaw for inservice staff development are the following:

Jigsaw, Type I: Individual Groups Report to the Class

Take any relevant reading matter, such as an article from a professional journal or part of a chapter from a book, and divide the reading into sections. Give each section to a different group of three to seven persons. (If you have more groups than sections, assign some sections to more than one group.) Ask the group to read, discuss, and prepare to summarize that section for the other workshop members (time depends on the length of each reading: 20–40 minutes).

You may want to guide reading and thinking of the groups with questions you have prepared. Here is an example prepared for a workshop of twenty-six participants divided into four groups. Each group took one part:

**Reading Questions for "Cooperative Professional
Development" by Allan A. Glatthorn, 1987.**
Educational Leadership, **45:31–35.**

Directions for Each Group:

- Read the part of the article assigned to your group.
- When all members of your group have finished reading, use the questions for your part to guide your discussion.
- Then plan a short (3–4 minutes) presentation of the main points of your section.
- Your workshop leader will give you materials to make a visual aid to illustrate your ideas.

Part I: pp. 31–32 to middle of column 3 (stop at "Curriculum Development")

1. What does the author mean by "cooperative professional development?"
2. Describe the process and purpose of professional dialogue.
3. Make one more question about this section and answer it.

Part II: pp. 32–33 "Curriculum Development"; and p. 34 "Action Research," columns 2 and 3

1. What does the author mean by "curriculum development"?
2. What is meant by "action research"?
3. Make one more question about this section and answer it.

Part III: pp. 33–34 (stop at "Action Research")

1. List nine characteristics of peer supervision.
2. List five major functions of peer coaching.
3. Make one more question about this section and answer it.

Part IV: pp. 34–35

1. What are the supportive conditions for cooperative development?
2. What is the suggested specific process for implementation?
3. Make one more question about this section and answer it.

Visuals for Group Presentations: Although groups can be asked to give a verbal summary only, more group interaction and processing of the material may happen if a product—some visual referent—is created by the group for the presentation.

Jigsaw, Type II: Expert-Groups Jigsaw   In this Jigsaw variation, each group studies a different part for presentation, then regroups into teams where each member has studied a different part. Rather than a large group presentation, each member in the small group is responsible for conveying the information each has studied to the other group members. After individual presentations within the small groups, the entire group is asked to show its grasp of the material by taking a written group test (discussion allowed), answering an oral quiz with Numbered Heads, or creating some group product that shows its grasp of the material. See Appendix A at the end of the chapter for an example of Three-Part Jigsaw Readings with questions for small groups and a follow-up group test.

Jigsaw, Type III: Same Reading, Jigsawed Questions   Promoted by the Johnsons (1989), this is probably the simplest Jigsaw structure to transfer to classroom practice. It is particularly useful in an introductory workshop. However, it usually involves more planning and synthesis by the trainer to summarize longer articles or otherwise condense reading material to the appropriate length. Two examples follow.

READING WITH JIGSAW QUESTIONS: EXAMPLES

(For staff development. These are printed small here to conserve space. If using them in staff development, you can decrease reading time and increase first-time comprehension by printing them in larger type, double spaced. This will help in budgeting precious staff development time.)

Using Cooperative Learning in the Language Class*

Language teachers have always been interested in ways to encourage students to use the target language. At one time, such use would be considered "practice" of grammar and vocabulary already presented and drilled in class. Opportunities for practice would most likely be withheld until considerable teacher-directed activity had taken place.

Now, however, opinions are changing about when and how to encourage student interaction. Recent research in language acquisition suggests strongly that learners acquire *more* language by using it in communicative situations as early as possible. Language teachers are challenged more than ever to devise activities that encourage participation by all students, even at the beginning levels, while maintaining class control and a clear sense of purpose.

Quite recently, much useful information has come from "cooperative learning" as used in regular in K–12 content classes for native English speakers. Cooperative learning as developed and studied by Aronson and his colleagues (1978), the Johnsons (1987), Kagan (1990), Slavin (1981, 1989b), and others ensures more consistently successful group work through carefully planned classroom management techniques for the teacher. Currently, programs in California and other states are making serious commitments to cooperative learning strategies in their teacher staff development and program development for limited English speakers.

Two important task goals in cooperative learning are:

a) building *interdependence* among group members, so that they willingly help and seek help from each other; and

b) promoting *individual accountability,* so that each student willingly takes responsibility for part of the task, and there are no "free riders" who let the rest of the group do all the work.

One procedure that promotes both interdependence and individual accountability is "Jigsaw Reading Questions," a technique promoted by cooperative learning pioneers David and Roger Johnson. In this technique, members of a group all receive the same reading, which may be assigned in class or given as homework the night before. After reading and discussing the assignment in their groups, each group member is given a different slip of paper with a question or set of questions about the reading.

Students each read their questions aloud to the group, who must discuss the questions and come to agreement on the best answer for each. Each student then writes the answers under the questions s/he has read aloud.

When the group has finished answering all the questions, members then tape their answers together, sign the completed product (which signifies that all agree on the answers) and turn it in to the teacher or put it up on the wall for inspection and comparison with other groups' products.

Teachers using this technique regularly report better overall understanding of class readings by all the students and increased cooperation within groups.

---

*By J. W-B Olsen, 1988. Permission granted to duplicate for staff development.

"Using Cooperative Structures in the Language Classroom"
Questions on the Reading

Note: You should be reading and discussing this article in groups of no fewer than three people and no more than six. Start by cutting or tearing this question sheet along the dotted lines. Give each question (A, B, and C) to a different person. If there are more than three people, have group members "double up" so that two people are responsible for one question. Each person reads his/her question aloud to the rest of the group. Group members should listen to, not read, each other's questions. Members then discuss the question and come to consensus. When all three questions have been discussed, each person writes the group answer to his/her question. Answers are then taped together, signed by all parties indicating agreement, and turned in to the teacher or posted on the wall to compare with other groups' products.

A. Why are language teachers interested in promoting interaction among students? (Discuss this question with your group. When everyone agrees on an answer, write it here.)

· ·

B. What does COOPERATIVE LEARNING from native speaker K–12 content teaching have to offer second language teachers? (Discuss this question with your group. When everyone agrees on an answer, write it here.)

· ·

C. Describe the steps of a Jigsaw Reading. What kinds of readings might a language class use? (Discuss this question with your group. When everyone agrees on an answer, write it here.)

· ·

"Cooperation in Adult Learning"*

At an Adult Basic Education (ABE) Institute, Dr. Robert Fullilove (1986), Director of the Professional Development Program at University of California, Berkeley, described a current project. He and colleagues in the Mathematics Department noticed that African American and Hispanic students studying math followed the same pattern as these students did in other departments in the University. They failed in large numbers.

In an effort to find out the cause of such a high failure rate among these two minority groups, a research project was undertaken in which the researchers looked at another minority group that had dramatic success at the University—the Asian students. In order to find out differences in these three groups relating to their studies, the researchers investigated the interaction patterns and the study habits of the groups.

The findings showed that all three groups interacted with their own ethnic groups socially in much the same way. But there were differences in their study habits. At study time, the Hispanic and Black students "holed up" alone. They studied conscientiously, going over material repeatedly. However, they tended to avoid asking for help lest they give the appearance of weakness. The Asian students, on the other hand, formed study groups. They took turns explaining material to the others, and they critiqued one anothers' presentations. When one student was able to solve a problem that the others couldn't do, that one student was responsible for teaching it to the others. When none of the students could solve a problem, they sought out their Teaching Assistant for help. Their view of getting help was not that it showed weakness but that it was necessary for survival.

As a result of the research findings, Dr. Fullilove's group set up Workshops for Black and Hispanic students in math. At first the students waited too long to attend the Workshops and they continued to fail. Eventually, they began to join the Workshop at the beginning of a semester. In the Workshops, they were given strategies for studying, and the most important strategy was the one that the Asian students were using so effectively: group studying. In the Workshops, the philosophy was that the institution does not have to make special allowances for minority students. Nothing less was demanded of them than of the other students. They were told that they were going to be taught how to be honor roll students and most of them did learn the strategies needed to achieve that goal.

Since the onset of the Workshops, Black and Hispanic students have dramatically improved their achievement in math. There is now an 80 percent success rate at the freshman level, and 82 percent of Black and Hispanic students who have taken the Workshop complete Calculus with an average grade of 2.9 (B−).

Several pilot projects have occurred in San Francisco Bay Area high schools with large minority enrollment. These projects affirm that this process works with less able students as well as those at the top.

From a report by Peggy Doherty, Assistant Director, San Francisco Community College District, Centers Division, written for her faculty. Permission granted to print here and to reproduce for staff development.

Questions on the Reading "Cooperation in Adult Learning"

Note: You should be reading and discussing this article in groups of no fewer than three people and no more than six. Start by cutting or tearing this question sheet along the dotted lines. Give each question (A, B, and C) to a different person. If there are more than three people, have group members "double up" so that two people are responsible for one question. Each person reads his/her question aloud to the rest of the group. Group members should listen to, not read, one another's questions. Members then discuss the question and come to consensus. When all three questions have been discussed, each person writes the group answers to his/her question. Answers are then taped together, signed by all parties indicating agreement, and turned in to the teacher or posted on the wall to compare with other groups' products.

A. Our reading describes a study of different student groups at the University of California, Berkeley. Who was studied and why? (Discuss this question with your group. When everyone agrees on an answer, and all questions have been discussed, write the answer to your question here.)

. . . .

B. List three or more findings for the UC, Berkeley study. (Discuss this question with your group. When everyone agrees on an answer, and all questions have been discussed, write the answer to your question here.)

. . . .

C. What implications do the findings of this study have for our students? (Discuss the question with your group. When everyone agrees on an answer, and all questions have been discussed, write the answer to your question here.)

. . . .

Investigating Other Cooperative Techniques: Structures for Processing the Information

People not only have to get information, they have to process it—to have a chance to reflect on it. Three structures facilitating this are Think-Pair-Share, Group Product, and Mixer Review.

Think-Pair-Share: This activity is also good for preview—or review at the end of the session. See Chapter 1 for a description of the steps.

Group Product: This is good for long-term synthesis of complex ideas. It can be used with assigned roles. Group products might include a written report, a group presentation such as a skit or several related oral reports, or a visual such as a bulletin board, a mural, a poster, or overhead transparency.

Setting a time limit for discussion, planning, and execution of the visual product also encourages interaction and hastens crystallization of ideas. It should be stressed that the point of making a visual is not to create a masterpiece, but to capture quickly the main points. (Marks' [1989] article ''Poster Presentations'' makes a number of helpful suggestions and comments on this point.)

A poster (made with marking pens on large pieces of newsprint) has several advantages. It is a product that several group members can work on at once. It can remain posted in the staff development room for the rest of the workshop as an ongoing reminder of certain basic points—and perhaps be posted as a reminder in future workshops.

An overhead transparency (groups use colored pens on clear transparencies) has the advantage of being a copy-able size. You can make Xerox paper copies of the transparencies from each group so that everyone has a permanent record of the information.

If possible, assign more than one person to present the information distilled by the group. This encourages more interaction between members. You may want to assign roles of leader, recorder, poster maker, and presenter through Numbered Heads, or tell groups to choose their own roles, making sure that everyone contributes. See Rhoades and McCabe (1989) for suggestions on types of cooperative group roles.

Mixer Review: On the following page is a description handed out in staff development together with an example.

Mixer Review

Purpose: Participants cooperatively review material previously studied together.

Procedure:

a. Participants form two lines, facing each other; OR, they form two concentric circles, the inner circle facing outward, the outer circle facing in.

b. Each person should be facing a partner in the other line or circle.

c. Partners discuss the first item on their question sheet. They may use notes, old readings, or listen in on other pairs if they ''get stuck.'' When they come to a mutually agreed-on answer, each writes it down on his/her sheet.

d. At a signal from the leader, one line or circle ''moves down one'' so that everyone is now facing a new partner. New partners answer question two, using the same procedure as in *c*.

e. The same procedure—''moving down one''—is repeated for each new question, until the sheet is completed.

f. When all questions have been completed in this manner, participants resume their seats and the leader leads a discussion of the answers.

Example: Mixer Review Questions*

(Note: these were questions amply discussed in a previous class.)

1. List two or more characteristics that make Inservice Staff Development different from university-based teacher education.

(*possible answers:* immediately relevant, at the convenience of the students, for a particular population, often conducted by peers)

2. What does the term "transfer of training" mean?

(*possible answer:* teaching behavior learned in staff development that is regularly and appropriately applied in the classroom)

3. Name two or more characteristics of cooperative learning.

(*possible answers:* heterogeneous learning groups, activities to promote individual accountability, and positive interdependence)

4. Name two or more advantages of cooperative learning

(*possible answers:* peer teaching/learning; attention to social aspects of communication)

5. List two or more ways that coaching is different from evaluation
(*possible answers:* is developmental, is initiated by teacher to be observed)

6. In studies of effective staff development described by Joyce and Showers (1983), four general methods of staff development were examined. What were they? How was transfer of training most successfully achieved?

(*answer:* theory presentation, demonstration, practice and feedback, follow-up—especially coaching. Transfer most successfully achieved using *all four*—coaching is an essential ingredient, but need the other components as well.)

7. List as many cooperative structures as you can remember that we've done in class so far. When you've made your list as complete as you can, go back and identify the purpose of each activity. (Think about the specific content and about the social dynamic.)

Note: this is one of many ways that participants were asked to continually review activities and put them into a larger personal framework. In any course, particularly an intensive one, this is an important ongoing consideration.

8. The activity in which you are now engaging—at this very moment—is a Mixer Review. What are some purposes of a Mixer Review? What do you see as some of the advantages? The disadvantages? How might you use a Mixer Review strategy in your class?

(*possible answers: purpose*—more peer teaching/review opportunities; *advantages*—energizer, easy to get info from many; *disadvantages*—noisy, takes space; *uses*—reviewing any important content information; practicing short interchanges in a language class)

Developed by J. W-B Olsen for a course entitled "Cooperative Learning in the Language Classroom" for the TESOL Summer Institute, San Francisco State University, 1989.

Explore Social Considerations

There is paradox here. Those most experienced with CL emphasize the importance of developing good team social skills (Johnson and Johnson, 1989; Kagan, 1989). Yet those new to CL may be more interested in the mechanics of the cooperative structures. There is much new information to digest, and "how to" information on CL structures is often the first stated priority of the trainee.

In the format presented in this chapter, it is unlikely that in the first sessions the presenter will be able to make more than passing reference to development of interactive group skills and social process. Though certainly any presenter/facilitator needs to be monitoring and processing behavior of the staff development groups and adjusting the workshop accordingly. It is my opinion that not many of the participants will be able to consciously attend to the additional layer of social process, at first. Too much else bids for attention.

The reader should be aware that opinions among trainers/facilitators differ sharply on when and how to integrate social skills into cooperative learning staff development, and other staff developers might approach workshop presentation rather differently. The needs and interests of the participants play a major role here in workshop design. Are the participants teachers/counselors/administrators of elementary school, high school, college/university, or adult education students? Do they work primarily with language development, or with content subjects and language together? Are they in bilingual, second language, or foreign language programs?

This chapter reflects my background as a teacher as well as a teacher trainer. There is stated recognition of the need for attention to social processing at all levels, but more attention has been paid here to the mechanics of arranging interaction for language practice and the assimilation of content appropriate for older students.

While teachers of younger students will benefit from many of the activities in this chapter, they will also need to learn in their workshops how to attend more strongly to the development of social skills very early in their classroom work with cooperative learning. See Chapter 5 for some specific examples of activities for social processing for younger students.

The challenge of integrating content and process with ample attention to development of social skills is one reason why staff development for CL should be considered an ongoing project—say, three to five years—and why follow-up coaching becomes such an important factor for ultimate success.

Plan for Ongoing Growth

In the last few decades, ESL educators have focused attention on the learner and the language. Teacher-researchers have explored ways of discovering, describing, and meaningfully addressing the complexities of both learner and language. Second language educators have taken into account how language is acquired in actual classroom practice.

Only quite recently has much mention been made of other factors in the educational process—that teachers, as well as students, should grow. The *Teacher Development Newsletter* (1985) from the International Association of Teachers of English as a Foreign Language (IATEFL) addresses this well. Stimulation and support for professional growth should come from the community of faculty and administration in the school itself (Johnson and Johnson, 1989; Joyce et al., 1983, 1987, 1989; Joyce and Showers, 1983; McRel, 1989).

Instead of the terms "teacher training" or "staff development," the larger rubric of "school improvement" is currently in use to suggest the more complex texture of what is required to effect meaningful, positive change. Cooperative structures, based on cooperative principles, are useful ways of introducing and developing new ideas in a more positive, less isolating atmosphere.

Research and anecdotal evidence show that the most effective staff development incorporates collegial support over an extended period of time. The now classic studies of Joyce and Showers (1980, 1983) show that the most effective inservice has all of the following four components:

1. presentation of theory relevant to staff development,
2. demonstration of appropriate methodology supported by the theory,
3. practice and feedback by participants (cf. "microteaching"),
4. follow-up with support groups and peer coaching.

Interest in peer support (Glatthorn, 1987; Gould and Letven, 1987) and in particular, coaching, developed in many educational settings in the mid- to late 1980s. Coaching is currently a component of an increasing number of staff development programs. Along with the study of the theory and practice of the new teaching approach is study of the theory and practice of coaching, as well.

The Coaching Guide: What Is Coaching?*
Example of Materials

Peer Coaching is classroom observation and supportive feedback by colleagues who have agreed to work together on particular teaching skills. Peer Coaching relationships are usually reciprocal—that is, partners observe and give feedback to each other. Coaching partnerships are often used to build individual confidence in trying new techniques—and staying with them until they are mastered. Ideally, coaching partners begin by working on techniques learned together in staff development so that they start with a reference point clearly common to both. Coaching can also be used to "fine tune" general teaching skills. It is a development process used for exploring, developing, strengthening, and refining teaching skills while developing stronger ties among faculty members. Peer Coaching is collegial in nature, neither supervisory nor evaluative.

Some staff development programs use **Expert Coaching.** This involves individual observation and feedback by the trainer or by mentor teachers with extensive staff development and experience in the skills to be developed. Expert Coaching sometimes precedes or is used in tandem with Peer Coaching. Programs using Expert Coaching are strongly urged to use Peer Coaching.

Some programs also use **Administrative Coaching**—observation and feedback by a supervisor—but this approach is easily confused with formal evaluation or clinical supervision and should be approached with extreme caution if the objective is to foster a school climate where faculty take an active part in their own development and growth.

Why Coaching?

Transfer-of-training studies show that regular, planned follow-up is necessary for new methods to become part of the teacher's natural repertoire. Coaching is highly recommended as an important part of that follow-up. Coaching partners take their training together and work together after the training to develop and refine their skills with the new methods. Many teachers report the usefulness of having a partner for planning, discussion, mutual observation, and general support.

*Developed by Judy Winn-Bell Olsen for staff development, unpublished.

Of course, effective implementation of any new ideas and processes—be they CL, or coaching, or anything else, depends on several factors. One is **administrative support.** Joyce and others (Garmston, 1989) recommend strongly that administrators be involved from the beginning—that they receive the initial staff development with the teachers, and in some cases participate in follow-up appropriate to their needs, as well. Some districts now have peer coaching projects for administrators to work on administrative concerns (Gibble and Lawrence, 1987).

Another critical factor is **willingness of teachers to risk** trying and persisting with something new. Joyce and McKibbin (1982) have classified ''growth states'' of teachers, with suggestions for which faculty to encourage most in early stages of staff development or any school improvement project. The growth states include:

- *The Omnivores,* who are always ready to try something new. These individuals appear to overcome obstacles readily and do not carry emotional charges preventing them from profiting from a great variety of activity. They do not waste energy on complaining.
- *The Active consumers,* people who are ''out there'' making use of all that is offered. Active consumers are often leaders and project-accomplishers.
- *The Passive Consumers,* people who can be drawn into new projects with effort, becoming good committee members, but who rarely look for or initiate new activities.
- *The Resistants,* individuals who tend to be threatened by anything new. They may present pockets of negativity. They should not be grouped together in training or involved in first-year staff development. Success is more likely if the strongest teachers are used to build a nucleus before trying to incorporate the others.
- *The Withdrawns,* who are difficult to engage. Like the resistant and the passive consumers, they can drain the trainer's energy.

Edwards and Stout (1989) suggest that staff projects begun slowly with only the most committed faculty may pull in less enthusiastic faculty in the second and third years, as positive results emerge and enthusiasm spreads. Staff developers note that the most significant changes in teacher attitudes and beliefs come *after* they begin using a new practice successfully and see changes in student learning (Guskey, 1989).

But a continuing danger is that trainers may forget how it feels to be a novice trying something new. It can be a particular problem when they have been working with staff development for some time and are continually dealing with new mixed groups of old-timers and novices together. Also, it is not always clear who is or will be feeling discomfort with a new procedure or philosophy. Many an old-timer in the school system has collided with changing professional expectations and felt once again the discomfort of the novice in unfamiliar territory. In staff development, written reassurances, as well as verbal ones, may be helpful.

Notes on Trying New Kinds of Group Work*

If you've never done group work before, it may feel a little scary. That happens to all of us—even the most experienced practitioners. If it's happening to you, here are some things to tell yourself as the activity gets underway and your stomach begins to flutter:

- It may take more than one "try" on one day before everyone (students *and* teachers) really knows what to do and gets into the activity smoothly. *That's okay*—it *will* happen. Just persist, pleasantly.
- When groups are doing their tasks, use the time to assess them unobtrusively as you circle the room. Listen in on groups, make mental notes on what needs review, and adjust your plans as necessary for the next steps.
- As you circle the room, make mental note of what is most troublesome (in content *or* group process) and who has the most trouble, for later work with the whole class or with individuals. Step in with help only if absolutely necessary—encourage group members to help and encourage each other.
- ESL teachers: When pronunciation is less than perfect, remember that it isn't perfect in a choral drill, either.
- Before beginning a group activity in ESL requiring cooperation, have the class practice appropriate phrases (such as those for clarification and encouragement) to use with each other in their groups.
- Remember that students improve over time—particularly when they know they will have responsibility for making themselves understood. That means that the activity type that you try should be done many times, with different content, for optimum success.
- When things go well with a new activity, pat yourself on the back: you're an innovator!
- When they don't go so well, keep smiling and try again in a few days.
- Think about what you did in the activity—could you add more steps, change the order of procedure, use less or more new material, change the pace?
- Ask a colleague to observe and "coach" you—that is, give helpful, supportive, encouraging suggestions. Before the observation, outline what you're trying to achieve and the steps you've planned to achieve it, so your observer has something to follow and respond to.

---

*Judy Winn-Bell Olsen. Permission granted to copy for staff development use.

Conclusion

Teacher development, like student learning, should be ongoing. CL principles and structures, applied to inservice and other school improvement activities, can develop a climate that encourages continued growth and support for faculty and administration as well as for students.

Reports from schools well into CL attest that change does not happen overnight. But stronger, more able, more collegial faculties are developed with patient persistence and attention to the guidelines outlined above (Red and Shainline, 1989).

When dealing with any school innovation, Kohonen (1988) suggests that we remind ourselves that profound change is often gradual, using the motto "TTT"— "Things Take Time."

That's a reminder that we can recognize and smile at—a message to close some meeting with, perhaps. Another appropriate closing is attributed to Paolo Freire (1970), who insightfully comments that no one educates another. Nor can one educate oneself alone. Persons are educated in communion with one another, in the midst of the world's influences.

Acknowledgements Particular thanks to several colleagues whose perspectives have helped clarify my own: Carole Cooper of the Cooperative Learning Implementation Project (CLIP), Redwood City, CA; Ann Lippincott and Margarita Calderon of the MultiDistrict Training of Trainers Institute (MTTI), Santa Barbara, CA; K. Lynn Savage, Christine Bunn, Peggy Doherty, and Bill Shoaf, San Francisco Community College District (SFCCD), and Jane Yedlin, New England Multifunctional Resources Center (NEMRC), Providence, RI.

Appendix

**A-B-C Jigsaw Readings
on Cooperative Learning**

A. Cooperative Learning: Management Considerations and Some Reasons Why It Is Important*

In some circles, the term "cooperative learning" is used for any kind of loosely structured group or pair work. ABE and ESL teachers report varied degrees of success with such work, depending on the willingness of students to interact and cooperate and teacher's instinctive abilities to guide and encourage the students to do so.

However, cooperative learning as developed and studied by Aronson and his colleagues (1978), the Johnsons (1987), Kagan (1990), Slavin (1981; 1989a) and others ensures more consistently successful group work through carefully planned classroom management techniques for the teacher. Well-structured cooperative groups actually provide the teacher with more "crowd control," rather than less, and more time for assessment and interaction with individual students. The key is in the planning and structuring of heterogeneous groups, fostering group spirit and interdependence with a variety of tasks, and rewarding appropriate academic and social behavior.

These management techniques usually require inservice teacher training and follow-up for effective transfer into regular, appropriate classroom use. Is CL really worth the investment of time and effort? Many school districts in California and elsewhere think so. Currently, there is particular interest in districts with changing ethnic populations, as teachers and administrators deal with new dimensions in diversity.

Properly structured cooperative learning fosters behavior that educational psychologists term "prosocial." Students cooperate more readily, are more able to see others' points of view, have more positive feelings about themselves, school, and other students who are intellectually, physically, or ethnically different.

Cooperative learning structures are particularly helpful to many non-white ethnic groups whose social and learning styles are traditionally more cooperative than competitive. Achievement scores of many Black and Hispanic students suggest that they are not responding well to competitive modes that have traditionally dominated "white majority" education. However, studies of cooperative classrooms show tremendous gains for these students.

*Judy Winn-Bell Olsen for Jigsaw Reading Activity in Staff Development Workshops

In studies by Slavin and Oickle (1981) of inner-city school junior high classrooms, a twelve-week pretest–posttest study of gains in English grammar proficiency showed CL to produce significant gains over traditional classroom structures. Black students in cooperative classrooms showed nearly nine times the gain of those in traditional classrooms, while white students showed double the gain of those in traditional classrooms. Other studies show comparable results.

Also of interest here is a study by Fullilove (1986), mathematics professor at the University of California, Berkeley. After observing that the performance of Asian students was consistently better than that of African Americans or Hispanic students at UC, Berkeley, Dr. Treisman, a colleague, conducted a survey of the three cultural groups, trying to pinpoint reasons for their successes and failures. Among the factors examined were motivation, academic preparation, family support, family income, and study habits.

Only one factor was found to make a significant difference in Treisman's survey: cooperative study habits. The Chinese students found study mates and met together regularly with routines for review and study. The Hispanic and Black students shared social lives, but did not study together.

B.   Some Studies on Academic Benefits of CL*

Classroom tasks structured for cooperative learning provide greater and more varied opportunities for student interaction with each other and with the information to be learned. More task-based student interaction provides more opportunities for students to have information clarified for them by their peers, more opportunity for students to develop their own speaking skills, greater frequency and variety of practice with the subject matter, and more time on task.

Eliot Aronson and associates (1978) compared social studies classrooms using the Jigsaw model of cooperative learning with classrooms using regular competitive classroom approaches. In their study of 300 students at five schools in Austin, Texas, cooperative classrooms showed much higher average post-test scores than the "regular" social studies classes. (All had studied the same unit on colonial America and both groups had equivalent pretest scores.) Aronson observes: A very important aspect of Jigsaw is: The low-achieving children benefit from the high-achieving children; the high-achieving children are not hampered by the low-achieving ones.

Johnson et al., (1981) in completing a meta-analysis of 109 studies comparing the relative effects of cooperative, competitive, and individualistic learning situations on achievement found that results strongly indicate that cooperative learning promotes higher achievement than competitive or individualistic instruction. The average student in a cooperative situation performs at approximately the eightieth percentile of students in competitive and individualistic situations. These results hold for all age levels, for all subject areas, particularly for tasks involving various kinds of problem solving, categorizing, and guessing-judging-predicting.

A wealth of other studies has consistently shown cooperative learning structures producing tremendous gains over traditional structures for low achievers and middle achievers, and scores at least as good and usually better than traditional structures for high achievers. In other words, nobody loses.

Why is this so? Extensive studies of student motivation by the Johnsons and others show that the greatest incentive to achieve comes from peer encouragement and support. Cooperative learning features a variety of structured teamwork tasks, with group and individual rewards for academic achievement and improvement and cooperative group behavior.

And what of older, nontraditional students? In the past twenty years, nearly all the studies of cooperative learning have been with K–12 or college students. Research on the effects of cooperative group work with ABE/ESL students has just begun: Preliminary reports from a two-year project at Simon Fraser University which included ABE and adult ESL, show the following:

a.   ABE students stated strong preferences for the cooperative mode of learning over the more traditional modes in which they had previously failed;

b.   ESL students (mostly Asian) stated preferences for cooperative learning, "once they had gotten used to it."

*Prepared by Judy Winn-Bell Olsen for Jigsaw Reading Activity in Staff Development Workshops

C. Some Historical and Demographic Reasons for CL Importance*

Changes in our economy and society continue to accelerate. While the nation took about a century to develop from an agriculture-based economy to an industry-based economy, it has moved from an industry/labor base to an information/management/service-based economy in the last thirty years.

In 1950, information-related jobs accounted for 17 percent of the workforce; in the 1980's, 66 percent of our jobs deal primarily with information and/or other people. Of twenty million new jobs created in the 1970s, 5 percent were in manufacturing and almost 90 percent were in information, knowledge, or service. Scientific and technical information available to us currently doubles every five years, often rendering previous information obsolete before it is barely recorded, much less learned.

Far fewer jobs now require autonomous individuals in farm or factory settings. Far more complex interpersonal skills are required as workers interact in a variety of ways, often in a variety of jobs within a single worker's lifetime, with many different people. Multinational corporations require new levels of cooperation in international business agreements, where machine parts manufactured in several countries may be assembled in the United States or elsewhere for markets all over the world.

These accelerated changes have enormous implications for educators. We must enable our students to learn how to learn for themselves in a wide range of settings. We must also prepare them to get along in a variety of job-related social settings. Recent figures show that more than half the U.S. workers who are fired from their first job are fired because of lack of social skills, not lack of job skills. In other words, they can do the work, but they can't get along with their co-workers. Why not?

Among the factors cited are societal changes. The American student population is becoming increasingly urbanized and less consistently socialized as traditional family modes change. Studies of cooperativeness in urban and rural settings in many parts of the world show that children raised in urban settings give less value to the prosocial behaviors of sharing, helping, caring, and cooperating. And the trend toward urbanization is worldwide. In 1800, 2.4 percent of the world lived in urban centers; in 1900 urban population was about 10 percent, by 1950 it was 25 percent.

At one time, cooperative behaviors were taught and valued as children were raised in traditional family settings. Now, with single-parent families common and most parents working, there is not the time or—in many cases—the continuity necessary to promote these values to the same extent as before. Whether or not teachers want to add social values to the lengthy list of what they must teach, they may in

*Prepared by Judy Winn-Bell Olsen for Jigsaw Reading Activity in Staff Development Workshops.

fact be in the best position to model, encourage, and reward such values through cooperative learning structures.

According to Spencer Kagan, we must prepare our students to be flexible—to be prepared to work under a wide range of economic and social task and reward structures. Economic success—at both the individual and company levels—will come by transforming competitive task and reward structures into cooperative structures.

Well-structured cooperative learning will provide that preparation.

(Information from Toffler [1970] *Future Shock;* Naisbitt, [1982] *Megatrends,* and Kagan, [1990] *Cooperative Learning Resources for Teachers.)*

Questions for Jigsaw Readings on Co-op Expert Group A*

1. According to our reading, group work is more consistently successful when it is carefully

2. The key to better management of groups is in:

a.

b.

c.

3. In what places is there considerable interest in inservice staff development and follow-up in cooperative learning? Why?

4. Give three or more examples of the prosocial behavior that properly structured cooperative learning fosters.

5. Describe the study by Slavin and Oickle (1981). What implications does it have for us?

6. With your group, write another question about the information in your reading.

OR

Rewrite any or all of the questions above to make them more thought- and discussion provoking.

*From previously unpublished staff development materials by J. W-B Olsen and J. Yedlin.

Questions for Jigsaw Readings on Co-op for Expert Group B*

1. According to our reading, cooperative learning tasks provide _____ more _____ opportunities for students to _____ with each other and with the information to be learned.

2. List at least three benefits of increased task-based student interaction.

3. List at least two findings of Aronson's study of the social studies classroom, as described in your reading.

4. A survey of 109 studies indicates that cooperative learning promotes higher achievement than _____ or _____ instruction.

5. For whom does cooperative learning provide the greatest gains? (List at least two groups)

6. With your group, write another question about the information in your reading.

OR

Rewrite any or all of the questions above to make them more thought provoking and discussion provoking.

*By J. W-B Olsen and J. Yedlin

Questions for Jigsaw Readings on Co-op Expert Group C*

1. Choose the best word:
Our economy and society are changing (more/less) rapidly than before.

2. In the last thirty years, our economy has moved from an _____/
_____ base to an _____/_____ base.

3. Our reading states that "far more complex interpersonal skills are required" of today's workers. Give three or more reasons why.

4. What are at least two societal changes described in the reading?

5. Two or more implications of these changes for educators?

6. With your group, write another question about the information in your
reading.

OR

Rewrite any or all of the questions above to make them more thought provoking and discussion provoking.

*By J. W-B Olsen and J. Yedlin

Part I

1. According to studies by Johnson and others (1989), the greatest incentive for students to achieve comes from:
    a.   their teachers
    b.   their peers
    c.   their families
    (answer: b)

2. Studies of student performance in cooperative learning classrooms vs. traditional competitive classrooms show:
    a.   increased academic performance in cooperative classrooms
    b.   increased liking for classmates in cooperative classrooms
    c.   increased self-esteem in cooperative classrooms
    d.   increased liking for school in cooperative classrooms
    e.   all of the above
    f.   some, but not all of the above
    g.   none of the above
    (answer: e)

3. What is the most common reason for first-time job holders to be fired from their jobs?
    (lack of social skills)

4. What kind of group composition has proved best in cooperative learning?
    (heterogeneous)

5. List two kinds of students who have made significantly greater academic progress in cooperative learning classrooms than in regular, competitive classrooms, according to many studies.
    (minority students; low achievers)

6. List two or more changes in the workplace that require increased cooperation by today's worker.

7. Your district is planning to start an innovative language development program for ESL students, and is looking for possible models to adapt.

*Designed by Judy Winn-Bell Olsen for Jigsaw Reading Activity

Outline a ten-minute presentation to the program planners on why the program should be based on cooperative learning models. What specific arguments and evidence would you use?

8. With your group members, make at least one more question which will integrate the information from your three readings.

Part II

a) At this moment, you are participating in a Jigsaw activity designed for staff development. Think now about using Jigsaw in a class of ESL students of intermediate, advanced, or mixed levels, or a mainstream class with some native speakers and some nonnative speakers. What source materials might you use in designing a Jigsaw activity? (Think about existing texts, not about writing your own. Think about dividing the reading into different parts. Think about making questions for each part for the expert groups, and questions to integrate the information on home-team worksheets.)

b) In this workshop, we have sped through this Jigsaw activity in a very short time. Think about how long such an exercise would take with your students. How many class periods? You should probably plan on an Expert Groups Jigsaw taking at least five days if your classes are about an hour long. If it takes that much time, what makes it worth doing?

REFERENCES

ARONSON, E., N. BLANEY, C. STEPHAN, J. SIKES, and M. SNAPP. 1978. *The Jigsaw Classroom.* Beverly Hills, CA & London: Sage.

COOPER, C. 1990. Personal communication.

COOPER, C., L. ROBERTSON et al. 1990. *Training Manuals in Cooperative Learning. V1: Staff Development; V.2: Coaching; V.3: Implementation.* Redwood City, CA: Redwood City Cooperative Learning Implementation Project, Redwood City School District.

EDWARDS, C., and J. STOUT. 1989. Cooperative learning: the first year. *Educational Leadership,* 47, no. 4: 38–41.

FREIRE, P. 1970. *Pedagogy of the Oppressed.* New York: Seabury Press.

FULLILOVE, R.E. 1986. Sealing the leaks in the pipeline: Improving the performance and persistence of minority students in college. Report on *The Professional Development Programs Mathematics Workshop.* Berkeley, CA: University of California.

GARMSTON, R.J. 1989. How administrators support peer coaching. In R.S. Brandt (ed.), *Coaching and Staff Development, Readings from Educational Leadership,* Alexandria, VA: ASCD Publications.

GIBBLE, J.L., and J.D. LAWRENCE. 1987. Peer coaching for principles. *Educational Leadership,* 45, no. 3: 72–74.

GLATTHORN, A.A. 1987. Cooperative professional development: Peer-centered options for teacher growth. *Educational Leadership,* 45 no. 3: 31–35.

GOULD, S., and E. LETVEN. 1987. A center for interactive professional development. *Educational Leadership,* 45, no. 3: 49–53.

GUSKEY, T.R. 1989. Staff development and teacher change. In R.S. Brandt (ed.), *Coaching and Staff Development: Readings from Educational Leadership.* Alexandria, VA: Association for Supervision and Curriculum Development Publications.

JOHNSON, D.W., and R.T. JOHNSON. 1989. Social skills for successful group work. *Educational Leadership,* 47, no. 4: 29–33.

————. Learning from colleagues: Cooperative learning among adults. In training handbook *Cooperative Learning for the Teacher Educator.* San Jose, CA: San Jose State University School of Education.

JOHNSON, D.W., G. MARUYAMA, R.T. JOHNSON, D. NELSON, and L. SKON. 1981. Effects of cooperative, competitive, and individualistic goal structures on achievement: A meta-analysis. *Psychological Bulletin* 89: 47–62.

JOYCE, B., R.H. HERSH, and M. MCKIBBIN, 1983. *The Structure of School Improvement.* New York: Longman.

JOYCE, B., and M. MCKIBBIN. 1982. Teacher growth states and school environments. *Educational Leadership* 40: 36–41.

JOYCE, B., C. MURPHY, B. SHOWERS, and J. MURPHY. 1989. School renewal as cultural change. *Educational Leadership,* 47, no. 3: 70–83.

JOYCE, B., and B. SHOWERS, 1980. Improving in-service training: The messages of research. *Educational Leadership,* 38: 379–385

————. 1983. *Power in Staff Development Through Research on Training.* Alexandria, VA: Association for Supervision and Curriculum Development.

JOYCE, B., B. SHOWERS, and C. ROLHEISER-BENNETT. 1987. Staff development and student learning: A synthesis of research on models of teaching. *Educational Leadership,* 45, no. 2: 11–29.

KAGAN, S. 1990. *Cooperative Learning Resources for Teachers.* San Juan Capistrano, CA: Resources for Teachers.

————.1989. A structural approach to cooperative learning. *Educational Leadership,* 47, no. 4: 12–15.

KOHONEN, V. 1988. Address to the CATESOL Bay Area Regional Conference, October 1988.

MARKS, J. 1989. Poster presentations in teacher training courses. *The Teacher Trainer: A Practical Journal,* 3, no. 3: 17–18. Canterbury, England: Pilgrims English Language Courses.

Mid-Continent Regional Educational Laboratory (McREL) 1983. Coaching: A powerful strategy for improving staff development and in-service education. In *Opening Doors: An Introduction to Peer Coaching.* Alexandria, VA: Association for Supervision and Curriculum Development.

NAISBITT, J. 1982. Megatrends. New York: Warner Books.

OLSEN, J. W-B. 1988. Focus on the teacher. Presentation at International TESOL and Puerto Rico TESOL Conferences.

RED, C., and E. SHAINLINE, 1989. Teachers reflect on change. In R.S. Brandt, ed., *Coaching and Staff Development: Readings from Educational Leadership.* Alexandria. VA: Association for Supervision and Curriculum Development.

RHOADES, J., and M.E. MCCABE. 1989. *Simple Cooperation in the Classroom.* Willits, CA: ITA Publications.

SLAVIN, R.E. 1981. Synthesis of research on cooperative learning. *Educational Leadership,* 39: 655–60.

————.1989. Here to stay–or gone tomorrow? *Educational Leadership,* 47, no. 4: 3.

————.1989. Research on cooperative learning: Consensus and controversy. *Educational Leadership,* 47, no. 4: 52–54.

SLAVIN, R.E., and E. OICKLE. 1981. Effects of learning teams on student achievement and race relations.: Treatment by race interactions. *Sociology of Education,* 54: 174–80.

Teacher Development Newsletter. 1985. Teacher Development Special Group of the International Association of Teachers of English as a Foreign Language (IATEFL) Whitstable, England.

TOFFLER, A. 1970. *Future Shock.* New York: Random House.

Trivial Pursuit © 1981. Horn Abbot Ltd. Bay Shore, New York: Selchow & Righter Co.

BIBLIOGRAPHY OF COOPERATIVE LANGUAGE LEARNING AND ACQUIRING ENGLISH

Roger E. W-B Olsen

Reviews of research in cooperative learning during the 1980s came largely from David and Roger Johnson, Shlomo Sharan, and Robert E. Slavin and initially focused largely on examining and organizing research that supported cooperative over competitive and individualistic learning. In 1980, Sharan and Slavin published reviews in the journal *Review of Educational Research* and the Johnsons in *Psychological Bulletin.*

The Johnson's emphasized elements or characteristics that contribute to the positive effects of cooperation, such as interdependence and heterogeneous grouping. Sharan emphasized Group Investigation research, establishing that CL was appropriate for complex, "higher-order thinking" subject material, even at the graduate level. Slavin emphasized somewhat more the validation of certain marriages of procedure with specific curriculum. These reviews gave considerable research-based support to CL during the 1980s and no doubt stimulated additional inquiry. The number of journal articles, dissertations, and program evaluation documents on CL more than doubled between 1979 and 1989.

The 1980s closed with three new mega-reviews, annotated on the following pages, of CL research by the Johnsons, Sharan, and Slavin.

This bibliography is organized into three sections: publications relating mainly to cooperative learning, publications concerned mainly with students acquiring English, and a group of general interest titles.

I. Cooperative Learning Section
    A. Mega-reviews
    B. Selected Research
    C. General Methodology and Overviews of Cooperative Learning
    D. Methodology: Specific Lesson Plans, Strategies, Suggestions, and Techniques

II. Students Acquiring English Section
    A. Selected Research About Students Acquiring English
    B. General, About Students Acquiring English
    C. Cooperative Learning and Students Acquiring English: Research, Techniques, and Strategies

III. General Education, Methodology, and Classics

Mega-reviews

SHARAN, S. 1980. Cooperative learning in small groups: Recent methods and effects on achievement, attitudes, and ethnic relations. *Review of Educational Research,* 50: 241–71.

SLAVIN, R.E. 1980. Cooperative learning. *Review of Educational Research,* 50: 315–42.

JOHNSON, D.W., G. MARUYAMA, R. JOHNSON, D. NELSON, and L. SKON. 1981. Effects of cooperative, competitive, and individualistic goal structures on achievement: A meta-analysis. *Psychological Bulletin,* 89: 47–62.

JOHNSON, D.W., and R.T. JOHNSON. 1989 *Cooperation and Competition: Theory and Research.* Interaction Book Company, 7208 Cornelia Drive, Edina, MN 55435. 253 pp. This *tour de force* uses meta-analysis procedures to analyze over 1,000 studies of cooperation in schools K–12, adult, and college level. They include journal articles, dissertations, and project evaluation reports—not how-to publications or overviews of cooperative learning. Special attention is given to comparing the effects of cooperation with competition and specific factors (elements or characteristics) that make cooperation more effective, such as heterogeneous grouping, individual and group accountability, and interdependence.

SHARAN, S., (ed.). 1990. *Cooperative Learning: Theory and Practice.* New York: Praeger Press. This is an impressive collection of scholarly articles addressing many issues in cooperative learning, especially group investigation methods with complex skills and knowledge (see "low-consensus information" in Chapters 1 and 5), or "higher-order thinking skills."

SLAVIN, R.E. 1990. *Cooperative Learning: Theory, Research and Practice.* Englewood Cliffs, NJ: Prentice Hall. 187 pp. Summarizes the literature using "best evidence," literature survey, and meta-analysis methods to show conditions where CL contributes to achievement and other outcomes. Slavin also relates CL to research in kindred fields such as cognitive psychology, developmental psychology, education, and educational psychology to examine why CL works. Approximately half the text is comprised of lesson plan material that may be reproduced for classroom use. Intended for preservice education courses.

Selected Research

ARMSTRONG., B., D.W. JOHNSON, and B. BALOW. 1981. Effects of cooperative versus individualistic learning experiences on interpersonal attraction between learning-disabled and normal-progress elementary school students. *Contemporary Educational Psychology,* 6: 102–9.

COHEN, P.A., and J.A. KULIK. 1981. Synthesis of research on the effects of tutoring. *Research Information Service,* 39: 227–29.

JOHNSON, D.W., R.T. JOHNSON, and G. MARUYAMA. 1983. Interdependence and interpersonal attraction among heterogeneous and homogeneous individuals: A theoretical formulation and a meta-analysis of the research. *Review of Educational Research,* 53: 5–54.

JOHNSON, D.W., R. JOHNSON, J. JOHNSON, and D. ANDERSON. The effects of cooperative vs. individualized instruction on student prosocial behavior, attitudes toward learning and achievement. *Journal of Educational Psychology,* 68: 446–52.

KAGAN, S. 1977. Social motives and behaviors of Mexican-American and Anglo-American children. In J.L. Martinez (ed.), *Chicano Psychology.* New York: Academic Press.

MARTINO, L., and D.W. JOHNSON. 1979. Cooperative and individualistic experiences among disabled and normal children. *Journal of Social Psychology,* 109: 177–83.

NEVIN, A., D.W. JOHNSON, and R. JOHNSON. 1982. Effects of groups and individual contingencies on academic performance and social relations of special needs students. *Journal of Social Psychology,* 116: 441–59.

SKON, L., D.W. JOHNSON, and R. JOHNSON. 1981 Cooperative peer interaction versus individual competition and individualistic efforts: Effects on the acquisition of cognitive reasoning strategies. *Journal of Educational Psychology,* 73: 83–91.

SLAVIN, R.E. 1983. When does cooperative learning increase student achievement? *Psychological Bulletin,* 94, no.3: 429–45.

————. 1981. Synthesis of research on cooperative learning. *Educational Leadership* (May 1981): 665–59. This is an overview of methods and research at the turn of the decade. It also provides descriptions of team learning methods and possible other uses.

SLAVIN, R.E., and E. OICKLE. 1981. Effects of learning teams on student achievement and race relations: Treatment by race interactions. *Sociology of Education,* 54: 174–80.

SMITH, K., D.W. JOHNSON, and R. JOHNSON. 1981. Can conflict be constructive? Controversy versus concurrence seeking in learning groups. *Journal of Educational Psychology,* 73: 651–63.

————. 1982. Effects of cooperative and individualistic instruction on the achievement of handicapped, regular, and gifted students. *Journal of Social Psychology,* 116: 277–82.

————. 1984. Effects of controversy on learning in cooperative groups. *Journal of Social Psychology,* 122: 199–09.

WEBB., N. 1988. Small group problem solving: Peer interaction and learning. *International Association for the Study of Cooperation in Education Newsletter,* 9, nos. 3 & 4: 11–12.

General Methodology and Overviews of Cooperative Learning

ARONSON, E., N. BLANEY, J. SIKES, C. STEPHAN, and M. SNAPP. 1975. Busing and racial tension: The jigsaw route to learning and liking. *Psychology Today* (February 1975): 43–50. This is an early, "classic" description of Jigsaw with detailed discussion of technique developed, instructional challenges encountered, and outcomes realized.

ARONSON, E., N. BLANEY, C. STEPHAN, J. SIKES, and M. SNAPP. 1978. *The Jigsaw Classroom.* Beverly Hills, CA & London, UK: Sage Publications. 193 pp. This classic how-to text details procedures for using Jigsaw. Each team member learns different information while in "expert" groups, then teaches "home" team members.

BRUBACHER, M., R. PAYNE, and K. RICKETT. 1990. *Perspectives on Small Group Learning.* Oakville, Ont.: Rubicon Publishing Co. [Distributed in the U.S. by Dominie Press, Inc. P.O. Box 910449, San Diego, CA 92191; (619) 481-3838]. 342 pp. A collection of 25 descriptive articles address CL theory, rationale, process, application, and implementation.

COHEN, E.G. 1986. *Designing Groupwork.* New York: Teachers College Press. 184 pp. This is an introductory text about groupwork: group processes, dynamics, leadership, and management. Cohen places special emphasis on ways to equalize status and participation among group members who may be heterogeneous for achievement, status, race, SES, or ethnicity.

COOPER, H.M. 1979. Pygmalion grows up: A model for teacher expectation, communication, and performance influence. *Review of Educational Research,* 49: 389–10. A succinct and thorough analysis of the effects of teacher expectations on student achievement.

DAVIDSON, N., (ed.). 1990. *Cooperative Learning in Mathematics: A Handbook for Teachers.* Reading, MA: Addison-Wesley. 409 pp. Twelve articles by seventeen teachers who use CL to teach mathematics at grade levels primary through college. Content ranges from basic skills to algebra and The Calculas. Real-class examples include narrated classroom discussion, problems and possible solutions, and CL structures that are used to teach mathematics.

JOHNSON, D.W., and R.T. JOHNSON. 1987. *Learning Together and Alone: Cooperative, Competitive, and Individualistic Learning* (2/e). Englewood Cliffs, NJ: Prentice Hall. Provides theory and models for using CL in the classroom. Emphasizes principles of CL, group processes, and social skills. A college-level text on group process and management.

JOHNSON, D.W., R.T. JOHNSON, and E.J. HOLUBEC. 1986. *Circles of Learning: Cooperation in the Classroom* (rev. ed.). Interaction Book Company, 7208 Cornelia Drive, Edina, MN 55435. 88 pp. A concise overview to help parents, teachers, and administrators understand what CL is. Cooperation is compared to competitive and individualistic structures. It describes eighteen steps or stages for lesson planning, addressing selection of content, and four basic CL elements (positive interdependence, individual accountability, forming groups, and teaching prosocial skills).

JOHNSON, D.W., and F.P. JOHNSON. 1982. *Joining Together: Group Theory and Group Skills.* Englewood Cliffs, NJ: Prentice-Hall. 510 pp. This is a social psychology text on group dynamics, group theory, and group skills. Many of the activities use CL principles—for example, assigning roles.

JOHNSON, D.W., and R.T. JOHNSON. 1987. *Leading the Cooperative School.* Interaction Book Company (see Johnson et al., 1986). 279 pp. "To qualify as a cooperative school, cooperation must dominate both student and faculty life." This quote from the first chapter summarizes the premise of this leadership manual for changing schools into cooperative structures and for maintaining them once established. Theory and research are intermingled with advice and specific suggestions of activities to build and maintain colleagiality. (Thanks to Peggy Doherty for her review of *Leading the Cooperative School.*)

———. 1989. Social skills for successful group work. *Educational Leadership*, 47, no. 4 (December 1989/January1990). Emphasizes the importance of social skills and ways to stress them.

SCHNIEDEWIND, N., and S.J. SALEND. 1987. Cooperative learning works. *Teaching Exceptional Children* (Winter 1987): 22–25. A nontechnical overview of cooperative learning strategies, such as Jigsaw and other group approaches, with practical suggestions for using them in the classroom: establishing guidelines, forming groups, arranging the classroom, developing cooperative (prosocial) skills, evaluation, and confronting problems.

SHARAN, S., P. HARE, C.D. WEBB, and R. HERTZ-LAZAROWITZ (eds.). 1980 *Cooperation in Education.* Provo, UT: Brigham Young University Press. A collection of articles to describe various aspects of CL, such as "A Group-Investigation method of cooperative learning in the classroom" by S. Sharan and R. Hertz-Lazarowitz.

SHARAN, Y., and S. SHARAN. 1989. Group investigation expands cooperative learning. *Educational Leadership*, 47, no. 4: 17–21. This is a nontechnical overview of Group Investigation, a brief history, planning considerations, stages of implementation, and a miniresearch review of effects on achievement, social interaction, and teachers.

SLAVIN, R.E. 1987. How student learning teams can integrate the desegregated classroom. *Integrated Education*, 15: 56–58.

———. 1990. *Cooperative Learning: Theory, Research and Practice.* Englewood Cliffs, NJ: Prentice Hall. 187 pp. Summarizes the literature to show conditions where CL contributes to achievement and other outcomes and which elements may be key characteristics.

Approximately half the text is comprised of lesson-plan material that may be reproduced for classroom use.

―――. 1987. Cooperative learning and the cooperative school. *Educational Leadership,* 45, no. 3: 7–13. Discusses cooperative learning methods and conditions when cooperative learning is effective; explores *why* cooperative learning works ("Students are often able to translate the teacher's language into 'kid language' for one another."); describes several methods or procedures, and looks at ways to begin building cooperative schools.

SLAVIN, R.E., N.A. MADDEN, and R.J. STEVENS. 1989. Cooperative learning models for the 3 Rs. *Educational Leadership,* 47, no. 4: 22–28. Describes team learning programs that are integral to year-round instruction in basic skill areas of math and language arts: team assisted individualization (TAI) and cooperative integrated reading and composition (CIRC). Includes principal features, the basic instructional plan, and relevant research on CIRC and TAI.

SLAVIN, R.E., S. SHARAN, S. KAGAN, R. HERTZ-LAZAROWITZ, and R. SCHMUCK (eds.). 1985. *Learning to Cooperate, Cooperating to Learn.* New York: Plenum. Includes historically important articles, including N. Webb's "Student interaction and learning in small groups: A research summary" and S. Kagan's early discussion on structures entitled "The dimensions of cooperative classroom structures." Other articles address basic concepts, group dynamics, learning to cooperate, and so forth.

Methodology: Specific Lesson Plans, Strategies, Suggestions and Techniques

ANDRINI, B. 1989. *Cooperative Learning & Mathematics: A Multi-Structural Approach.* Resources for Teachers: 27314 Paseo Espada #202, San Juan Capistrano, CA 92675; (714) 248-7757. 166 pp. Describes eighteen structures and then chains or sequences structures into "multistructural lessons." The lesson plans include duplicatable student activity pages and cover eight math topics from kindergarten through eighth grade. The topics are number, measurement, geometry, patterns and functions, statistics, probability, logic, and algebra. Each topic (except algebra) has a lesson for primary, intermediate, and upper grades, so the book covers K–8 math.

DAVIDSON, N., and P.W. O'LEARY. 1990. How cooperative learning can enhance mastery teaching. *Educational Leadership* (February 1990): 30–34. This article shows how to use cooperative learning with "mastery teaching." Different structures can be used at various stages of the mastery teaching lesson (anticipatory set, setting objectives and purpose, presentation, checking for understanding, guided practice, independent practice, closure and evaluation) and discusses parallels between principles of cooperative learning and Hunter's "instructional theory into practice (ITIP)" learning principles (motivation, practice, retention, transfer, learning styles, and extending thinking).

DISHON, D., and P.W. O'LEARY. 1985. *A Guidebook for Cooperative Learning: A Technique for Creating More Effective Schools.* Cooperation Unlimited, P.O. Box 68, Portage, MI 49081. 132 pp. A clear, step-by-step guide to implementing the Johnsons' "learning together" approach, emphasizing basic principles, planning steps, and the teacher's role.

KAGAN, S. 1989. *Cooperative Learning Resources for Teachers.* Resources for Teachers (see B. Andrini, 1989). 306 pp. This is an extensive manual with lesson plans and explanations of CL, especially the structural approach. Updated annually, it includes sample lesson material across the curriculum, including "whole language," mathematics, social studies, and science topics, with structures like Co-op Co-op, Jigsaw, and STAD. Duplicatable (blackline master) pages contain activity sheets, management charts, and award certificate forms. Special attention is devoted to specific structures.

KAGAN, S. 1989. The structural approach to cooperative learning. *Educational Leadership* (December1989/January 1990), 47, no. 4: 12–15. A concise overview of the structural approach includes descriptions of fifteen structures and some of their uses academically and socially. For example, some structures are more appropriate for drill-like review tasks and others are more appropriate for developing awareness; and structures can have different social functions. Includes suggestions for developing multi-structural lessons and a strategy for getting started using structures in day-to-day teaching

KAGAN, S. 1990. *Same–Different: Holidays Edition.* Resources for Teachers (see B. Andrini, 1989). 78 pp. Same–Different materials are A/B information sheets (discussed in Chapter 5). Students are to find differences between picture pairs without looking at each other's picture. *Same–Different: Holidays* covers fourteen holidays and each picture has twenty differences.

LYMAN, F. 1989. Rechoreographing: The middle-level minuet. *The Early Adolescent Magazine,* 4, no.1 (September/October 1989): 22–24. This description of Think-Pair-Share includes classroom scenarios, different kinds of response modes, and several useful variations of TPS, such as Think-Pair-Share-Think-Share and Think-Pair-Share-Write-Share.

McCABE, M.E., and J. RHOADES. 1989. *The Nurturing Classroom: Developing Self-Esteem, Thinking Skills, and Responsibility Through Simple Cooperation.* ITA Publications, P.O. Drawer 1599, Willits, CA 95490-1599; (707) 459-6100. 357 pp. This is a combination trainer and trainee manual, giving more attention to details than to general theory or research. In addition to numerous lesson activity plans throughout the main body of the text, there are fifty-seven additional pages of lesson plans and a six-week (thirty-day) sample implementation schedule in the appendices. Special attention is given to ways to incorporate thinking skills into lessons.

SCHNIEDEWIND, N., and E. DAVIDSON. 1987. *Cooperative Learning, Cooperative Lives.* Dubuque, IA: Wm. C. Brown. 538 pp. A detailed, step-by-step manual for implementing CL. Activities have been selected to emphasize student awareness of cooperation as well as to demonstrate formats for cooperative lessons such as Board Games, Cooperative Card Games, Creative Controversy, Group Project, Jigsaw, Group Grade, Learning Center, Research Project, Partners, Peer Teaching, and Treasure Hunt. Content includes social studies (e.g., the American underground railroad in the 1800s), social issues (e.g., mothers in the work force), and global education (e.g., jobs with peace).

SLAVIN, R.E. 1980. *Using Student Team Learning* (rev. ed.). Baltimore: The Center for Social Organization of Schools, The Johns Hopkins University. Complete instructions for STAD and TGT; descriptions of TAI, CIRC, and other methods.

STONE, J.M. 1989. *Cooperative Learning & Language Arts: A Multistructural Approach.* Resources for Teachers (see B. Andrini, 1989). Based on Kagan's structural approach, Stone has chained or sequenced structures to create multistructural lessons—CL and language arts.

Selected Research About Students Acquiring English

ADDISON, A.A. 1988. Comprehensible textbooks in science for the non-native English speaker: Evidence from discourse analysis. *CATESOL Journal 1,* no. 1 (November 1988): 49–66.

ARTHUR, B., R. WEINER, M. CULVER, Y.J. LEE, and D. THOMAS. 1980. The register of impersonal discourse to foreigners: Verbal adjustments to foreign accent. In D. Larsen-Freeman (ed.), *Discourse Analysis in Second Language Acquisition.* Rowley, MA: Newbury House.

BEJARANO, Y. 1987. A cooperative small-group methodology in the language classroom. *TESOL Quarterly,* 21, no. 3 (September 1987): 483–504.

BROCK, C. 1986. The effects of referential questions on ESL classroom discourse. *TESOL Quarterly,* 20, no. 1: 47–60.

CHAMOT, A.U., and J.M. O'MALLEY. 1987. The cognitive academic language learning approach: A bridge to the mainstream. *TESOL Quarterly,* 21, no. 2 (June 1987): 227–49.

COLLIER, V.P. 1989. How long? A synthesis of research on academic achievement in a second language. *TESOL Quarterly,* 23, no. 3 (September 1989): 509–31.

HAMAYAN, E.V., and G.R. TUCKER. 1980. Language input in the bilingual classroom and its relationship to second language achievement. *TESOL Quarterly,* 14, no. 4 (December 1980): 453–68.

KUTRAKUN, S. 1989. The main factors causing LEP students to be at risk in content area classes. *WAESOL Newsletter* (Washington Association for the Education of Speakers of Other Languages), 14, no. 2 (Spring 1989): 2–3,8.

LONG, M.H. 1981. Input, interaction, and second language acquisition. *Annals of the New York Academy of Sciences,* 379: 259–78.

LONG, M.H. 1983. Linguistics and conversational adjustments to non-native speakers. *Studies in Second Language Acquisition,* 5: 177–93.

LONG, M.H., and P. PORTER. 1985. Group work, interlanguage talk, and second language acquisition. *TESOL Quarterly,* 19, no. 2: 207–28

LONG, M.H., E. BROCK, G. CROOKES, C. DEICKE, L. POTTER, and S. ZHANG. 1984. The effect of teacher's questioning patterns and wait-time on pupil participation in public high school classes. Technical Report No. 1, Center for Second Language Classroom Research. University of Hawaii at Manoa.

OLSEN, R.E. W-B. 1989. A survey of limited English proficient (LEP) student enrollments and identification criteria. *TESOL Quarterly,* 23, no. 3 (September 1989): 469–88.

PICA, T. 1988. Interlanguage adjustments as an outcome of NS–NNS negotiated interaction. *Language Learning,* 38, no. 1 (March 1988): 45–73.

PICA, T., R. YOUNG, C. DOUGHTY. 1987. The impact of interaction on comprehension. *TESOL Quarterly,* 21, no. 4: 737–58.

SCHINKE-LLANO, L.A. 1983. Foreigner talk in content classrooms. In H.W. Seliger & M.H. Long (eds.), *Classroom Oriented Research in Second Language Acquisition.* Rowley, MA: Newbury House.

General About Students Acquiring English

California State Department of Education, Office of Bilingual Bicultural Education (ed.) 1986. *Beyond Language: Social & Cultural Factors in Schooling Language Minority Students.* Sacramento, CA: California State Department of Education. 343 pp.

————*Schooling and Language Minority Students: A Theoretical Framework.* Los Angeles, CA:

Evaluation, Dissemination, and Assessment Center, California State University at Los Angeles. 218 pp.

―――*Studies on Immersion Education.* Sacramento, CA: California State Department of Education. 184 pp.

CRANDALL, J. (ed.). 1987. *ESL Through Content-Area Instruction: Mathematics, Science, Social Studies.* Englewood Cliffs, NJ: Prentice Hall Regents.

KELLER, E., and S.T. WARNER. 1988. *Conversation Gambits.* Hove, UK: Language Teaching Publications (35 Church Road, Hove, BN3 2BE).

KRASHEN, S.D., and T.D. TERRELL. 1983. *The Natural Approach: Language Acquisition in the Classroom.* Englewood Cliffs, NJ: Alemany Press/Prentice Hall Regents.

Cooperative Learning and Students Acquiring English: Research, Techniques, and Strategies

BASSANO, S., and M.A. CHRISTISON. 1988. Cooperative learning in the ESL classroom. *TESOL Newsletter,* 22, no. 2: 1,8–9.

COEHLO, E., L. WINER, and J.W-B OLSEN. 1989. *All Sides of the Issue: Activities for Cooperative Jigsaw Groups.* Englewood Cliffs, NJ: Alemany Press.

MCGROARTY, M. 1989. The benefits of cooperative learning arrangements in second language instruction. *NABE Journal,* 13, no. 2 (Winter 1989): 127–43.

OLSEN, J.W-B. 1987. *Communication-Starters and Other Activities for the ESL Classroom.* Englewood Cliffs, NJ: Alemany Press.

―――. 1984. *Look-Again Pictures for Language Development and Lifeskills.* Englewood Cliffs, NJ: Alemany Press.

PALMER, A.S., T.S. RODGERS, and J. W-B OLSEN. 1988. *Back and Forth: Pair Activities for Language Development.* Englewood Cliffs, NJ: Alemany Press.

General Education, Methodology, and Classics

ALLPORT, G.W. 1954. *The Nature of Prejudice.* Reading, MA: Addison-Wesley.

BLOOM, B.S. (ed.). 1956. *Taxonomy of Educational Objectives, Handbook 1: Cognitive Domain.* New York: David McKay.

BUDD-ROWE, M. 1974. Pausing phenomena: Influence on the quality of instruction. *Journal of Psycholinguistic Research,* 3: 203–23.

DEUTSCH, M. 1949. A theory of cooperation and competition. *Human Relations,* 2: 129–52.

DEWEY, J. 1957. *Experience and Education.* New York: Macmillan.

GOODLAD, J.I. 1984. *A Place Called School: Prospects for the Future.* New York: McGraw-Hill.

JOYCE, B., and M. WEIL. 1972. *Models of Teaching.* Englewood Cliffs, NJ: Prentice-Hall. (Cited in Bejarano, 1987: 488).

INDEX

Authors

Subjects